Rethinking Life

SUNY series in Contemporary Italian Philosophy
—————
Silvia Benso and Brian Schroeder, editors

Rethinking Life
Italian Philosophy in Precarious Times

Edited by
Silvia Benso

Published by State University of New York Press, Albany

© 2022 State University of New York

All rights reserved

Printed in the United States of America

No part of this book may be used or reproduced in any manner whatsoever without written permission. No part of this book may be stored in a retrieval system or transmitted in any form or by any means including electronic, electrostatic, magnetic tape, mechanical, photocopying, recording, or otherwise without the prior permission in writing of the publisher.

For information, contact State University of New York Press, Albany, NY
www.sunypress.edu

Library of Congress Cataloging-in-Publication Data

Name: Benso, Silvia, editor.
Title: Rethinking life : Italian philosophy in precarious times / Silvia Benso.
Description: Albany : State University of New York Press, [2022] | Series: SUNY series in Contemporary Italian Philosophy | Includes bibliographical references and index.
Identifiers: ISBN 9781438488158 (hardcover : alk. paper) | ISBN 9781438488172 (ebook) | ISBN 9781438488165 (pbk. : alk. paper)
Further information is available at the Library of Congress.

10 9 8 7 6 5 4 3 2 1

To Erik Aren,
A most joyful companion
Through our times of isolation and solitude

Contents

Acknowledgments   ix

Epidemics, Precariousness, and Vulnerability: Introductory Remarks
toward a Rethinking of Life   1
   Silvia Benso

Part One: Confronting Disaster

1. Cassandra's Details: Coronavirus and the Course of Globalization   25
   Luisa Bonesio

2. Improvising Self-Expression in the Time of a Contingency that
Has Eliminated Contingency   39
   Alessandro Bertinetto

3. Out of the Choir: Bodies Inclined on the Playboy   53
   Lorenzo Bernini

4. Metaphor as Illness? Life, War, and a Linguistic *Pharmakon*   71
   Alberto Martinengo

Part Two: Vulnerability, Care, and Responsibility

5. "The Lungs that We All Are": Rethinking Life in the Times
of a Pandemic   91
   Olivia Guaraldo

6. Necropolitics, Care, and the Common Elia Zaru	107
7. Lacking Beings Luca Illetterati	119
8. Vulnerable Existences Caterina Resta	133
9. Life and Useless Suffering: Responsibility for Others and the Impossible Theodicy Rita Fulco	145

Part Three: Rethinking Life

10. Greek Zèn: Living Starting from the Origin Alessandra Cislaghi	161
11. Life and the "Black Swan" Enrica Lisciani-Petrini	177
12. What Finitude Does Not Say: Rethinking Life beyond Nihilism Roberto Mancini	191
13. Writing Life: Biography, Autobiography, and the Remainder Claudia Baracchi	203
14. With the Finitude of Life beyond the Phenomenon: Phenomenology, Hermeneutics, and a Metaphysics of the Finite Ugo Perone	217
Contributors	229
Index	235

Acknowledgments

This edited volume was conceived in early spring 2020, at the time of the first lockdown due to the Covid-19 pandemic. During that period, I was on a research leave in Salzburg, Austria, where I had accompanied my son Erik who was in the middle of his first academic year as a baroque violin student in the program of *Alte Musik* at the Mozarteum Universität. Suddenly and without warning, what was supposed to be a year of travels, lectures, meetings with colleagues, gatherings with friends and family, joyfulness and overall good times shockingly came to an abrupt end. Literally from night to day, on March 16, 2020 a nationwide stay-at-home order went into force in Austria. The quarantine measures had already become effective in Italy starting March 10—travel was banned except for work or family emergencies. For various reasons, we decided to stay put in Salzburg. The Alps, for centuries providing passes and passages between the two countries, became virtually impassable, planes were grounded, and national borders were reinstituted and closed. Salzburg, a mecca of music, artistic performances, concerts, outdoors café and markets, cosmopolitan tourism, went silent, emptied out of all human voices and sounds. It did not help that the forces of living nature, that *zoe* that continues imperturbably, took possession of the scene, that birds kept chirping and singing, that trees and flowers started their blooming season in the mildness of the spring days and with an abundance of smells and colors, that the river swelled with the melting snows and continued to flow, that the mountains stood majestic and solitary despite their closeness in the gleaming of the warming sun. Nor did it help that the aesthetic magnificence of the Baroque squares and buildings, empty of all human businesses and interactions, could now emerge in the purity of their forms, in the geometric harmony and beauty whose architectural rhythm carries the trace, if not the presence, of human beings, even when they are absent. All of a sudden and without mercy, everything seemed to fade in the melancholy of a time without change, in the monotonous repetition of days each equal to the previous one, within a magic castle in which we were captive—admittedly not a bad place to be; on the contrary, a place of extreme privilege and luxury, compared to other situations. Yet the gravity and precariousness of times fell heavily upon us. Everything seemed, felt on hold—not dead but suspended, disconnected, floating. If it had not been for the bells.

Salzburg is a city of many churches, of many bell towers, and, hence, of many bells. At every hour, in some cases even at every quarter, some bell tolls, alone or with others. Forged by the mastery of some blacksmith at times in some exotic country, each bell has a function characterizing it— each has, as it were, its individuality, its personality. Each even has a name. Even though similar, the bells are not identical, in terms of either material or role. Some are cast in iron, some in bronze, some mark the hours, some announce the convening of the community for religious functions, some invoke a prayer for the sick or dying, some simply toll, for reasons and with rhythms that remain mysterious to this writer. Three times a day, from the Glockenspiel, the bell tower on top of the archbishop's residence, a carillon with thirty-five bells plays a piece of classical music, a melody that stays the same during the day but changes with the liturgical seasons. Identity and difference; specificity and indistinctness; matter and sound; stillness and vibrations; joy and mourning; life and death; novelty and repetition—Salzburg's bells gather many contrasts within the polyphonic harmony of their tolling.

Thanks to the bells, during the pandemic sojourn the impersonal time of biological and natural life, of the *zoe* that goes on continuously, implacably, insensibly, even cruelly, became wrapped up, embraced, rhythmed by the interruptions brought up and signified by the sound of these hourly companions of a time otherwise lengthy, suspended, indefinite. Thanks to their recall of recognizable social activities (mourning, death, joy, gathering, celebrations) with which the bells resound and which perhaps they institute, and with which *zoe* is enveloped, not only did *zoe* retain an appearance of *bios* but also time as indefinite repetition opened up to the possibility of time as *kairos*, as interruption that allows for a swerve, a distance, a memory, a hope, a living and lively identity, a contact, a connection, a sociality— the ringing of a phone call from a friend or family on one of the social media available to us. The liturgy of the hours became origin, occasion, and blessing of diversity and difference, of markers and interruptions that presaged contacts and connections.

I am thankful to the tolling of the Salzburg's bells, which recalled me to the fact that, even in isolation, in physical and social distance, in the appearance of stillness and death imposed by the utter contingency of the pandemic, there is other—there is life, there are sounds, voices, contacts, community. May the tolling of the bells continue and turn into celebration, I thought—both of life and of those who have gone through life and have exited it, leaving a trace, an echo, a vibration, like the sound that fades and disappears after the last toll; yet the air remains the custodian of the resounding of such a presence.

I am especially thankful to my son, Erik, who, during our stay in Salzburg, made the endless hours of our suspended time full with the joyfulness of laughter and smiles, the cheerfulness and melancholy of the violin, the creativity of numerous artistic projects, the lightheartedness of many walks and bike rides through the countryside, wind in our hair, sunbeams in our eyes.

I am thankful to my spouse, Brian, and to my family in Italy, who made the forced geographical distance that separated us appear less burdensome through almost daily contacts via social networks, as if love and caring knew no barriers, as if bonds were stronger than difficulties, as if vulnerability were an occasion for closer connectedness.

I am thankful to Michael Rinella, Diane Ganeles, and the staff at SUNY Press, not only for their editorial competence, good-humored attitude, and enthusiastic backing of this volume but also for their constant support of the SUNY Series in Contemporary Italian Philosophy in which this book appears.

I wish to thank the anonymous reviewers who took time to read the initial version of the manuscript thoroughly and carefully and who offered important insights to help me make the volume a better work.

And last but not least, I extend my sincerest and deepest appreciation and thanks to the contributors of this volume for their prompt responsiveness, ongoing collaboration, and unending patience—even during extremely demanding and challenging times. Without them and their thinking, there would be no volume, the intersections of various aspects of life and death, sickness and health, care and responsibility would be less explored, and the rethinking of forms of life more aligned with the precarious times of our existence would remain less possible. Their thinking has been the thread that has let some philosophical life continue.

On April 1, 2022 Italy lifted the state of emergency due to the pandemic. The virus has not disappeared, the pandemic is not over, but the medical emergency seems to have ended. What has not ended though is our need to rethink the meaning of life in light of the experience we have undergone.

Silvia Benso
Scottsville, NY, April 2022

Epidemics, Precariousness, and Vulnerability

Introductory Remarks toward a Rethinking of Life

Silvia Benso

"Ci si abbraccia per ritrovarsi interi."
—Alda Merini[1]

Thinking within Precarity

There is no denying that the time we have recently inhabited has been—and will most likely be remembered as—a time of heightened instability, uncertainty, and general sense of disorientation. Everything has seemed pervaded by a precarity that has manifested itself at various levels, from health to politics to economics to family ties, jobs, social relations, and institutions. To what end is also somewhat (still) uncertain.

This volume gathers fourteen contributions written by Italian philosophers within the context of the specific form of contemporary precarity that has suddenly surrounded us in conjunction with the Covid-19 epidemic. Due to the epidemiological development of the disease, it was when it first reached Italy that the epidemic's impact and shocking effects began to escalate to the global level. Strung together by the pandemic, the chapters gathered in the collection vary greatly in terms of approach, content, style, inspiration, background, provenance, and the institutional affiliation of their authors. Some of the contributors are well renowned, long-established philosophical figures in the Italian academia, whereas others are junior thinkers with very active records of research, scholarship, and publications. Various stages of life—philosophical, professional, existential, and personal among others—are thus represented in the volume.

The heterogeneity of the contributions is fluidly yet solidly and richly held together by two features. First is a discursive form that, while being academically scholarly and rigorous in style, is deliberately agile and stripped of indulgences in excessive philosophical technicisms, textual commentaries, and bibliographical references. This sobriety results in an elegant, incisive, and direct prose of great effect and immediacy—a captivating, compelling, and at times moving narrative not difficult to relate to. Second, and more significant, is the candid, lucid, and explicit confrontation with a common theme of profound relevance carried out in conversations with an array of such diverse thinkers as Jünger, Sloterdijk, Hegel, Foucault, Agamben, Arendt, Esposito, Cavarero, Levinas, Sontag, Butler, Mbembe, Jankélévitch, Derrida, Preciado, Plato, Aristotle, and Merleau-Ponty, just to name a few.

Despite possible initial assumptions with respect to the likely content of the volume, the common theme of the collection is neither the 2020 pandemic per se nor the prolonged state of emergency that has resulted from such an epidemic outburst. Some Italian thinkers, most notably Giorgio Agamben, have hastily questioned the medically dictated restrictions imposed during the pandemic and have assimilated them to an oppressive state of exception by a biopolitical form of governance invested in the exaggeration, or even the invention, of the contagion.[2] The alleged goal of such a biopolitical move, which Agamben qualifies as "health terrorism," would be the deprivation of individuals of their personal rights and freedoms in the service of neoliberal, capitalistic, bioeconomic world forces of a despotic nature. References to biopolitical dispositives of governance as well as notions of contagion, disease, and the implications of the concrete ways (rules, ordinances, indecisions, failures) with which the Covid-19 pandemic has been managed certainly constitute the (more or less explicitly thematized) constant and, possibly, even inevitable background on which the chapters are situated. Yet the philosophical concern of the volume is oriented by an overall perspective that points *beyond* the pandemic—whether as a biopolitical or exquisitely biomedical event—toward a future that the present, with its epiphanies of precariousness, calls us to rethink and, possibly, reshape. Ultimately and jointly, the two elements—pandemic and precariousness—function, in this volume, as motivation, occasion, and framework or *cornice*, as we could say employing a term familiar to scholars of the *Decameron*, the masterpiece of Italian literature by Giovanni Boccaccio, which also unfolds in a time of epidemic.[3] The two circumstantial elements thus constitute simultaneously the context, subtext, and pretext within which to think or, better, to rethink that which is mostly affected by the pandemic yet does not end with it—that is, life.

By addressing life as its ultimate, shared theme, the volume touches therefore on one of, if not *the*, most characterizing features of human existence. In this sense, the volume is not at all rendered a merely occasional, opportunistic, or provisional work by the contingency of the coronavirus pandemic. On the contrary, its perspectives and interrogatives go well beyond the sociopolitical and medical contexts within which the chapters originate and are historically and geographically situated. The underlying conviction that emerges from the volume is that what is precarious is, in fact, not time—the time of pandemics we live in or any historical time—but life itself.

As stated above, life is, ultimately, the essential topic this book is about: life, living beings, the precariousness that is life itself, and the need—which possibly marks a radical change and even a transformational heresy within the current socioeconomic conceptual model—to rethink life, in a time of precarity (or, perhaps, in the precarity that the time of life is), as itself precarious. What will the implications of this be? How does the pandemic, what it represents and exposes—precariousness and, ultimately, vulnerability—call us to rethink a notion of life, and of living, that is capable of confronting and sustaining, even though not immediately defeating, the pandemic itself? How does an episode of morbidity affect a possibly fuller understanding of life or, even, the configuration of a fuller life? How can the pandemic, and the precariousness it exposes, be interpreted in terms that avoid nihilistic drifts as well as the reduction of life to the so-called bare life or naked existence? Can such a hermeneutic move be dared and sustained? And what would this require, and compel to, at the ethical, sociopolitical, and economic levels? As the gaze of the rethinking of life is stretched toward the future of a life that exceeds its current conditions, the volume is as much descriptive as it is deeply utopian insofar as it also presents political aspirations toward a different life and mode of collective living.

Italian Epidemiographies

The fact that life is marked by the radical precariousness of its exposure to a disease made more lethal with age; by a contingency that strikes unexpectedly, somewhat randomly, and even indiscriminately; and by a fundamental fragility that affects all human beings became painfully and unarguably clear to most, if not all, contemporary Italians at the emotional, experiential, and also practical levels—that is, beyond the abstractness of theoretical speculation and recognition—in the early months of 2020, as Lorenzo Bernini, Alessandro Bertinetto, and Alberto Martinengo among others vividly recount. In Italy, this was the time of the first lockdown and of ordinances such as the "*#iorestoacasa [#Istayathome]*" (March 10, 2020) and "*Chiudi Italia [Close Italy]*" (March 22, 2020) decrees. In a shocking and unprecedented way for contemporary people's experience, these ordinances by the government put a stop to all nonessential travel, gatherings, and activities. As mentioned above, Italy was the first Western and European country to be highly impacted—medically, politically, and psychologically—by the disaster that later became known as the coronavirus pandemic.[4]

Officially announced first in China as the cause of cases of "anomalous pneumonia" at the end of December 2019, the virus revealed its presence in Italy at the end of January 2020, when two Chinese tourists who had contracted the virus were hospitalized in one of Rome's main hospitals, the hospital for infectious diseases, Lazzaro Spallanzani. After the World Health Organization (WHO) proclaimed the global state of health emergency on January 30 due to the slow yet progressive spread of the infection outside of China, on February 11 the new sickness received its own name, soon to become sadly infamous: Covid-19—"Co-" and "vi-" to indicate the family of coronavirus, to which the virus belongs, "-d" to indicate (in English) the term "disease," and "19" to mark the year when the virus was detected. It was not until March 11, 2020, that the WHO elevated the health situation from the status of an epidemic to that of a pandemic. By that time, Italy had already been severely affected with respect to the number of cases. By that time, the virus too, like so many other aspects of contemporary life, had gone global—and no closing of points of entries, walls, or bans (against travel and travelers from specific countries) managed to protect against the spreading of the virus and, with it, its decentering, destabilizing effects on people's lives.

Epidemics as well as epidemiographists have abounded in the history of medicine and cultures even though previous infections may not have reached the classification of pandemics due to the absence of a globalized setting the way we have experienced it in our times. Within the Western world, already in its remote origins, the first book of Homer's *Iliad* begins with a description of the spreading of the plague among the Greeks; to them, the disease appears as vengeance, punishment, and even an expiation for an offense made against the god.[5] Later, Thucydides gives us an incomparable description of the Great Plague of Athens, the one that caused the death of perhaps the most charismatic Greek leader, Pericles. It is this account that, centuries later, inspires a similar description by the Roman poet Lucretius in book 6 of his *De Rerum Natura*. The scenes and actions of Sophocles' tragedy, *Oedipus Rex*, are also staged on the background of the curse of the plague ravaging Thebes, which Oedipus' search for a culprit is supposed to remedy until his final cry of both pain and recognition that the plague is due to nothing else except himself. Chronicles of the plague, which at times takes up the role of metaphor for a more general sociopolitical condition of spiritual or moral corruption and degeneration, appear in texts by authors of various geographical as well as historical belonging such as, still within Western literature, Daniel Defoe (*Journal of the Plague Year*), Edgar Allan Poe ("Shadow" and "The Masque of the Red Death"), Alexander Pushkin (*A Feast in Time of Plague*), and, probably best known to most philosophical readers, Albert Camus (*The Plague*).

In these and numerous other accounts, the disease is interpreted as originating from a variety of causes, invested with multiple ideological functions, and fulfilling an assortment of purposes within the economy of human existence—revenge on the side of the god(s), punishment, penitence and expiation, appeal to life, natural occurrence, utter meaninglessness, testing and unmasking of the true nature of the human being, annihilation of the sociopolitical reality as known or constructed, state of exception, epiphany of an endemic destiny of corruption and putrefaction, act of (divine or natural) providence, instrument of divine salvation, and so on. In many senses, through the ranges of responses and interpretations they originate, epidemics, symbolized in the idea of plague, open up the metaphysical question of the existence, nature, and role of the negative, as Rita Fulco highlights—a theme provocatively and masterfully explored in the 2012 volume *Metafisica della peste. Colpa e destino* [*Metaphysics of the Plague: Guilt and Fate*], by acclaimed Italian philosopher Sergio Givone.[6] Paraphrasing Paul Ricouer's famous statement, in his *Symbolism of Evil*, that "the symbol gives rise to thought," we could conclude that the plague too gives material to thought.

The hermeneutic frames of explanation and signification into which various narrative accounts insert epidemics are many—both in the past and in the present. Most literary accounts also provide a *theoria*, in the Greek sense of overview and representation, of anthropological and sociological reactions and responses to the disease—whether such reactions are a matter of ideological positions, behaviors, or emotions. Constant throughout the ages, these reactions and responses are not absent from our times either. A theater of human types is thus put on display in the various narratives—from negationists to alarmists, conspiracy theorists, opportunists, self-proclaimed scientists, indifferent, resigned, concerned, philanthropist, scared, combative, socialites, segregationists, isolationists, even fanatics uplifted by what is perceived as a test (of one's faith, courage, humanity, survival, and so on). Plagues—as well as the language used to describe such events, as Alberto Martinengo points out—become metaphors for so much more that occurs in life. They become some kind of litmus test for one's conditions of existence, for one's attitude and response toward life and what or who is encountered in it. And yet, as Olivia Guaraldo reminds us, there is a serious danger in the overmetaphorization of diseases: namely, the risk of erasing the fundamentally embodied nature of life and its experience, including the attitudes of the living, whose being alive depends on acts of embodied (individual and, even more, collective) sustenance, responsibility, and care.

Illustrative in this matter is, to remain within the realm of Italian literature and to the purpose of disclosing the metaphorical role played by the plague in terms of a representation of the variety of embodied human reactions, the description provided by Boccaccio with respect to the 1348 plague that ravaged through Florence as well as the rest of Europe. It will not be surprising that Boccaccio's account perfectly anticipates the contemporary attitudes in their gamut from initial shock to pandemic fatigue. Boccaccio begins his *Decameron* by retracing the origin of the epidemics in the East, highlighting the uselessness of all medical and social measures of mitigation and containment, describing the symptoms in those affected by the contagion and its transmission by some who bear no sign of it, noticing the leap from animals to human beings and vice versa, and remarking on the self-induced social and physical distancing to which most individuals resort in the hope of preserving their personal health. Following that, Boccaccio offers a few paragraphs that focus on the relinquishment or abandonment, on the side of the Florentines affected by the disease, of all previous standards and habits—of moral decency, of social norms and customs, of civic respect, of natural bonds and practices—which end up being brought to an extreme, whether by surplus or by deficiency. Epidemics bring about a situation of interruption, Boccaccio seems to indicate—human beings feel suspended, held on the verge of an abyss where everything is possible; and their customary, embodied habits, whether natural or conventional, are also suspended. The time of epidemics is a time of suspension, of awaiting where one does not know what one awaits—perhaps, one simply awaits the end, either of oneself or of the epidemic. That is, one awaits the suspension of the state of suspension. One awaits the time when one's embodiment returns to being an occasion for physical proximity, close bodily contacts, and embodied celebration.

As is the case in much of Europe, the Italian landscape is dotted with artistic memories that stand, often solitary in their monumentality, as embodied and collective markers of the passage of previous epidemics. Churches, chapels, fountains, columns, hospitals, paintings, and other products of creative expression were erected either to rejoice at the end of a contagion or to invoke its quick and forgiving passing. In addition to numerous chapels devoted to San Rocco (the saint protector from the plague), creativity in the times of plague is to be credited for famous artistic masterpieces such as the Church of Santissimo Redentore and the Basilica of Santa Maria della Salute in Venice, the Obelisk of San Domenico in Naples, the Church of Santa Maria in Campitelli in Rome, the Croce della Peste in Rho (near Milan), or the Pala della Peste by Guido Reni in Bologna, just to name a few. The epidemic origin of many such legacies had, however, faded in the Italian cultural memory as these artistic creations—sanitized of their origin and admired for their artistic splendor—became incorporated into the uplifting landscape of beautiful creative works from the past, with which they assimilated. At the onset of the 2020 pandemic, all this changes, and the landscape becomes a painful reminiscence of past epidemic outbreaks, almost like skin butchered by marks left by a disfiguring infection. At the same time, natural life continues its course, indifferent, oblivious, even strengthened, emboldened, renewed by the sudden absence of most human inhabitants, as if the pandemic might be the herald of a possible environmental redemption—dolphins are even sighted swimming in Venice's Canal Grande, whose usually murky waters have transformed into "water crystal clear enough to see fish swimming below."[7]

The Italian experience of the Covid-19 pandemic is filtered through two previous accounts of plague epidemics. Even though unthematized and hardly named in the chapters collected in this volume, these past contagions have sedimented in the Italian unconscious and powerfully and vividly resonate within the Italian collective imaginary while Italy passes through the twenty-first century-strain of the disease.[8] The chronicles of two past contagions occupy, in fact, a prominent place in two major works in Italian literature, and generations of Italian students have familiarized themselves with such texts, internalizing them to a great extent as they constitute mandatory readings during the impressionable years of everyone's high school education.

The first of such epidemics is the already-mentioned 1348 plague (the infamous Black Plague), which a group of ten wealthy Florentine youths (seven women and three men) attempt to escape, as the wealthy have often done and keep doing, by retreating to an idyllic farmhouse in the hills around Florence. To entertain themselves during the time of segregation, each person will tell the others a story, for ten days, thus narrating the one hundred novels that constitute the content of Boccaccio's *Decameron*.

Through literary fiction, one of the issues, among many, that Boccaccio's work brings immediately to the fore is the socioeconomic privileges and injustices of all epidemics and the related problems of the accessibility of the health system and the universal right to medical care—questions certainly pressing in the neoliberal, privatized health systems that have eroded the traditionally public nature of the Italian medical care structure.

The second famous epidemic is, for Italians, the 1630 plague that is incorporated in Alessandro Manzoni's *I Promessi sposi* [*The Betrothed*], whose account is based on original historical documents and reports such as a "*Storia della peste del 1630* [History of the 1630 Plague]" by Giuseppe Ripamonti, the *Ragguaglio* [*Report*] by Alessandro Tadino (a doctor and officer in the Tribunale di Sanità, the public health department) as well as various *grida*, the public health ordinances by the Milan government.[9] The novel is some sort of romantic tale in which love, lust, compassion, power relations, political denunciation of ill-governance, injustices and abuses, aspirations to political freedom, trust in the providential vision of history, and enlightenment ideals of rationality, planning, and good governance coexist. A major topic brought to the fore by Manzoni's account of the plague is the general difficulty in recognizing epidemics and the overall unpreparedness and disorganization of political governments and medical authorities in managing the spreading of infections.

The two epidemiographies provided by Boccaccio and Manzoni differ greatly in terms of the role of the epidemics within the narrative discourse that unfolds around them. Yet both accounts agree in terms of the general sense of precariousness that the plague spreads together with the contagion—in terms of the uncertainty in recognizing the disease, the indecision in devising and implementing measures of mitigation and containment, the confusion of ordinances and decrees, the ineffectiveness of the measures taken, the subversion of standard norms and behaviors, the upending of previous and future plans, the sense of fear and suspiciousness toward everything and everyone, the flimsiness of judgment that turns everyone into an expert and true experts into suspects, and the suspension of the overall customary practices of life. The plague (the infection) becomes a pestilence (a way of being and living).

Precarity and Life

One could argue, of course, that precariousness, the feature that epidemics highlight to a perhaps unprecedented degree, is a condition of human existence. Few are the elements of certainty, in human life—that we are born, that we are going to die, and a few other occurrences that Western philosophical ambition has tried to identify in what have been at times called transcendental conditions of existence or, more prosaically, facts of life. Ultimately, however, even the greatest certainty—death, considered so certain as to become the defining trait of the essence of human beings, characterized therefore as mortals—is truly a matter of deep uncertainty, perhaps the highest symbol of the overall precariousness that enfolds human existence. There is no way to ascertain ahead of time when and, moreover, how we are going to die, whether death is a blessing, a punishment, or nothing at all, how life after birth is going to unfold, and so on. Even with respect to some few alleged certainties then, there is no assurance, firmness, or security. Uncertainty reigns sovereign, one could say, and, with it, the precariousness of human life—a precarity that renders human existence fragile, unwarranted, unexpected, vulnerable and that, ultimately (and nevertheless), is also the source of perennial surprise, unlimited openness, and the wonder that, for the Greeks, gives birth to philosophy.

In its morbidity, certainly the epidemic raises questions of death and mortality, as Elia Zaru's considerations on necropolitics remind us. As various other chapters in the volume point out though (for example, Luca Illetterati's), precariousness is not necessarily tied to death and mortality. Precarity is rather connected to humanity and its life conditions. We undergo conditions of precarity well before we die. We are precarious because we are alive. That is what the epidemic brings to the fore. It is not by coincidence that, for the ancient Greek thinkers—Heraclitus, Plato, Aristotle, but also later thinkers such as Epicurus and even Epictetus—balance, that is, lack of precarity, the stability that is brought about by the harmony of life conditions, whether anthropological or cosmic, was considered a divine feature, a godly affair, which for humans translates into a metaphysical as well as an ethical-political aspiration or ideal, often equated to health, well-being, and happiness. As the ancient thinkers promptly acknowledge though, only the gods (or perhaps not even them, as Illetterati provocatively suggests) can be truly happy—complete, satisfied, without needs, lacks, wants, or even desires. Can a human life, marked by precarity, be full, complete, and happy? What does it mean to live a full life under the sign of precarity?

It is not necessary to be versed in reading Heidegger and his reflections on Greek *techne* and the *Gestell* to acknowledge that the dream of modern science and technology, at least from Bacon and possibly even before, has been precisely that of somehow trying to mitigate, to rein in uncertainties, precariousness, and unpredictability. As Luisa Bonesio poignantly hints in some passages of her chapter, the desired mastery is sought by exploring and establishing patterns of behavior through statistical analyses, by projecting such patterns into the future through computational modeling, and, ultimately, by devising mechanisms of control and even manipulation of such projected models whose predictability is presented as, almost, certain—or, at least, as the most probable.

The dream is built on friable grounds, though, and undergoes repeated attacks whose memory of defeats is often obliterated (or conveniently overlooked). The loss of historical memory, at (most?) times more ideological than accidental, fuels the recurrent delusion of constant progress—itself a feature of the modern conception of history—whereas what we may have is, more appropriately and as early eighteenth-century Italian thinker Giambattista Vico reminds us, repeats, returns, steps forward accompanied by various steps backward, pauses, cycles, detours, blocks, and arrests. The struggle to eliminate precariousness seems endless because it is, most likely, impossible. Then precariousness is revealed as the marker of human existence, especially when understood in the sense of vulnerability (as for Guaraldo) or exposure to an excessiveness, an exceedance that constitutes life while life itself cannot contain it (as for Roberto Mancini, Claudia Baracchi, and Ugo Perone).

To expose, in our times, the fundamental exceedance of life to itself—its vulnerability to something that is itself living—on some indefinite day and through vectors that, despite all contact tracing, are hard to identify conclusively, a novel, invisible, miniscule, undetectable virus enters our vital universe. Its devastating effects progressively suspend those fragile mechanisms we had created to govern the uncertain. Ironically, the arrival of that virus too had been predictable and predicted—but the dream of control, turned into the delusion of omnipotence, made us blind, and we ignored the signals. As we slowly discovered (and keep discovering despite our difficulties to reckon with this and our repeated, and regularly frustrated, attempts at renewed investigations), the day and first vector of the viral entry—its origin—remain for the most part unspecified, likely unspecifiable, and possibly not unique as is perhaps the case for all origins, which may very well be better understood as plural rather than singular. Does the virus call then, as Perone asks, for a different metaphysics of the origins, for a different metaphysics altogether? Or is life simply a matter of biopolitics and of its counterpart, necropolitics? Is biopolitics, which has become one of the currently dominant philosophical paradigms to address life, sufficient to capture the richness of the phenomenon of life, especially of life marked by a precariousness the virus certainly exposed but does not create?[10]

The virus has a highfalutin name—coronavirus, the virus with a crown. In this, it is like death, which, in medieval iconography, was also often portrayed wearing a crown. The most deadly form of contagion our history has possibly recorded, the Black Plague of 1348, is also known as the Black Death, thus establishing a line of continuity between contagion, death, and sovereignty. Who or what is sovereign, though? Is it death, in its being the universal and therefore democratic Grim Reaper? As Zaru reminds us, we all die, but not everyone dies benefitting from the same privileges of care and support. Or is the virus sovereign, whose level of infectiousness is certainly somewhat uniformly high but whose morbidity, whose ability to bring death, varies dramatically among the population based, at least partly, on various demographics, thereby creating novel discriminations and exposing and reinforcing customary ones, as Bernini observes? Certainly, this novel virus becomes sovereign in terms of dictating our conditions of life, as the title of a well-timed and fortunate book by Italian philosopher Donatella Di Cesare, *Il virus sovrano*, appropriately acknowledges.[11] The virus becomes the sovereign not only with respect to our scientific and technological projects, whose plans of containment miserably collapse while the parallel push to find a vaccine (and a cure) grows commensurately, but also and moreover in relation to our daily lives with their complexities and stratification (political, economic, legal, educational, artistic, and medical to name a few), which the virus brings to a halt.

With a vitalism and a vitality, with a strength of life (its own life), that are impressive in their being both evident (the virus affects millions) and sly (it affects us in ways, organs, and through channels and variants that are still unmapped), the coronavirus forces us to rethink our conceptual structures, our modes of existence and of what, with some pansemantic arrogance, we have gotten used to consider as life (whereas it is only, ultimately, the life of the human being). All of a sudden, we, Western thinkers for the most part heirs of the legacy of the Enlightenment—even when critical of it—and its ideals of clarity, transparency, rationality, and scientificity; we, who considered ourselves invincible because, thanks to science, we have conquered unimaginable spaces (from the Moon to Mars to the genetic modification of organisms); we, whose medical knowledge has defeated and, at times, completely eradicated deadly diseases like smallpox, hepatitis C, and even AIDS; we, whom the economic capitalistic and neoliberal system has convinced that at the center is always us or, rather, me, with my caprices advertised as primary needs, with my desires, in truth fabricated by the market economy, upheld as assertions of freedom and rights; we, perennially caught between Prometheus and Sisyphus; we, the self-proclaimed masters of the universe have found ourselves displaced, unprepared, fearful, confused, and, what is most remarkable, vulnerable—an observation that becomes the starting point or the necessary conclusion of many of the chapters in the volume.

We have discovered that the invisible—that little virus that is both nowhere and everywhere—is more powerful than the visible. Its strength has brought the entire world to its knees. It does not cut deals to anyone, it upends, it subverts our plans, gestures, and institutions while at the same time it exposes the injustices of our times (which are, in a way, the injustices of many, when not of all known epochs so far) thereby, once again, challenging our established notions of justice. Only the ancient and revered notion of truth, now somewhat considered obsolete, may have had a perhaps equally revelatory power. Life has come to a halt—or must be made to come to a halt through various, repeated political interventions known as "lockdowns"—because of the power of the virus, which either has imposed an end to the physical existence of many people or has forced us to a self-imposed suspension of our cohabitation and shared activities in the hope of stopping the vitalistic spreading of the virus by enforcing rules of physical social distancing. In ways and at levels that are too many to list, we have been exposed to, reminded of, and confronted with the precariousness of our existences—of our lives. "Stay at home," "Shelter in place" have been the recurrent invitations that have resounded around the globe. What about those who do not have a home or a shelter, though? Or for whom home is not a safe shelter? Or for whom staying at home is not a viable option (essential workers, medical personnel, and so on)? The precarity of life is internally multiplied.

Life—what is it? Western thought, of Platonic descent (or, at least, influenced by a certain Platonist interpretation that may not entirely correspond to what may emerge from a close reading of Plato's dialogues), has presumed that it could encapsulate the meaning of things within univocal concepts—fixed, eternal, and unrelated, easier to manipulate, control, and administer because they are contained within well-defined boundaries that map reality according to oppositions and dualisms marking delimitations as well as exclusions. Among such long-standing dualisms are beginning and end, inside and outside, friend and enemy, peace and war, truth and falsehood, mind and body, good and bad, up and down, vertical and horizontal, subject and object, culture and nature, male and female, self and other—and these are only a few. The task of thinking—a task that, as a matter of fact, is the outcome of a somewhat presumptuous and arrogant self-imposition—has thus become the identification of such concepts, their isolation, and the clarification of their meaning conceived, at the same time, as both originary and final, as primal cause and goal. As Perone adroitly observes, the so-called forms or essences were therefore conceived with the goal of providing us with an insight into the core of reality.

The notion of life too has been subjected to such schematism and, for a long time, philosophy has searched for its essential meaning and for the essential meaning of the subject, the human self that has arrogantly situated itself at the heart (or rather, at the apex) of life. Thus, through a complex and articulated process that unfolds across over two millennia of intellectual and cultural history, life—by which is generally meant human life, and here the anthropocentrism of this entire millenary project is disclosed—was for the most part made to coincide with the time of corporeal existence or earthly occupancy of the human subject, and *zoe* was opposed to *bios* (with limitations Alessandra Cislaghi and Claudia Baracchi explore). The time of life-*bios* has then been seen as delimited by two other notions that act as boundaries and limits, namely, birth and death. As if life began with birth and ended with death, which therefore would be the opposite of life.

This conviction neglects, dismisses, or outright denies, however, that death is not the opposite of life (for some, including Socrates, death is rather the entry into real life) but rather, if anything, the opposite of birth. It is birth and death that constitute the two opposite limits of existence as we know of it, as Mancini notes. Life is, in itself, much more complex and comprises birth as well as death, health as well as illness, joy as well as despair, laughter as well as tears. Life is ambiguity, multiplicity, plurality of forms and perspectives that at times follow one another, at times coexist, at times intertwine in inextricable plots, at times even fight with one another, and, in all cases, refer to some other, to a relationality that is foundational of life. The fundamental ambiguity and interrelationality constitute the substrate of our tenuous attempts at disentangling some possible threads we may follow: the search for joy, the escape from pain, the consolation that strives toward holding everything together (consolation derives from the Latin *cum*, together and *solus*, the whole) without anything getting lost. Life is complexity, complicity, interrelatedness, and relationality. Its human subject, the human self that tries to find its way in the bundle of relations cannot be declined, as the modern, (neo)liberal, individualist tradition has taught, in its self-proclaimed isolation—I, me, mine, to me, for me—but must rather be conjugated, that is, inclined and stretched in various directions that pull it toward others and reveal thereby its exposure, its vulnerability, and its exceedance.

It is to the theme of vulnerability that most of the chapters in the volume refer in the effort to rethink life in the aftermath of the pandemic, as if vulnerability and exposure to the other were the pandemic's greatest truth, that which it reveals, to which it recalls and even compels. Vulnerability is the notion that the authors stubbornly, courageously, impressively refuse to overcome, sidestep, or even overlook; that to which they relentlessly return; that which they attentively attend to from their geographical, institutional, and experiential positions across Italy—from Turin to Trieste passing through Pavia, Verona, and Padua; from Milan to Messina traversing Pisa, Macerata, and Salerno. In the various chapters, vulnerability gets to be articulated in a series of concepts that underlie, accompany, and expand such a notion once it is recognized as a fundamental marker of life. Thus, the discourse moves to attention to the body and to the formulation of an embodied subjectivity; to the concept of relationality and its anthropological as well as ethical and socio-political ramifications; to the notions of responsibility and care as fundamental correlates of a vulnerable, relational, and embodied subjectivity; to the need to stretch temporal considerations to include not purely the present in its immediacy but also the future (ours, our children, future generations, the world) as well as the past (ours, our elderly, history); to the call for social and environmental justice as ways to correspond to a renewed subjectivity and understanding of life; to the need to understand the constitutive elements of human life in terms that go beyond and yet are fundamental (such as the environment) to what such a human life would be; ultimately, to the demand, which comes from life itself, to conceive of life in terms that exceed what life shows itself being.

This Volume: An Overview

This volume has been organized in three parts. Part One, "Confronting Disaster," is the most explicitly concerned with the coronavirus pandemic. Far from being merely expository though, it offers a philosophical contextualization of the disease in terms of theoretical considerations of both its place within the horizon of modern technology and its impact on various practices of daily life regarded as entryways into broader speculative reflections. The first chapter in this part is by Luisa Bonesio, a scholar of aesthetics, landscapes and the environment, and geophilosophy. In "Cassandra's Details: Coronavirus and the Course of Globalization," Bonesio analyzes the epochal relevance of three crucial events in technological modernity, namely, the sinking of the *Titanic*, the attack on the Twin Towers, and the coronavirus pandemic, which she philosophically interprets as prophetically revelatory of the violence as well as the precarity of Western techno-economic globalization. As is the case for the Greek figure, Cassandra, even though correct in their predictions, such prophecies nevertheless go unheard, resisted with incredulity and feelings of powerlessness.

The next chapter, "Improvising Self-Expression in the Time of a Contingency that Has Eliminated Contingency," is by Alessandro Bertinetto, a scholar trained in German Idealism and hermeneutics with research interests in aesthetics, philosophy of art and music, and image theory. Moving from an account of his personal musical experiences during the pandemic, Bertinetto offers a reflection on the implications of musical expression and rhythm for affective and intersubjective life and focuses on the connection between improvisation as an artistic practice and improvisation as a central feature of human life. In a situation like the one imposed on many by the Covid-19 epidemics—a situation that can be rightly considered as a deprivation of spaces of free interaction with the contingencies of life—human beings rely on their ability to invent the rules of their practices, including expressive practice, through their performances: an ability that nourishes artistic creativity, such as the "music from the balconies" during the early lockdown in Italy.

The personal perspective, which finds the author segregated in a condition of physical isolation associating all Italians during the harshest months of the lockdown, is the point of entry also for the following chapter by Lorenzo Bernini, a major voice in the Italian gender and queer debate with interests ranging from classical political thought to psychoanalysis to contemporary theories of radical democracy, feminist philosophies, and critical race theories. In "Out of the Choir: Bodies Inclined on the Playboy," following an ironical yet poignant autobiographic opening, Bernini analyzes the pandemic as a reagent that enables a better observation of the biopolitical and bioeconomic dispositives that nourish and exploit hierarchies and inequalities having to do with class, age, gender, and race. Bernini privileges the lens of gender and sexuality as an apt way to focus the philosophical-political question of subjectivity emerging from the pandemic. With compelling clarity, Bernini highlights the role of the pandemic in exposing the (male) "hallucination" of "invulnerability" and points out the implications for bodies in "neoliberal technical-patriarchal societies."

Part One concludes with a chapter by Alberto Martinengo, a scholar in the hermeneutic tradition with interests for themes in the philosophy of metaphors. In "Metaphor as Illness? Life, War, and Linguistic *Pharmakon*," Martinengo focuses on the militarized metaphor of the disease as enemy and its fight as war—metaphors that have pervaded the narrative on the Covid-19 pandemic—and highlights some examples of the use of such a metaphor within political rhetoric. Martinengo wonders about the possibility of speaking of disease outside some recourse to linguistic figures. Explicitly engaging Susan Sontag's metaphors of cancer, he proposes a philosophical-political reconsideration of the metaphor of sickness.

Part Two, "Vulnerability, Care, and Responsibility," deepens the focus of analysis introduced by the previous chapters by considering how the pandemic calls for a reconceptualization of subjectivity understood in the context of embodiment, relationality, vulnerability of embodied life, care of the body, responsibility, and body politics. Metaphoric applications to the notions of life, death, and illness, already a theme in Martinengo's chapter, are a critical concern also for Olivia Guaraldo, a political theorist who, after studying the thought of Hannah Arendt, works on investigating the theoretical and political relations between Italian feminist philosophy and Anglo-American gender theory. In "'The Lungs that We All Are': Rethinking Life in the Times of a Pandemic," Guaraldo warns against the political and moral dangers of the use of metaphors to address life, death, and illness, and focuses instead on a consideration of life in its material and embodied form for which vulnerability becomes a fundamental feature of the human—a feature that can hardly be expressed by metaphors. The experience of Covid-19 reveals in fact that there is no "enemy" that can be clearly identified, and we are all equally vulnerable (even though we are not equal). The pandemic thus offers an unprecedented occasion to reflect in extremely concrete terms on the concept of shared vulnerability and on care as a "viewpoint," a notion that Guaraldo explores at length as an alternative to the state's militarized discourse in its response to the pandemic.

The theme of the vulnerability of the body and its care is continued in the following chapter by Elia Zaru, whose research focuses on the crisis of modernity in contemporary debates. In "Necropolitics, Care, and the Common," Zaru reflects on the concept of necropolitics understood as the power over death exercised, within the current pandemic, by deciding which lives are worth saving and which are not. Against neoliberal necropolitics, Zaru discusses the idea of a "biopolitics from below" centered on the notions of vulnerability, care, and the common, which he considers as a possible solution to restore dignity to all lives injured by the ongoing search for profit that is proper to neoliberal economies and their biopolitical practices.

The reflection on the vulnerability of human existence continues with a chapter by Luca Illetterati, whose primary research interests include German Idealism, especially Hegel, a philosophical understanding of nature, and the philosophy of translation. In "Lacking Beings," Illetterati argues that for living beings, being is living—that is, an action, a dynamics in which the living being consummates itself in order to continue being itself. Need and lack belong to life and cannot be understood as defective moments whose overcoming would restore life to some prior positivity or future fulfillment. Ultimately, Illetterati claims, life is not different from the negativity that manifests itself in the need and lack interwoven with life's way of being. Negativity is one and the same with life and a mark of life's powerful fragility.

The theme of fragility underlies also the following chapter by Caterina Resta, whose work focuses on contemporary continental philosophy and, more specifically, on questions of the deconstruction of the subject, the notion of the human, technology and nihilism, and geophilosophy (especially in the context of globalization, the Mediterranean, and Europe). In "Vulnerable Existences," after exploring how the twentieth-century search for "true life" and "the new human being" mutates into the necropolitics of the two world wars, Resta turns to a characterization of the contemporary human being as interdependent and vulnerable and argues for an assumption of responsibility toward one's vulnerability as the foundation to address meaningfully what Aristotle considered as the main task of politics, namely, living well together.

An explicit confrontation with the notion of responsibility preoccupies Rita Fulco, whose research interest centers on the theoretical, ethical, political, and religious entailments of the twentieth century with specific attention to the philosophies of Simone Weil, Emmanuel Levinas, and Italian theologian Sergio Quinzio. In "Life and Useless Suffering: Responsibility for Others and the Impossible Theodicy," Fulco begins with a phenomenological analysis of suffering that points to the impossibility of justifying it in the name of any theodicy, no matter how it may be configured. Focusing on the notions of neighbor and stranger, Fulco identifies vulnerability as the primal feature of the humanity of the human and indicates the call to collective responsibility as the most appropriate way to address the care for suffering and vulnerability at a level that intersects life and political institutions.

Life and its possible meanings and possibilities, introduced at several points in the previous chapters under the rubrics of vulnerability, responsibility, and care, are the themes that gain center stage in Part Three, "Rethinking Life." In not always conspicuous or explicitly declared ways, this part also offers critiques and alternatives to biopolitical conceptions of life focused on bare or naked life (*nuda vita*) as well as to possible nihilistic drifts in front of the disaster. Part Three opens with a chapter by Alessandra Cislaghi, a scholar educated in the Italian hermeneutic tradition of Luigi Pareyson and whose research interests span from philosophy and theology to the question of the human, the notion of the self and embodied subjectivity, and the hermeneutics of myths. In "Greek Zèn: Living Starting from the Origin," through an analysis of Greek philosophical and theological sources on the notion of life, Cislaghi points to the idea of life as an inexhaustible source, spring, and origin that allows for a regeneration of vital energy (*zoe*) via a second birth into individual existence (*bios*). A reading of the Edenic myth aimed at highlighting multiple levels and interpretations of the state of nature enables Cislaghi to argue against Agamben's concept of "bare life" and in favor of the recognition of the value of the fullness of living.

The topic of life is explored further by Enrica Lisciani-Petrini, whose scholarly interest centers on the intertwining of philosophy, politics, the humanities, and artistic movements in view of developing a philosophy of everyday life. In "Life and the 'Black Swan,'" Lisciani-Petrini intersects the precarity of embodied life in its concrete and organic dimensions with the theme of the existential finitude of life. The aim is to delineate a perspective wherein living beings are no longer seen in light of a delusional eternity but rather in the backlight of an unavoidable precariousness that makes them, with an expression from Jankélévitch, ever more "precious."

The notion of the finitude of the human condition is also a major concern of the chapter by Roberto Mancini, whose research interests include the dialogical theory of truth, the anthropology of human rights, the ethics of common good, and the development of a new economic model. In "What Finitude Does Not Say: Rethinking Life beyond Nihilism," Mancini criticizes the nihilistic ground of various philosophies of finitude that in different ways oppose life to particular living beings as they regard death as an experience that annihilates the living. Mancini advocates instead for a conception of life that carries within itself the aspiration to a form of harmony or fulfillment that does not coincide with death or the end but instead is linked to an immemorial past as well as to an unexpected future, thus opening the horizon toward dimensions that go beyond the particular individual human being.

The theme of precariousness as the underlying condition of life that, far from constraining life, opens it to dimensions of excess and the beyond is addressed in the chapter by Claudia Baracchi, a scholar of ancient philosophy whose research interests focus on ethics and the question of nature; philosophy in relation to myth, poetry, and theater; and Asian (especially Indo-Vedic) traditions. In "Writing Life: Biography, Autobiography, and the Remainder," Baracchi explores the implications of the writing of life, especially in the mode of (auto)biography, with the aim of showing the shortcomings of the biopolitical paradigm and its constitutive dichotomies. Precisely because (auto)biographical narrations are incapable of grasping elusive life, because the "documents of life" are ultimately destined to document their own finitude and remain open onto life's excess, they may begin to disclose, Baracchi argues, that the animal does not fall outside political life but rather grounds it, that *bios* is not without *zoe*, that ethics is not without bodies, and that the "I" is not without "we," even as nameless multitude.

The theme of the excess and exceedance of life over all possible descriptions (biopolitical as well as phenomenological or of other kinds) continues in the last chapter of Part Three—which is also the conclusive chapter in the volume—by Ugo Perone, whose philosophical research has been devoted to subjectivity, time, memory, feelings, and the relation between philosophy and religion. In "With the Finitude of Life beyond the Phenomenon: Phenomenology, Hermeneutics, and a Metaphysics of the Finite," Perone phenomenologically underscores the double feature of finite life, that is, both its consistency and its fragility due to the essential connection with the no-longer and the not-yet or nonbeing. This is a dimension that escapes phenomenology and can only be accessed through hermeneutic reason, which is open to the exceedance of reality and the beyond. Perone argues for a renewed metaphysics that can be compatible with modernity while remaining capable of understanding finite life in its transcending elements.

Conclusion

As the reflections collected in this volume thematize, the pandemic demonstrates and compels to acknowledging that life is precarious, vulnerable, and fragile. The chapters also underscore, however, that life is mostly or irremediably precarious when it is lived not as togetherness (which is possible even at a distance) but as isolation (which is different from solitude), when life is reduced to naked existence in the forgetfulness of its dimensions of exceedance toward alterity, the others, and the beyond. The consistency and solidity of life—which are not its fixity or stability—come from the recognition of its relationality, interconnectedness, interdependence, and, ultimately, solidarity (which, in the volume, is evoked through the notions of collective responsibility and communal care) that binds the parts into a whole—neither a homogeneous (or integrated) nor a fragmented (or disjoint) whole but rather something more similar to a choir made of unique, recognizable voices whose singing to life soars in the form of chorales and collective hymns. These songs would be elevated in and as celebration of communal life, which means both life together and the togetherness of life. In this way, life could never be exhausted or exhaustible in one, single, and separate dimension but, rather, would always be open to some other and, therefore, precarious as for its (limited) power and yet powerful through its (precarious) collective extensiveness. In other words, it would be a life that is always in movement, in contact, affective and affected, flowing, living life, life that is alive and never rests, life that goes on and must go on—as we have heard repeatedly in the current times of precarity due to Covid-19—not alone but together, because life is greater than any of its life forms. Yet life needs each and all of them as they are what life itself is.

Notes

1. The meaning of this sentence by Merini oscillates between "We embrace each other to make ourselves [or one another] whole again," "We embrace to become whole," "We embrace each other to find ourselves [or one another] whole again," "We embrace to be made whole once again," and "We embrace each other to find out that we are still whole." That is, the semantic ambiguity and multiplicity points to the interrelatedness of self and other in the activity of making (or finding or confirming) ourselves (or oneself or each other) whole—a holistic act that happens only together and as the result of an activity (a making) that is also and simultaneously an acknowledgment and recognition (a finding, a confirmation).

2. See Giorgio Agamben, *A che punto siamo? L'epidemia come politica* (Macerata: Quodlibet, 2020) and *Quando la casa brucia* (Macerata: Giacometti & Antonello, 2020).

3. Giovanni Boccaccio, *Decameron*, trans. G. H. McWilliam (New York: Penguin, 2003).

4. On the disaster as a form of de-centering, see Maurice Blanchot, *The Writing of the Disaster*, trans. Ann Smock (Lincoln: University of Nebraska Press, 1995).

5. It should be noted that, in the past, the term "plague" was often generically used to denote epidemics that were in fact possibly due to other highly contagious and deadly diseases. Thus, based on the reported symptoms, the plague of Athens was, most likely, a typhus epidemic, whereas the so called Antonine plague was probably a measles or smallpox outbreak.

6. Sergio Givone, *Metafisica della peste* (Turin: Einaudi, 2012).

7. See https://abcnews.go.com/International/venice-canals-clear-fish-coronavirus-halts-tourism-city/story?id=69662690.

8. Whereas the epidemic Boccaccio described—as well as the one portrayed by Manzoni—was properly an instance of plague, which is caused by a bacterium (the bacterium *Yersinia pestis*), the coronavirus pandemic cannot be considered a form of plague as it is caused by a virus instead.

9. Alessandro Manzoni, *I Promessi Sposi*, trans. Brice Penman (New York: Penguin, 1983). The 1630 plague afflicts Milan on the heels of the descent into the Duchy of Milan, then under Spanish domination, of the army of the German landsknechts on the way to help militarily solve the political question of the dynastic succession of the Duchy of Mantua.

10. Such a paradigm, which characterizes, for example, the so-called Italian Thought or Italian Theory, has currently become so prevalent that it has often but inappropriately been interpreted by some scholars as a marker capable of rep-

resenting the entirety of Italian philosophy—as if the whole could be exhausted in one of its parts.

11. Donatella Di Cesare, *Il virus sovrano: L'asfissia capitalistica* (Turin: Bollati Boringhieri, 2020).

Part One
Confronting Disaster

One

Cassandra's Details

Coronavirus and the Course of Globalization

Luisa Bonesio

Faced with the unexpected coronavirus pandemic, which has spread very rapidly and has affected the world on a planetary scale, the predominant trends of thought have instantly imploded while the mantras of world unification in the name of capital have turned to defensive positions or have been repeated in an increasingly unconvincing way. Within this context, a hermeneutics of some turning-point events of the twentieth century may be illuminating in order to understand the necessary thread that connects such occurrences in a catastrophic crescendo as well as offer an almost didactic explication of the unsustainability of the model of mundialization (*mondializzazione*) that has unfolded ever since the beginning of the twentieth century.

The symbolic events (*eventi-simbolo*) at the core of the hermeneutic reflection I propose here are the sinking of the *Titanic* (1912), the collapse of the Twin Towers (2001), and the coronavirus pandemic (2020). Like the details of a prediction by Cassandra—the Trojan priestess of Apollo cursed to utter accurate prophecies yet not to be believed—these three events appear as true cornerstones in an unconsciously self-destructive course pursued by the dominating cultural—but, truly, economic—model; that is, the model of Western globalism and its compensatory ideologies.

The intention of the considerations that follow is neither to advance nor to hope for future scenarios, but rather simply to take note of a movement in crescendo toward a point of no return. This course of development, whose point of no return might have already been crossed, is marked not by mere events but by a specific symbolism that recapitulates the details of all possible individual analyses and liquidates, at least for now, most of the political and social imaginaries (*immaginari*) advanced in the last decades.

The Power of the Elementary: Technology and the Titans

Ernst Jünger is perhaps the most visionary twentieth-century interpreter of modernity. In his 1951 *The Forest Passage* (*Der Waldgang*), he sketches an unsurpassed analysis of technological automatism understood as primer for the inevitability (*fatalità*) of disasters.[1] In automation, the liberation of human beings from fatigue and repetitiveness turns into cession of autonomy and freedom. The impersonal dangerousness of this abdication is displayed in the case of accidents, where the space for human autonomy and initiative is almost always drastically reduced. When it takes up the aspect of inevitability, as it happens in technological modernity, fear becomes terrifying, Jünger remarks. The well-known example that is analyzed in his text is the sinking of the *Titanic*, caused by collision with an iceberg. The *Titanic* was a luxurious transatlantic liner, an emblem of modern power; it carried, up to the ineludible catastrophe, a cosmopolitan, wealthy, and elegant society in a cruise around the world—sort of an anticipatory icon of other condominium ships, accurate and fatal reproductions of mass society, big numbers, and the desire to escape by finding always and again the same things. At the time of its happening, the sinking of the *Titanic* caused much emotional stirring. Yet, it neither marked the end of these kinds of activities, nor did it call into doubt the model of the world that had created it and for which it stood as symbol. The sinking was simply read as a mere accident of technology.

Those who had sufficient interpretative ability could have nevertheless fathomed the quite evident, ominous portent of that catastrophe, starting with the name that had been proudly and superstitiously given to a ship that was the supreme creation of technology. Many years later, with respect to the modern faith in the demiurgic power of technology—which is an exemplary expression of the nihilistic will to power initially underscored by Nietzsche—Jünger remarks that "in the end, the Titans are not sufficient as was demonstrated in augural form by the sinking against the iceberg of the ship that had been named after them. Very rarely does Cassandra deal with details in the same way as she did then."[2]

Technological human beings are idolatrous, though, and have de-divinized the world, turning it into a globe that can be dominated in all its corners; they do not raise questions from a point of view that remains external to their own ideologies. An instructive revelation of modernity's unlimited will to power within a world that has lost or, even better, has destroyed its religious and metaphysical points of reference was the ship's name, *Titanic*. Ever since its outset, the twentieth century, which is the century of iron and fire, of enormous destructions, of the rush to overcome all limits and level all forms of thought that do not adapt to the politically correct and to conforming globalization, had received a clear symbolic warning that nevertheless remained unheeded.

There is no reason to recall what the 1900s have brought, including global wars, genocides of populations, massacres of nature, consumerism, poverty, policies of global power and annihilation of cultures and civilizations, and homogenizations that have been imposed via bombs as well as glamour. Yet, the sinking of the *Titanic* already contained all elements of criticism and potential dissolution of that which would then unfold, escalate in power, and detail itself with related, increasing blindness concerning the catastrophic course imposed on the Earth and its inhabitants (including those living beings that have no active say in any of this).

This is not all that happened, though. The *Titanic* prolonged and reproduced itself, with abundance of details, in all big contemporary cruise ships. These democratic and cosmopolitan quarters currently have more reassuring and Disney-inspired names than their progenitor (*Celebrity Reflection, Carnival, Fantasia, Oasis of the Seas, Concordia, Royal Princess*, etc.); they navigate the seas and oceans of the world carrying multitudes of people from all parts and origins; they loyally (yet paradoxically, given that it should be leisure time) duplicate modalities, proximities, and alienations of the mass situations from which their guests would like to escape; and, in addition, they replicate lifestyles, views, and pictures of the world whose ability to match those repeatedly seen before departure is tested and verified during the cruises. It is a paradoxical and yet revelatory logic, in which the image of something functions as the standard to which the world has to conform. It is the world reduced to an image, as analyzed by a fundamental thinker of the twentieth century such as Martin Heidegger.

Now, with the coronavirus pandemic, these big cruise ships and, what is more, even airplanes have come to a halt. What, together with them, has come to a stop is the very ideology of traveling, of being continuously on the move, of never being anywhere. This ideology finds in the virtuality of "surfing" the internet its quintessential and deepest truth, namely, the vaporization (*vanificazione*) of the world, the annihilation of the Earth, of nature, and of cultures through their digital replacement, the portability of devices, hyper-reality, the instantaneousness in which everything has already been seen, everything is replaceable, ephemeral, interchangeable. Cruise ships too have suddenly become (or have revealed themselves to be) claustrophobic spaces of unwanted cohabitation, or they have become floating lazarettos rejected from all harbors. They have disclosed the profound truth of our time, that is, the impossibility of escaping the truth unless one recognizes it, fake sociality, and a superficial statelessness very similar to a generalized *Truman Show*.

In the abovementioned essay, Jünger also dwells on another aspect that fear can assume and then spread around in a world that is hyperconnected, dominated by techno-science, and feels self-deceptively safe. This other aspect is the contagion and the train of related manifestations and figures. Jünger writes:

> A man may join the realms of rigorous knowledge and ridicule earlier spirits who were so terrified by Gothic schemas and infernal imagery. Yet he will hardly suspect that he is caught in the same chains. The phantoms that test him will naturally conform to the style of knowledge, will appear as scientific facts. The old forest may have become a managed woodland, an economic factor; yet a lost child still strays in it. Now the world is a battlefield for armies of microbes; the apocalypse threatens as it always did, only now as the doing of physics. The old delusions continue to flourish in psychoses and neuroses. Even the man-eating ogre can be recognized again through his transparent cloak—and not only as exploiter and taskmaster in the bone mills of our times. More likely he will appear as a serologist, sitting among his instruments and retorts and pondering how to use human spleen or breastbone to produce marvelous new medicines.[3]

This is not all, though. Jünger prophetically notices how, in a Europe that is divided, humiliated by the catastrophe of World War II, where the American colonization of the collective imaginary and of the economy begins to appear, the very ideas of freedom, human dignity, and spirituality will undergo transformations, ideologizations, instrumentalizations, and persecutions such as those that find a disquieting and precise fictional anticipation in George Orwell's dystopian yet incredibly clairvoyant narrative. In a world that is dominated by the ideology of political correctness and humanitarianism, by an idea (of an abstractly Enlightenment nature) of humanity, of the emancipation of habits and customs—an ideology that is nevertheless fundamentally and necessarily uninterested with respect to the conditions of survival that are about to be set in place for oneself and the planet—Jünger foresees how, within such a world, besides the weapons of planetary destruction and the "accidents of technology," microbes (and thus the contagion), which are unperceived due to their infinitely small dimension, and medicalization will play an increasingly larger and more capillary role in our societies and their collective imaginary. A few years later, Ivan Illich too will argue in similar terms in his fundamental *Medical Nemesis: The Expropriation of Health*.[4] The reasons for such an increased role of microbes and medicalization have to do with the fact that morbidity (or the fear of it) will grow, thereby creating increasingly greater and more capillarily diffused dependencies and weaknesses. This constitutes a form of power that may terrorize or heal, make one live or let one die—the case is that of an all-pervasive biopolitics, in which anyone is an object and a dependent, an experimental ground void of transcendence. In some phases, biopolitics will be able to explicate its power openly—a power that only a minority will have the intellectual and spiritual instruments to understand in its deeper meaning.

What remains to be dealt with is the supporting background of all the considerations above. From a philosophical point of view, it is the materialistic immanentization through functional economic regimes that enables the sanitary short circuit of the unified world. From an environmental perspective, it is the *Titanic* blindness that subverts, perhaps irreversibly, the possibility of further human dwelling on the Earth. Appealing to the numerous works in this area, starting with the scientific predictions on the limits of growth and development by the Club of Rome (1972), has been useless. The fundamental studies by Serge Latouche have been marginalized and ignored.[5] The late pleas by Greta Thunberg have been unsuccessful, even when she symbolically puts on stage the very powerful (yet, perhaps, as matter of fact, naïve and ephemeral) image of the young girl who unarmed fights in the crusade for the awakening of the superpowers. Useless have been the religious appeals for a battle which, next to the establishment of good mass practices, would require a total change of paradigms. But the techno-economic powers have no intention of implementing such a change, in what Vandana Shiva has qualified as an age of violence and shallowness, which is the emanation of an abstract and uprooted mind.[6]

The coronavirus pandemic has displayed aspects, though, that might be capable of undermining the representation of the ineluctability of globalization as it is currently carried out, on the one hand, in economic ultraliberalism and the financialization of the world and, on the other, through the construction of narratives based on the extraordinary possibilities of global tourism, (chosen or imposed) emigration, the joyful homogenization of glamour, fashion, the ephemeral, consumerism, unawareness, and deresponsibilization. This is a concrete horizon in which the globalist model displays its falsity and unsustainability insofar as it does not take into account the main subject of this possible evolution, that is, the Earth (the topic at the core of the reflections by Jünger, Shiva, Panikkar, Latouche and many others) and the crucially constitutive role played by cultural differences, which are swept away with elementary violence by the economic and cultural globalist model.

The Collapsed Towers of Mundialization

Evidently keeping in mind the stultification in which the majority of globalized humanity has fallen after the sinking of the *Titanic*, Cassandra returns to her instructional task almost a century later, in 2001, on the occasion of the collapse of the Twin Towers—the site and monument of the global trade. Her warning is accurate also in terms of geopolitical localization, namely, the United States, busy with destructuring the planet in the name of market logics and geopolitical calculations. There occurs, here, a shift of the world axis from Europe to the United States, which had already been responsible for the nuclear bombs dropped on the Japanese civil population and for innumerable wars causing destabilization on a global level. The event of the collapse of the two towers has been highly spectacularized by media all over the world. Ever since its happening, it has also been legitimately beclouded by various interpretative doubts, which have been supported by an unwieldy series of questions and incongruences.[7] Here though, I will consider the event of the collapse of the Twin Towers only in its explicit, symbolic aspect within the new global world. I will do so on the basis of Jean Baudrillard's essay "Requiem for the Twin Towers," contained in his book *The Spirit of Terrorism*.[8]

The spectacular sequences of the planes crashing into the two identical towers, site and emblem of the organisms of international trade, have appeared, on the one hand, as some sort of hyper-real simulation and, on the other, as symbol for the fragility of globalization and its myths. Paradoxically, such fragility became most explicit in the official version of the dynamics of the event and in its "staging" in the frames of the video clips that have immortalized it. The sensation of "unreality" comes, according to Baudrillard, from the overwhelming symbolism of the event—the doubled symmetry of the two towers, the attack in two stages by two planes—which has prolonged the terrifying aspect of the happening in all its details. "The collapse of the two towers is the major symbolic event"[9] because it is their symbolic character that has been made a target. Baudrillard writes, "It was, in fact, their symbolic collapse that brought about their physical collapse, not the other way around. As if the power bearing these towers suddenly lost all energy, all resilience; as though that arrogant power suddenly gave way under the pressure of too intense an effort: the effort always to be the unique world model."[10] What disappears is the symbol of the omnipotence of the North American and globalized West, of a world and a planet caged in the omnipresent network of global marketing, of the forced acceleration of transformations and information. Such a world does not tolerate diversity (the twinness of the towers is the symbol thereof), is still and always pushed by the tragic Faustian drive toward the infinite on a finite planet and, in a manner that has by now become constitutive, confuses virtuality and reality, glamour and infantilization, technological power and ignorance, micrometric control and blindness.

The unimaginable accident that comes from the air expresses all the uncertainty that, starting with the industrial revolution, such a vital element—the air—carries: miasmas, darkening of the sky, pollution, diseases that spread due to their being borne by the essential vital element, up to the "terror from the air" of the military gases that Peter Sloterdijk describes so efficaciously.[11] Climate changes, progressive poisoning, the ideal and literal suffocation of the world and nature come from such an artificialized, disturbed, uncertain, and potentially lethal atmosphere.

Not even this renewed warning by Cassandra, which has been so clear in so many ways, has been met by the West with a questioning of itself and its violent "growth models," which are considered the creation of "free and emancipated human beings" who only make rational choices and consider the imposition on the world of such choices as their moral imperative. The towers of the World Trade Center were the emblem of a rationality that completely identifies with the reasons of commercial trade, of goods, of that kingdom of Quantity whose "signs of the times" have not yet been understood.[12] As Baudrillard writes, "Shaped in the pure computer image of banking and finance, (ac)countable and digital, they were in a sense its brain, and in striking there the terrorists have struck at the brain, at the nerve-center of the system. The violence of globalization also involves architecture, and hence the violent protest against it also involves the destruction of that architecture."[13]

Their collapse, according to Baudrillard, constitutes a symbolic failure of the claim to represent the only possible model of life, a failure of a hierarchy of values that decrees the subordination of a large part of the world and, moreover, the failure of an unacceptable contempt for sacredness and nature. Baudrillard too reaches a similar conclusion to the one traced earlier by Jünger. He writes, "Very logically, and inexorably, the increase in the power of power heightens the will to destroy it. But there is more: somewhere, it was party to its own destruction. [. . .] T]he rejection of any system, including internal rejection, grow[s] all the stronger as it approaches perfection or omnipotence. [. . .] T]he West, in the position of God (divine omnipotence and absolute moral legitimacy), has become suicidal, and declared war on itself."[14] Moreover, it is as if that event also manifested "a kind of agonizing revisionism in respect of the established positions of modernity, in respect of the idea of progress and history—a kind of rejection not only of the famous global technostructure, but of the mental structure of the identification of all cultures and all continents in the concept of the universal."[15] That is, a rejection of mundialization, of homogenization in the name of the Enlightenment and the Dollar[16] with its explicit assertion that its power will last eternally (a *"Novus Ordo Seculorum,"* a new secular order at the base of a pyramid with the divine eye at its top—if one wants to speak of details).

The Invisible That Comes from Afar

It is, again, Jünger who notes that, in the current epoch, fear is tied to situations and objects different from the past. He writes: "This is the style of the period, behind which the spirit of the Earth is hidden. Objects change. Once, the image of the plague was that of a woman cloaked in black; now, one observes microbes and even tinier forms. And one fears other kinds of collective death."[17] In other words, Jünger connects the appearance of especially troubling epidemic manifestations with a disturbance of the human relation with the Earth and nature—a relation that needs to be reestablished. "Is fever a disease or is it rather a morbid symptom, a symptom that shows us how the body wishes to restore a lost balance?"[18]

Let us analogically extend Jünger's consideration to the Earth, whose balances are subverted, which is robbed and violated in all possible ways, which is conceptualized merely as a standing reserve to the avail of Enlightenment-based, rationalist, individualistic human beings and at the disposal of an ideology (actually, a real creed) of unlimited economic and productive growth for which the United States are the most extremist representatives. Under such an extension, the coronavirus appears as Cassandra's latest warning with respect to the phenomena produced by our relation with the

Earth. Among them are the upheaval to the point of no-return of natural as well as cultural balances. The former form of upheaval is a phenomenon that affects humanity in its entirety in an analogy with the ideology of unlimited growth and the disappearance of borders and ecological specificities, that is, the alleged cross-species transmission or "species jump" which is the presumed origin of all viruses. The latter includes mundialization, the pandemic circulation of goods, and the homogenization of values in a general economicism.[19] Not last in such a set of warnings is the specific dimension of the agent, namely, its invisibility. It is no longer the physical mass of the iceberg that mocks the *Titanic* powers. It is no longer a "terroristic" event in its Hollywood-style hyper-reality. Now it is an invisible, nonrepresentable, deceitful disease that manifests itself in the tragic, everyday reality of each and every one, which is therefore unsettled as for rhythms, affections, and habits. It reveals itself in death, and, moreover, in the impotence (or insufficiency) of all our previous "magics" such as technology, medicine, consumption, sociality. Most of all, it presents itself in an immobility for which the world, built and liquefied in the ideal of the perennial mobility of everyone, of the goods, of tourism, of passing fancies, now suddenly becomes alien and impassable, remote, and nonrefundable via virtualization.

What is on stage is biological horror, which Jünger had foreseen ahead of his times as a form of "covert intrusion of the heteroclite," which provokes the greatest terror when it manifests itself as life "affected and threatened at its genetic level, that is, more in depth than in specific individuals."[20] Jünger ties this dimension to biological experimentation, to its increasing relevance and diffusion, which constitutes the entry into a new dimension of the history of the Earth. It is as if the veil of matter were to move. With respect to some monstrous mutations observed in the form of living beings found in industrial drains, he writes, "It is evident that life is here affected and threatened at its genetic level, that is, more in depth than in specific individuals."[21] Jünger acknowledges the ineluctability of research and experimentation, which are, in part, the responses to the messages of evolutionary unrest provided by the Earth, which is an intelligent organism; but he also recognizes the horror that humanity faces when human beings are not guided by respect, measure, and prudence. In other words, the Earth responds to the various historical forms of humanity and discloses various and diverse possibilities. Yet the desire for unlimited control and power which, in our contemporary times, is enacted at the planetary level can only generate catastrophic effects, which are recognized in a reticent and always belated way. It is still the case of *Titanic* blindness, of the Faustian will to unlimited overcoming, even when this is wrapped up in the reassuring semblances of the world made available on the screen, in a leisure trip, or in the aestheticized food that we consume. Behind immediate presence, universal communication, and encounters, mass communication and social media leave the stage open to the ghosts of a world that is minutely controlled by technological networks, in which the imaginary too is homogenized and preformed. This is accompanied by a constant lowering of collective awareness and intelligence, which is dissolved in a babbling made of acronyms, likes, and emoticons, in a chattering that liquidates and phantasmatizes encounters and communities, and in the repetition of mantras reassuring that one is in the right. In this world, public opinion could never come to the realization of the seriousness of the no-return situation; and the few voices that are aware and dissonant have been ridiculed and marginalized. To the knowledge of the masses, Italian fashion blogger Chiara Ferragni, who was ranked first on the Forbes "Top Fashion Influencers" list, surpasses degrowth economist Serge Latouche or ecosophy theologian Raimon Panikkar. Analogously, the hyper-real pornography of food representation eclipses the poverty and hunger of most of the world, even of those close to us. Furthermore, very few give up a world trip whose goal is to replicate the pictures already taken by millions before them—pictures that are all the same, narcissistic, with already preset color deforming effects, as if to habituate us to a nightmarish reality, to a world that replaces itself, its natural or historical colors with the hues of a dystopic and crazy reality.

The great repressed of our contemporary epoch is the care (*custodia*) of the Earth understood as a planet with extraordinary manifestations and potentialities for life. The artificialization that modern technology has pursued serves a univocal project, namely, to control the world, exploit nature unlimitedly, liquidate those cultures and societies that do not conform to the Western model, uproot oneself and others in the name of economic profit, of forms of domination that, to succeed, need homogenization through various means, from wars to hunger, from induced terrorism to the social media, from genetic engineering to glamour, from the "politically correct" to deforestation and the annihilation of all traces that are not homogenized.

Yet, within the context of this will to power in its purest state, the signs of unrest multiply at the level of the imaginary. In the novel *Dissipatio H. G.*, which not by chance takes place in Chrysopolis (a *nomen omen*, a name that is a sign for Zurich, the capital of finance), the main character aspires to commit suicide but then renounces. When he reemerges from the cave where he had wanted to take his life, he discovers that human beings have disappeared without leaving any trace except for their manufactured products and objects; at the same time, animals begin to repossess places, and nature starts flourishing. As Morselli writes, "The end of the world? It's one of the jokes of anthropocentrism, which describes the end of the species as implying the death of vegetal and animal nature, the very end of the Earth. The fall of the skies [. . .]. Come on, you know-it-all and presumptuous people, you were thinking too highly of yourselves! The world has never been as alive as today when a certain species of bipeds has stopped inhabiting it. It has never been as clean, sparkling, and cheerful."[22]

In our case too, one of the effects of the coronavirus has been that, while humans have been confined in closed spaces, nature has begun to reappropriate places. The level of pollution has decreased and, with it, noise and traffic. Many activities that generate effects that put the life of many—both humans and other beings—at stake have been reduced or come to a halt. Animals have seized the territory again and wander through towns and villages in groups. Nature, which has been attacked for long, now breathes; and, if we are not sick, we breathe with her.

Yet, this will only last for a little while, unless techno-economic humanity is capable, in *extremis*, of changing horizon, paradigms, and values and of acknowledging its falsity and blindness. As Jünger argues, "Only if we change our perspective can we understand what would otherwise remain inexplicable, namely, the failure of intelligence not due to oppositional elements but rather because of its own internal goals."[23]

Terror in the Air

"The twentieth century will be remembered as the age whose essential thought consisted in targeting no longer the body, but the enemy's environment. This is the basic idea of terrorism in the more explicit sense."[24] Peter Sloterdijk develops an atmospherology as part of his theoretical project *Spheres*, an impressive and fascinating philosophical *summa* of the representations of the Earth and the philosophical history of globalization. He observes that a catastrophic epochal change takes place through the technology used for war purposes during World War One. The use of lethal gases during battles brings about a change in human consciousness. Starting with the battle of Ypres (1915) in West Flanders, when German soldiers unleashed chlorine gas on their enemies, breathing may mean death rather than life. Unlike the morbidity brought about by industrial pollution ever since the beginning of the industrial world, this new consciousness is triggered by the suddenness of the effect. The twentieth century commences with an irreversible "'explication.' In other words: the revealing inclusion of the background givens underlying manifest operations."[25] That is, the twentieth century begins with the awareness of the artificial and invisible dangers introduced into the environment by technology and industry. The elements that enable life are transformed into potentialities for danger. Nature itself may become a deadly "environment," and breathing may turn into an accomplice in the annihilation of one's own life. Using the fundamental elements of life (air, water, soil) in order to attain a (economic, commercial, or military) profit at all cost is, properly, terrorism; it is the project of reducing the Earth to a globe infinitely available for technical, economic, and imperialist manipulations. Sloterdijk claims that terrorism is neither a random accident nor the result of resented violence; rather, terrorism is modernity. The increasing "explication" that the environment undergoes so that a uniform model of life may be imposed is "the knowledge of modernized extermination."[26]

With the battle of Ypres, what disappears is the thousands-year-old perception of the atmosphere and the world. Symbolically, this also marks the end of any possible harmony. What begins is the age of air conditioning. The meaning of greenhouses that, ever since their appearance, had been the spaces for universal expos becomes clearer and more detailed. One of such greenhouses is the Crystal Palace in London—the archetype of an architectural typology that enjoyed a long-lasting fortune until it transformed itself into an ideal emergency space for the cure of the coronavirus, with a precise and cruel symbolic shortcut. This transformation in terms of its use is one more instance of Cassandra's details. The violent globalization of the world has not been halted by the terroristic attack on its imperial emblem; the insidious ubiquity of a virus that hides in our very own breath joins within itself—all the way down to its symbols, imaginaries, food, and spirituality—the theme of the subversion and poisoning of nature with the *hybris* of the humongous animal holocaust and the liquidation of cultures in the name of the only one, the single one (*l'unico*). What it joins though, it also unmasks. That there were no sufficient masks to protect the population from the contagion but also that there are no more arguments for the umpteenth misrepresentation of a blind will to power is perhaps Cassandra's latest, most instructive, and final warning.

Translated from Italian by Silvia Benso

Notes

1. Ernst Jünger, *The Forest Passage*, trans. Thomas Friese (Candor, NY: Telos Press, 2016).

2. Ernst Jünger, *Die Schere* (Stuttgart: Klett-Cotta, 2015); Italian trans. Q. Principe, *La forbice* (Parma: Guanda, 1996), 124.

3. Jünger, *The Forest Passage*, 49.
4. Ivan Illich, *Medical Nemesis: The Expropriation of Health* (New York: Pantheon, 1982).
5. Among Latouche's fundamental works, see Serge Latouche, *The Westernization of the World: Significance, Scope and Limits of the Drive towards Global Uniformity* (Cambridge, UK: Polity Press, 1996).
6. Vandana Shiva, *Earth Democracy: Justice, Sustainability, and Peace* (Berkeley, CA: New Atlantic Books, 2005).
7. A serious reflection on the phenomenon of the so-called "conspiracy theory," which also emerged in the twentieth century, is in order. Beyond the assessment of its specific interpretations, such a theory displays the widespread perception that things "do not add up" to a rational explanation in a period of maximum scientism and technocracy, when the power over the world escapes the control of the people, busy with "self-expression" on the social channels.
8. Jean Baudrillard, *The Spirit of Terrorism*, trans. Chris Turner (London: Verso, 2002).
9. Baudrillard, *The Spirit of Terrorism*, 43.
10. Baudrillard, *The Spirit of Terrorism*, 44.
11. Peter Sloterdijk, *Terror from the Air*, trans. Amy Patton and Steve Corcoran (Los Angeles: Semiotext(e), 2009).
12. The reference is to René Guénon, *The Reign of Quantity and the Signs of Time*, trans. Lord Northbourne (Hillsdale, NY: Sophia Perennis, 2001).
13. Baudrillard, *The Spirit of Terrorism*, 41.
14. Baudrillard, *The Spirit of Terrorism*, 45–46.
15. Jean Baudrillard, "Paroxysm: Interviews with Philippe Petit," in *Jean Baudrillard: Selected Writings*, ed. Mark Poster (Stanford: Stanford University Press, 2001), 281.
16. One should perhaps phrase this better as: "the quite explicit symbolism and the will to last eternally as represented on the dollar bills."
17. Ernst Jünger, *An der Zeitmauer* (Stuttgart: Klett-Cotta Verlag, 1959); Italian trans. Alvise La Rocca and Agnese Grieco, *Al muro del tempo* (Milan: Adelphi, 2000), 164.
18. Jünger, *Al muro del tempo*, 59.
19. On this, see the many works by Latouche and Panikkar.
20. Jünger, *Al muro del tempo*, 223.
21. Jünger, *Al muro del tempo*, 223.
22. Guido Morselli, *Dissipatio H. G.* (Milan: Adelphi, 1977), 26.
23. Jünger, *Al muro del tempo*, 204.
24. Sloterdijk, *Terror from the Air*, 14.
25. Sloterdijk, *Terror from the Air*, 9.
26. Sloterdijk, *Terror from the Air*, 16.

Two

Improvising Self-Expression in the Time of a Contingency That Has Eliminated Contingency

Alessandro Bertinetto

Prologue: Music from the (Real and Virtual) Balconies

A few days after the sudden and unforeseeable lockdown due to the Covid-19 emergency, Italians felt the need to express their desire for the human contact that they had lost through live music. Unable to resort to the usual forms of sociality, they spontaneously chose to express themselves—in the sense of letting themselves out—from their homes to recreate community through music. From simple singing, sometimes accompanied by a guitar, to solo exhibitions and improvised music groups put together through "social distancing"—as has been erroneously called what is actually a form of physical, and not necessarily social, distancing—music from balconies and windows has been one of the primary forms of expressing the need for social aggregation, physical distancing notwithstanding.[1]

Musicians, and artists in general, make up one of the social groups that have been hit the hardest economically by the effects of the pandemic. Generally poorly protected by the norms that are ordinarily in force in contemporary Italy, due to the pandemic, artists have been suddenly deprived of the possibility of exercising their professions, performing in public, and giving lessons. With greater or lesser success, the internet has certainly been able to replace, partly and in some cases, the possibility of performing music for an audience and of teaching music even though through the mediation of home computer screens. Indeed, my own experience with the online piano and clarinet lessons my daughters were able to take advantage of during the lockdown months, thanks to the generous availability of their teachers, was truly rewarding. These weekly lessons restored an important vital rhythm to their lives—as well as to mine and my wife's. The everyday rhythm of our lives, both at work and at home, was completely disrupted due to the unexpected state of emergency. These lessons have been a way to provide organization to our time.

The possibilities offered by digital technology and, in particular, by the internet have certainly constituted an *Ersatz*, a substitute also for some forms of musical performance as well as for other artistic forms, sometimes with unexpectedly positive results in terms of expressive effectiveness. Like in other areas of social life (academic webinars come to mind), the possibility of connecting with people located in different parts of the globe has favored forms of communication and interaction that had not been conceived of before the pandemic. The state of emergency has forced reactions capable of resolving some of the problems it has generated. And, in this way, it has forced us to be creative.

The University of Padua, in the persons of Marina Santi and Alessandro Fedrigo, organized Pansodia for the 2020 Unesco International Jazz Day (April 30).[2] Not being able to bring together artists and the public in the city of Padua to celebrate jazz music through concerts, conferences, and workshops, as it had usually been done during the past seven or so years, the event organizers invited musicians and scholars from all over the world to produce short videos with performances and talks that were then postproduced and assembled. In this way, a collective performance lasting almost 9 hours was created, which was then broadcast during a 24-hour period on YouTube (where it is still available).[3] It has been a sort of (in some cases, artistically very successful) "music from the balcony" on a global scale. I, too, participated in this event and, later, I will say some words about the performance I offered.

Musical Expressiveness, Rhythm, and Time

First, though, I would like to focus on two notions I have already mentioned in the prologue to this short chapter (which is indeed also a bit improvised, in order to cope somehow with its subject matter); namely, *expression* and *rhythm*. Expression and rhythm are two fundamental aspects of life. They are also two fundamental aspects of art, both as part of life and as a means of presentation and performative reflection on fundamental aspects of life.

Expression concerns the possibility of putting the self in communication with the world, articulating the affective life in the sense of a mutual attunement between organism and environment. *Rhythm* is the articulation of the dynamic flow of biological and social life, which, through the morphological configuration of the existent, produces forms of ontological and behavioral organization: a regularity open to change and variation which is the structural "physiological" basis, at the same time, of subjective and social habits and of the normativity that rules human practices.

Music stands out among the arts as being particularly capable of expressive and rhythmic creativity.[4] Music gives voice to affective life, is capable of exploring it in depth not only by "painting" emotions in sounds, but also by activating in the listener affects and emotions that can encourage the sharing of one's own intimate subjective experience on an intersubjective level. In this regard, among the many theories about musical expressiveness that are available within the contemporary philosophical debate, I consider the "person theory" particularly compelling because it accounts for the power of music to generate expressive interactions.[5] Person theory explains the recognition of the specific expressiveness of a piece or musical performance as based on attributing a personal character to music thanks to the way in which listeners respond affectively to the expressive affordances generated by sound articulations. Listening to music, understanding its expressiveness, means having a kind of personal relationship with and through music. This relationship allows us to explore the emotional life, often in an unconscious way; and this is one of the reasons why the listening experience is particularly rewarding, even when we experience sad or melancholic music. In addition, this also seems to be one of the reasons why the experience of musical expressiveness is often intensified in a qualitative sense by joint listening. In such cases, we share with other listeners the emotional interaction we have with music and this amplifies the role of empathy for the experience of musical expressiveness.

The intersubjective dimension of musical expressiveness is also made possible via the way in which music rhythmically organizes its sonic forms, thereby engaging listeners with each other by keeping them close to the groove traced by music and, in addition, also possibly organizing their cooperation in many kinds of daily activities (this phenomenon is called "entrainment" and nowadays is very much studied in psychology of music).[6]

The state of emergency due to Covid-19 has been a contingency that has eliminated ordinary possibilities of spontaneous interactions with contingency.[7] As such, it has suddenly both blocked the usual possibilities of expression and broken the rhythm of daily life, while also hindering artistic possibilities of expression and their impact on this rhythm. Therefore, the "music on the balconies" phenomenon can be explained, at least in part, with the need to restore, at a particularly hard time for individuals and communities, a public space for a joint expressiveness capable of offering a "common sense" to the crisis of sense provoked by the Covid-19-related state of emergency. "Music from the balconies" (but also some new forms of musical creativity enabled by the internet) has been a way to restore a bit (and a beat) of rhythm to existence thanks to a spontaneous outburst of musical expression. This could be understood as a confirmation of the fact that Nietzsche's idea that the world makes sense as an aesthetic phenomenon[8] must be interpreted not so much (or, at least, not only) as a form of aestheticism (the reduction of life to a rather meaningless art), but as a comprehension of the fact that art gives sense to life. The life-meaning activity performed by art is based on the different ways in which art creatively organizes our senses—with which we build our relationship with the world and with others—and offers human beings the possibility of performing forms of self-understanding.[9] Due to its ability to overcome physical distances through sounds (an ability that, as Kant argues, can also make it an element of disturbance, if used in inappropriate ways),[10] music is particularly capable of aggregating human beings who are otherwise forced to keep their distance from one another. The aggregative function takes place thanks to rhythm and expressiveness and by virtue of the power music has to stage the emotional life. This role seems to be particularly important at a time when the ordinary habits that shape the rhythm of our daily life—including the ability to produce and experience art—have been so profoundly altered.

In this respect, another specific feature of music seems to be particularly relevant: that is, the intrinsic relation music has with time. Indeed, in addition to the possibility of overcoming spatial distances, expressing emotions, and allowing for expressive interactions, music is not only articulated temporally, but it is also an articulation of temporality through sounds (and through structured, meaningful silences). In other words, music is able to structure and organize (our sense of) time. Music allows the self to experience the temporal articulation, shaped expressively, of its inner life.[11] Through the structural articulation of time by means of repetitions and variations as well as through the shaping of the listeners' memory, music may overcome temporal distances, re-establishing and creating connections that offer ways of reconstructing the unity of subjective and intersubjective experience. This possibility is increased by technical reproduction, which enables us to bring past sounds into the present via recording and broadcasting.

Furthermore, music's ability to organize the temporality of experience also involves the thematization of a sense of the future through the configuration of a directionality that seems to acquire the dimension of a project to come. In other words, the temporal organization of experience, which reconstructs a link between past and present, also opens up the utopian "not-yet," thereby giving a sense, a direction to the present by pointing it towards an imaginative goal that organized sounds can make us portend. Evoking the utopianism of Ernst Bloch's philosophy of music seems particularly appropriate here.[12]

The forms of musical performance improvised during the Covid-19 lockdown through the creation of a distanced or virtual copresence of performers and listeners have certainly had, from the very beginning, a bitter taste of nostalgia (in the sense of romantic *Sehnsucht*) for a lost reality. They have been the sign of an absence that aspired to be filled. What was previously a given has now become a utopia—the present utopia of recovering, in the future, a lost past, perhaps even in new or different ways.

Yet, more generally, in an interrupted time suspended between the regularity of a past that has been swept away by Covid-19 and an uncertain future that is more than ever unknown and not programmable, we have turned to music as to a possibility for recovering a sense of our disrupted experience, for reconnecting the present to our past—for example, thanks to songs that reactivate the memory, and the desire, of a social sharing—thus reconstructing a fabric of daily habits and offering possibilities for the future: for example, by showing that, despite everything, the sense of reciprocal belonging of individuals, beyond their own balcony, beyond their own village, and beyond their own country has not vanished. The issue was and is that of rethinking or, rather, re-performing a sense of the present as a possibility of a future.

Coping with the (Extra)Ordinary: Improvisation as Human Practice

Music plays an important role in terms of structuring and restoring our subjective and intersubjective experience, and this role has emerged with particular force during the lockdown. In light of these claims, I think that it could be particularly enlightening to address, even though within the limits of this short chapter, a specific musical and, more generally, artistic practice that is deeply rooted in our everyday practices: that is, the art of improvisation.

The role that improvisation has played, and continues to play, in this period of strong transformation imposed by dramatic, unforeseen events, has certainly exceeded the artistic sphere. Indeed, the Covid-19 pandemic has forced everyone to improvise in order to respond to the state of emergency. Never is the need to react in situated, responsive, and adaptive ways so strong and urgent as within a context of this kind. On a global scale, human beings have found themselves having to change rules and habits of behaviors and practices in order to react adaptively to an entirely unprecedented event that has interrupted their ordinary lives.

Behavioral and social norms and habits that regulate human practices are always effective if, and only if, they are capable of adapting themselves plastically to a reality in continuous, though often slow, transformation. Plastic adaptation implies self-transformation. Hence, the point is that the norms and habits of human practices are effective if they are able to transform themselves. Otherwise, they remain abstract patterns that are incapable of being effectively and efficaciously realized and are instead always useless and often harmful. In situations of state of emergency such as the one we experienced in 2020, changes were very rapid and called, and still call, for equally rapid responses. This extraordinary situation required the rules of our practices adequately respond to such an unexpected event.

As argued in a recent article I co-wrote with Georg Bertram from the Freie Universität Berlin,[13] a crucial aspect of the rationality of human practices is its ability to transform itself in relation to what happens in the natural and social environment, as happens paradigmatically in improvisation. This is not in the sense that human beings must continuously invent the modalities of their behavior *ex nihilo*. This is not how improvisation works. Improvisers do not invent everything on the spot. Rather, through repeated exercise, they acquire skills and competences of which they make use in their performances. This set of competences builds an embedded and embodied "know-how"[14] articulated in behavioral habits that are continually tested in different performance situations, thus shaping them and contributing to their continuous (trans)formation. In other words, not only is the improvisational performance made possible by competence, but competence is, in turn, generated through performance. Performers are compelled to be creative in order to respond to unforeseen concrete circumstances of the performance situations in which they are involved.

This idea applies in a very general sense to all human practices and has important implications for understanding the natural evolution of the human species. In fact, the ability to adapt plastically to a constantly changing world, reacting responsively to environmental affordances, is key to understanding the specificity of human beings' rationality. If, in ordinary situations, behavioral habits are sufficient to regulate the interaction with the environment, if they prove capable of modeling themselves plastically to the concreteness of the reality in which they are applied, in extraordinary situations one is forced to invent different behavioral rules and to design new habits, new practical rules of action. This necessity can have unexpected creative implications.

Let us take as an example the case of schools and, in general, of teaching. As Eleonora Zorzi argues in her recent book *L'insegnante improvvisatore* (*The Improvising Instructor*),[15] a good school requires improvisation: not in the sense of a superficial, botched, insufficiently prepared teaching, but in the very different sense of a teaching intended as continuous formation (training) and *trans*formation, as the ability to intercept change and to negotiate in the situation, through interaction with all players involved, the most effective rules for acting and interacting within the dynamic and, in its concreteness, unpredictable context of school life.

Sometimes—as is happening in these months due to the Covid-19 emergency—this unpredictability is radical and dramatic. The emergency thus forces us to explore effective ways of behaving in the new situation. On the one hand, it requires attention to the specific nature of the situation. For instance, school homework must be sustainable, it must be adequate to the specific moment: it cannot demand excessive efforts from parents committed to coping with similar improvisations in the workplace. If homework is not suitable for the specific situation within which it is assigned, it is not feasible, and it cannot achieve what it proposes, namely, contributing to the children's education. This has always been true; today, it is simply more evident.

On the other hand, the Covid-19 emergency forces choices regarding teaching media as well as methods of knowledge construction and dissemination. Today, at all levels of the educational system, from elementary schools to PhD programs, suddenly we find ourselves forced to review the practical rules of our profession as teachers and educators and to experiment with new solutions such as online teaching. We realize that human contact is fundamental, and we want to return to share physically the spaces of school and academy interaction. Yet we discover that some previously neglected technological possibilities can become important tools for teaching and researching because they are capable of building new ways of dialogue between teachers and learners, sometimes generating interesting forms of community. As good improvisers, we therefore try to seize this opportunity and creatively exploit even an unexpected dramatic event like the Covid-19 pandemic. The plastic adaptation of the habits that govern our practices to the unpredictable transformations of natural and social reality thus invites us inventively to explore new and good ways of (inter)action. Some of these ways will last even after the end of the emergency.

In short, in the extraordinary nature of an emergency that has affected schools as well as work and all aspects of everyday life, we can experientially understand what happens ordinarily in our everyday life: norms, skills, and habits may be effective if, in the specific situations of their application, they are able to intervene in a constantly changing reality. It is always the case that those who act in the contexts of everyday life interact with the participants in the situation and with the specific circumstances of their action: thus, action plans are not abstract schemes that must be "simply" realized. As Richard Sennett and Beth Preston have argued in different ways,[16] the work of human creative intelligence does not end with the preparation of action plans, nor are action plans completely configured before action: creative intelligence is fundamental for the action itself in its concreteness. Concrete actions are not mere executions of predetermined instructions that are valid regardless of the contexts of their application, and plans are not simply abstract predetermined instructions or rules; rather, they are developed through their interpretation in the situated and responsive (inter)action with and within the environment.

So, an emergency like the one we are experiencing on a global scale because of Covid-19 qualitatively intensifies the role of improvisation for human practices because such an emergency calls for radical, profound, and sudden changes. By forcing us to improvise, subverting many of our habits that are altered by the unexpected situation, the emergency we are experiencing makes us understand the role of improvisation for our daily lives.

This holds true, I think, even though the Covid-19 emergency is a contingent situation that makes it impossible or, in any case, very difficult to interact with contingency, as usually happens in an improvisation. Indeed, in a sense, this is true: the margins of freedom for our interactions with contingencies in the months of the lockdown were so narrow and constrained that we could not improvise anymore. And this impossibility has shown the importance of improvisation: "By asking citizens to suspend all 'unnecessary' activities, the authorities have brought to light everything that intrinsically defines social relationships: chance encounters, unforeseen exchanges, exposure to the unexpected. By enjoining individuals to concentrate on 'the essential,' we are basically returning to what we are most familiar with, warding ourselves off from that part of contingency that is the leaven of all human relationships. The disappearance of shared public space also corresponds to a disappearance of surprise."[17] Thus, the contingent and unexpected event of Covid-19 has somehow deprived us of that possibility of meeting unexpected contingencies in the creative way that seems to be a crucial aspect of the improvisational nature of human practices. However, even though for a certain period our possibilities of meeting and performing the unexpected as we did before have been strongly reduced, this situation has let us experientially understand the key role of improvisation for our life. As a consequence, we have tried to meet and perform the unexpected in new ways, responding to the emergent situation. Thus, it is true that many of the ways in which we were able to meet and perform the unexpected were, during the extremely constrained situation of the lockdown, very limited. But it is true as well that, by letting us see how important the encounter with, and the performance of, the unexpected is for our existence, this dramatically hard and unforeseen situation has forced us to experiment with *new* ways of creative interaction with the world. This may have, of course, positive and negative implications; but, for sure, it is an existential condition we have to deal with. Be as it may, the aspect I am interested in highlighting here is that, even in a context of general crisis for culture and artistic expression or, more radically, even in a time of repression and oppression of artistic creativity and aesthetic expressiveness, these have proved irreplaceable for human life.

Phenomena like the music from the balconies and other less ephemeral artistic inventions and performances have exhibited the ability of art—not only of professional "institutional" art, but rather of art as a particular way of making that, ensuing from everyday practices,[18] "invents the ways of making while making," according to Luigi Pareyson's compelling view.[19] In this way, art gives voice to that improvisational creativity that allows human beings to interact with the environment in both ordinary and extraordinary situations.

Performing Unexpected Interactions with Contingency

Let us now return to music as an art capable of articulating through sound the expression of our emotional life, thereby rhythmically organizing our temporal and social experience. Resuming the thread of considerations I carried out in the first part of this reflection, I can now cite, as an example of expressive musical improvisation in the time of the oppression of contingency, the performance that I offered for the aforementioned online event Pansodia, organized, as I already noted, by the University of Padua for the 2020 Unesco Jazz Day.[20]

As remarked above, Pansodia collected performance videos and short talks by musicians and scholars from different disciplines. I titled my contribution to the event "Improvisation on an Improvisation." The reason is this. In October 2018, I gave a presentation, interspersed with some musical performances, on the theme of "Improvising the Truth" as part of a series of lectures devoted to the philosophy of music and organized at the Ateneo Veneto in Venice by pianist and philosopher of music Letizia Michielon. One of the performances consisted in playing together with Mirio Cosottini the tune "Aurora Boreale" composed by Mirio Cosottini himself.[21] The piece consisted of a set of chords that I could play on the piano improvising their order, duration, dynamics, and voicing, while Mirio—a great musician and a great artist—improvised on the trumpet. The only additional rule we gave ourselves—and we gave it to ourselves at the very last moment, just as we were about to begin the performance—was that Mirio would play while walking slowly around the conference hall and the performance would end once he would return to the stage next to the piano. An intense and suspended atmosphere of musical participated contemplation was created in the magnificent sixteenth-seventeenth century Aula Magna of the Ateneo Veneto: what happened above all thanks to Mirio's creativity and his trumpet was a concrete example of how to "improvise the truth," and I always remember with pleasure the minutes of that musical interplay, in such a particular place.

When I was asked to contribute to Pansodia, after discarding some other performance possibilities I had been considering, I decided to recover the audio-video recording of that 2018 Venice performance and to interact, in the lockdown period, with a felicitous past in order to demonstrate that, despite the restriction of the possibilities for a creative confrontation with contingency, constraints and unexpected accidents can be exploited creatively. Playing the tenor sax (my preferred instrument for a few years now), I performed together with Mirio and with my past self, precisely improvising on that past improvisation. I videotaped this new performance with my Smartphone and included in the visual spectrum of the phone's camera also the PC screen broadcasting in streaming the recording of that Venice performance of "Aurora Boreale." I am certainly not an artist, and my technical skills as a saxophonist are *very* limited. Moreover, although the audio quality of the recording was not too bad at the end of the day, the technical conditions of my performance were certainly not optimal. Yet, in the end, I was satisfied with the idea and also a little with the concrete result of the performance. And so were Mirio and the friends who watched the video. Not being able, due to the lockdown restrictions, to interact live with other people[22]—not even from the balcony as my house is very isolated (certainly, in some ways, a significant advantage in that period)—I took advantage of the possibility of an artistic interaction across time that was offered to me by technology and made possible by Marina Santi and Alessandro Fredrigo's great idea. For me, it was a way of signifying my gratitude to the people with whom I had the privilege of interacting in making musical and philosophical experiences, and it was also a way to express my sense of nostalgia for a happy past in a present that aspires to a better future.

Of course, this kind of musical time travel is certainly not a novelty. Quite notably, the remaining three members of the Beatles (at that time; George Harrison also passed away some years later) put on a song together with the late John Lennon (who had died in 1980) on the occasion of the release of the documentary *Beatles Anthology* and the album *Anthology 1* (1995). Resuming a track recorded by John Lennon in 1977, they played with him, gathering the Beatles together again, even if only virtually. I do not want to compare myself to my favorite band, God forbid! And the two performances are very different. The Beatles piece is a song, whereas my performance was only an ephemeral improvisation on an ephemeral performance (even if it had been recorded). However, it was perhaps that famous artistic operation that gave me, even if unconsciously, the ideas of weaving, through a kind of homemade improvised mash-up, a link between the past and the present and of exploring an unforeseen possibility of shaping a sense for the present, thereby offering a moment of expressive sharing in a period of restriction of the possibilities of spontaneous interaction with contingency.

The point is that the unexpected forced me to look for possibilities for creative expression. Italians are particularly renowned for their ability to devote themselves to the art of getting by.[23] It is not always a good sign. And in this case, it certainly was not. The time of the Covid-19 emergency was and is dramatic for many people. But it has shown, once again, that the specificity of human beings' rationality is the creative ability to invent (the rules of their own) practices through their performances, and also to reorganize disrupted experiential orders and to shape possibilities for spontaneous self-expression in situations in which self-expression is radically limited. Certainly, the chances of the success of creativity cannot be taken for granted. But this insecurity, which also qualifies the success of aesthetic formativity, shows the importance of art as improvisational practice of inventing the rules of its making while making, that is, of performing the unexpected.[24]

Notes

1. See https://www.youtube.com/watch?v=EBByYjjvNzs.
2. See https://www.unipd.it/news/pansodia-2020-international-jazz-day-2020.
3. See https://www.youtube.com/watch?v=6cuwy8qAACM.
4. Obviously, music is not only this, being capable of the most daring and sophisticated intellectual constructions. But these two aspects are those on which I will dwell in these brief reflections.

5. See Jerrold Levinson, *The Pleasures of Aesthetics* (Ithaca, NY: Cornell University Press, 1996); Jerrold Levinson, *Contemplating Art* (Oxford: Oxford University Press, 2006); Jenefer Robinson, *Deeper than Reason: Emotion and Its Role in Literature, Music and Art* (Oxford: Clarendon Press, 2005). See also Alessandro Bertinetto, *Il pensiero dei suoni. Temi di filosofia della musica* (Milan: Bruno Mondadori, 2012) and "L'espressività nell'improvvisazione musicale," in *Grammatica della musica. Grammatica della percezione*, ed. D. Lentini and S. Oliva (Rome: il Glifo (ebook), 2016), 22–34.

6. See, for instance, Léa A. S. Chauvigné and others, "The neural basis of audiomotor entrainment: An ALE meta-analysis," *Frontiers in Human Neuroscience* 8, 776, PMC, https://www.ncbi.nlm.nih.gov/pmc/articles/PMC4179709.

7. Emmanuel Alloa, "Coronavirus: A Contingency that Eliminates Contingency," *Critical Inquiry*, https://critinq.wordpress.com/2020/04/20/coronavirus-a-contingency-that-eliminates-contingency/.

8. Friedrich Nietzsche, *The Joyful Wisdom*, in *The Collective Works*, ed. O. Levy (New York: Russell & Russell 1964), § 107, 145–47; Friedrich Nietzsche, *The Will to Power*, in *The Collective Works*, § 795, 239.

9. This would indeed be a way of bringing Nietzsche significantly closer to Hegel in the field of the philosophy of art. This is a hermeneutic operation that I believe is quite plausible. However, I cannot elaborate on this here.

10. Immanuel Kant, *Critique of the Power of Judgment*, ed. P. Guyer (Cambridge: Cambridge University Press, 2000), 207.

11. In this regard, the chapter that Hegel dedicates to music in his *Lectures on Aesthetics* is still truly illuminating. See G. W. F. Hegel, *Lectures on Fine Arts*, vol. 2, trans. T. M. Knox (Oxford: Clarendon Press, 1975), 888–958.

12. Ernst Bloch, *The Principle of Hope*, trans. N. Plaice, S. Plaice, and P. Knight (Cambridge: MIT Press, 1986).

13. Alessandro Bertinetto and Georg Bertram, "We Make Up the Rules as We Go Along: Improvisation as Essential Aspect of Human Practice?" *Open Philosophy* 3, no. 1: 202–21. https://doi.org/10.1515/opphil-2020-0012.

14. Gilbert Ryle, *The Concept of Mind* (London: Hutchinson's University Library, 1951), 25–61.

15. Eleonora Zorzi, *L'insegnante improvvisatore* (Naples: Liguori, 2020).

16. Richard Sennett, *The Craftsman* (New Haven: Yale University Press, 2008); B. Preston, *Philosophy of Material Culture* (London-New York: Routledge, 2013).

17. Alloa, "Coronavirus: A Contingency that Eliminates Contingency."

18. Michel De Certeau, *L'invention du quotidien. I. Arts de faire* (Paris: Gallimard, 1990). See also Alessandro Bertinetto, "The Birth of Art from the Spirit of Improvisation," *Quadranti*, 6, no. 1: 119–47.

19. Luigi Pareyson, *Estetica. Teoria della formatività* (Milan: Bompiani, 2010), 59.

20. Pansodia (including Pansodia) is retrievable here: https://www.youtube.com/watch?v=6cuwy8qAACM.

21. The performance, and the whole conference, is retrievable here: https://www.youtube.com/watch?v=YGsWZg2qZ5s.

22. Sometimes I had the pleasure of playing duets with my ten-year-old daughter, performing some easy pieces, she on the clarinet, and I on the piano.

23. See Alfred Sohn-Rethel, *Das Ideal des Kaputten* (Frickingen: Seutter, 2009).

24. I elaborated on the link between improvisation and Pareyson's notion of art as aesthetic formativity in Alessandro Bertinetto, "Improvvisazione e formatività," *Annuario filosofico* 25 (2009): 145–74, and Alessandro Bertinetto, "Formatività ricorsiva e costruzione della normatività nell'improvvisazione," in *Improvvisazione oggi*, ed. A. Sbordoni (Lucca: LIM, 2014), 15–28.

Three

Out of the Choir
Bodies Inclined on the Playboy

Lorenzo Bernini

Agreeing with Michel Foucault

Life is a recent invention, Michel Foucault claims in *The Order of Things*. It is the outcome of the epistemological break that has produced modernity.[1] Before this time, a form of knowledge like biology, whose object of study is life, was not possible; nor was it possible to have a theory of natural evolution, for which life is a subject that improves itself via self-reproduction through living beings.

For Foucault, modernity begins ultimately with the French Revolution and with Napoleon, with the ripening of the modern state as the guarantor of a market economy. According to Foucault's analyses, the invention of life is in fact paralleled by the invention of work, which is the object of that other form of modern knowledge that is economics. And when an epistemological break takes place in Foucault's theoretical path; when his thinking goes from the archeological stage of the 1960s to the genealogical approach of the 1970s; that is, when he moves from reconstructing the history of knowledge alone to reconstructing the history of the relationships between knowledge and power; briefly, when, about ten years after *The Order of Things: An Archeology of Knowledge*, Foucault writes *Discipline and Punish* and *The History of Sexuality 1: The Will to Knowledge*,[2] then what might have initially appeared to him as a contingency, namely, the simultaneous invention of life and work, emerges as the outcome of a form of government, itself typically modern, that is simultaneously biopolitical and bioeconomic.

To govern the life of the population in fact implies to guarantee not only its biological survival, but also its prosperity. Foucault dies at the beginning of the 1980s due to AIDS-related complications. Nevertheless, he has time to understand the form that such a government of life takes up within the neoliberalist regime that still belongs to us—it is a statistical and differential management that, far from producing uniformity and equality, nourishes and exploits inequalities.[3] As an archeologist, Foucault claims that "man," in the singular (and also in the masculine form; in *The Order of Things*, "man" is precisely the term he uses), is the subject of modernity and, at the same time, the object of the modern, humanistic forms of knowledge. Ultimately, it is man who lives and works (and speaks) and who, at the same time, knows life and work (and language). As a genealogist, however, Foucault realizes that the population, which is both subject and object of neoliberal biopolitics and bioeconomics, is made of human beings in the plural; that such human beings belonging to the population are dishomogeneous and unequal; that their lives do not count in the same way; that the safety, health, well-being, and wealth of some of them occur at the cost of the risk, disease, discomfort, and poverty of others.

Can one have doubts about such theses of this major French thinker? To agree with him, it suffices that one considers the social effects of the Covid-19 pandemic or, better, the governmental measures that have been implemented in the whole world, including Italy, to cope with it. In this chapter, I will reflect on this situation while privileging, among the many possible interpretative lenses, the registers of gender and sexuality. Before I get to that, though, I have three questions that I would like you, the readers, to consider: What has been your experience of the outburst of the pandemic and the state of emergency? How have you spent the lockdown time? How are you faring now?

Adriana Cavarero and the Privilege of Feeling Vulnerable

It is with some reticence (*pudore*) that I say this; yet, all things considered, I have fared well. Up to the time of writing this, the people who are dearest to me have been spared from the virus, and the same is true for me. Since the beginning, angst has taken for me the form of a very specific fear, namely, that my very old parents, who reside in Lombardy—the

Italian region most affected by the contagion—might become infected. I have certainly shared the mourning of some friends who have lost their parents, and I have partaken in the concerns for some other friends who have fallen sick (and then, luckily, have recovered). Yet, albeit within a very dramatic situation, I have been able to live the lockdown with a certain degree of comfort.

Those whose profession is to study and write are accustomed to isolation. Those who have a stable position within the Italian university benefit from fixed income. Those who, among such persons, have a good internet connection have been able to continue their work activities with ease via online modalities: meetings, lectures, seminars, conferences, exams, dissertation defenses. Through the same distance modalities, they have been able to continue meeting those who are dear to them: appointments, aperitifs, birthday gatherings—everything online. Last, those who have a home with sufficiently ample spaces have been able to rediscover the pleasures of domestic life in rhythms of existence suddenly made calmer in a time of living suddenly dilated. No more constant trips to give lectures at conferences; more time to devote to one's loved ones in order to feel them in proximity even when at a distance; silence in the streets and birds chirping (frequently punctuated, one must admit, with the sirens of the ambulances); online physical exercise classes; and so on. In short, we have discovered many ways to take care of ourselves. On my small, yet well-positioned home balcony, in front of my computer, during an invitingly mild spring, I have even gotten a bit of a suntan, as has rarely happened to me before.

In this experience of mine, I have not felt alone. I have felt isolated yet not lonely within a condition of serial isolation that, according to the media representation of the lockdown, appeared to affect all of Italy. Turning on the radio or the TV or surfing the internet was enough to feel "with company"; the slogan "*Io resto a casa,* I stay at home," the hashtag on social media, surfaced everywhere; everywhere proliferated interviews with famous and less famous characters who praised the virtues of their newly discovered contemplative life. Then, in the evening, there were the 6:00 p.m. flashmobs: everyone was locked inside one's home, and yet everyone was suddenly outside, on terraces and balconies, all together singing the Italian national anthem, elevating "a serenade for democracy," as Bonnie Honig has written citing Adriana Cavarero.[4]

In terms of having some company, I have not been deprived of philosophical reflections on this unprecedented situation. Among the most interesting of them in Italy, I would like to mention the revamping of feminist theories regarding relationality, care, and vulnerability; that is, regarding a conception of subjectivity alternative to the way in which the modern tradition, which is patriarchal, male, and male-chauvinist, has for the most part conceptualized the "man" of whom Foucault speaks. In an interview, Adriana Cavarero, for example, has highlighted that one of the effects of the pandemic has been an accentuation of the awareness of the vulnerability of oneself and others; that is, of the need for human beings to live in a compassionate community.

Paradoxically, however, caring for each other has taken up the form of distancing, of abstaining from contact among bodies. According to Cavarero, this unprecedented situation has also imposed a new hierarchy of perception and has allowed the voice, the vocal element, to prevail as the feature of recognition of the other's uniqueness.[5] Hence, the sense that Honig too has acknowledged in the 6:00 p.m. flashmobs: they are "a plural love song," composed of many unique voices, elevated "for that public happiness," that hanging out among people who are different, which "we especially miss while in physical isolation."[6]

Who more than me—with my being accustomed to the happiness of dialogues with the audience during conferences, with my being worried about my distant, elderly parents—could be sensitive to the call of such a plural singing, in which my voice could ideally join the voice of my parents? On the contrary, I abstained from such daily ritual—I remained out of the choir. I abstained not only due to allergy toward patriotism (had they sung "The Internationale," I might have thought about joining them). I abstained also because of my skepticism toward the rhetoric of the "I stay home" slogan; because of my diffidence toward the identification of myself in the remote work modality with the publicized image, broadcast by the media, of the Italians in lockdown (the Italians who stay home and go out on the balcony and sing). In other words, I abstained because of the bitter awareness that my possibility to be such an Italian, during the harshest months—at least until now—of the pandemic, is owed not only to the luck of not getting infected, but also to the privileges from which I benefit.

Giorgio Agamben on the Pedestal

I do not wish to be misunderstood here. I agree with Cavarero: the pandemic has rendered absolutely evident the inadequacy of that (even philosophical) male imaginary that represents the human being as a sovereign, unrelated, and independent individual; that is, as a calculating mind whose body is an accident (one can think here of Descartes, for whom the I is because it thinks!). For the human animal, as well as for any other living animal, the body is instead indispensable. We are, first of all, bodies; and, far from turning us into sovereign subjects, the body makes us dependent on the care of the other (since birth, because each of us is born from a woman's body and not from one's own thinking, *pace* Descartes). It is indeed true that the pandemic has presented a paradoxical situation, in which many of us have been asked to take care of others while remaining distant from them. Many of us could cultivate human relationships only at a distance, abstracting from the body or, better, relying on what are simply its partial manifestations: the voice in the long phone conversations with our dear ones; that form of avatar represented by our images framed in homogeneous rectangles during videoconferences; and so on. Are we sure, though, that this dematerialization of the human body has affected everyone in the same way? And that, when we move from theory to practice, it is easy to replace the male imaginary with another one? In truth, in the narratives of the pandemic, the subject of the patriarchal—unrelated, sovereign, bellicose—imaginary has proved not to be at all willing to yield to more fragile subjects that partake in kinder imaginaries.

To begin with, we could think of the proliferation of war-related metaphors that have been used all over the world by governmental sources as well as by the press. In this respect, Italy is no exception. In the briefings by the Italian prime minister, Giuseppe Conte; in the news released by TV channels and newspapers; in the comments during talk shows; and in posts and tweets on the social media, the SARS-CoV-2 has been described not only as a very contagious and potentially lethal virus, which it is indeed, but also as an invisible *enemy* against which the Italian people are fighting a *war*. The deceased—whose number was announced daily in a dispatch by the Protezione Civile, the Italian unit that deals with the prevention and management of national emergencies and disasters—have been collectively celebrated as if they were dead soldiers who, as it has been often repeated, had tried to withstand the disease as true fighters. Doctors and nurses have been described as being on the front line, in the trenches, in the role of the heroic avant-garde against the disease. The Italian national anthem during the flashmobs was dedicated to them, and the words of such an antiquated anthem leave no doubt: "Italian brothers (and, indeed, not sisters) . . . let us gather in cohort formation, we are ready to die, Italy has called us." Honig and Cavarero speak of a serenade to democracy and, certainly, there has been that aspect too. At the same time, though, these flashmobs have been an obedient response to the restrictive measures imposed by the government: the entire people like an army of disciplined soldiers willing to embrace any form of sacrifice, joining in "a cohort" without questions or objections. What jargon is more successful than the military idiom in neutralizing not only disobedience, but also critique?

Criticisms of the government too have been uttered, at times, with tones that are not only conspiratorial but also belligerent, in the name not of compassion toward vulnerability of oneself and others, but of resistance toward a state of exception perceived as having been proclaimed on purpose with the only goal of limiting our liberties. The most significant instance of such criticisms has raised some eyebrows also outside of Italy. In a series of essays on the "alleged epidemics of coronavirus," with scornful tones, Giorgio Agamben has come close to negationism when defining Covid-19 as "some kind of a flu."[7] He has also denounced the possibility of power abuses under the pretext of the medical emergency (which he has defined as "the lab where the new political and social assets awaiting humanity are prepared"[8] and as "an experiment [. . .] in which what is at stake is a new paradigm of government of human beings and things").[9] Moreover, he has prospected the possible degeneration of human relationships because of confinement and social distancing and the possible diffusion of a climate of mistrust and suspicion.[10] In addition to all this and above it all, though, Agamben has judged the rest of us from on high. He has mocked us—we who are confused and distressed, who are afraid of death, who care for our lives and for the lives of the people whom we love so much that we accept severe restrictions to the point of showing our thankfulness for them through our singing on balconies. Because the life that is at stake here is not bare or "naked life," as Agamben writes, but rather a life wrapped up with feelings, as for me is the life of my elderly parents. Agamben writes, "The first thing the wave of panic that's paralysed the country has clearly shown is that our society no longer believes in anything but naked life. It is evident that Italians are prepared to sacrifice practically everything—normal living conditions, social relations, work, even friendships and religious or political beliefs—to avoid the danger of falling ill. The naked life, and the fear of losing it, is not something that brings men and women together, but something that blinds and separates them."[11]

This position, to my mind, is one of the most fitting examples to describe the attitude that, in *The History of Sexuality 1: The Will to Knowledge*, Foucault calls "the speaker's benefit."[12] He uses this expression to criticize those intellectuals who limit themselves to preach, with contemptuous certainty, the refusal of what exists, as if this attitude were enough to free them from the condition in which the other social agents find themselves. Over the years, Agamben has assembled a major theoretical apparatus by re-elaborating, with great originality, concepts drawn not only from Foucault, but also from Hannah Arendt, Walter Benjamin, and Carl Schmitt (biopolitics, naked life, state of exception). In Agamben's most recent essays, this apparatus is deployed to remark on the reality of the pandemic without really examining it, without truly taking part in it (as if this self-distancing were possible). The effect of subjectivation produced by this attitude has been, to my mind, nothing else than the erection of a monument to himself, a pedestal on which to stand and assume the posture of a (certainly male) superman, neither compassionate nor empathic, who hallucinates his own invulnerability.

Indeed, we do need critique if we do not want to restrict ourselves to the contemplation (and vocalization) of our own vulnerability, which, by itself, runs the risk of reinforcing the privileges of some of us; if we, on the contrary, wish to denounce such privileges, that is, those dispositifs of differential vulnerability that Foucault already acknowledged and the pandemic has confirmed or even strengthened.[13] We need critique if we want to be vigilant regarding the forms of power that govern us, even during a state of emergency; if we intend to denounce their possible abuses; and, finally, if we wish to try to turn the crisis into a chance to resume thinking of social transformations and practicing them. Such a critique should, however, be sought elsewhere—neither in the comfort of our homes and on our rhetorical balconies nor on psychotic pedestals, but rather in the midst of the thing itself. That is, in that productive and reproductive world in which the virus does not stop circulating.

Paul B. Preciado and the Horizontal Worker

Already in 1977, while reflecting on her personal experience of cancer, and then in 1988, regarding the AIDS pandemic, Susan Sontag denounced the little empathy that is contained in the application of the metaphors of fight, victory or defeat (in addition to those of sin and expiation) to an illness. She also decried how this can be an obstacle to the healing process as it burdens the sickened person with feelings of guilt and the possible loss of the sense of one's own priorities.[14] Recuperating one's health depends not on the tenaciousness of the single person, but rather on the care that such a person receives, on the health resources that are available, and, ultimately, also on good luck. Paul B. Preciado is one of those who have given a testimony of their suffering through Covid-19. In a less-than-heroic article, rather than celebrating a victorious battle against the virus, Preciado narrates how the illness weakened him physically and intellectually; he then confesses how, once healed, he felt the "ridiculous" need to write a love letter to his former lover.[15] In an another article, written not much later, with reference to Foucault's thought and his retrieval by Roberto Esposito and Emily Martins,[16] Preciado claims that, now as well as in the past, the management of pandemics discloses, as if it were a reagent, not only the power structures at work in a society, but also the processes of subjectivation and the corresponding immunitary phantasies related to such structures.

Not unlike Cavarero, Preciado acknowledges that political modernity is founded on the ideal of the individual understood "as an immunized body radically separated, that owed nothing to the community." Cavarero would say that this invulnerable subject, which is seemingly neutral, is in fact sexually male. Preciado adds that such a subject is also heterosexual and white; and he reconstructs how the biopolitical management of epidemics has contributed to the construction of this subject, transforming diseases into an occasion to immunize society from those bodies that constitute the abjected reversal of the hegemonic individual. For colonial and industrial societies from the thirteenth to the eighteenth century, for example, "as a working and often racialized woman, a body outside the laws of home and marriage, who turned her sexuality into her means of production, the sex worker was made visible, controlled and stigmatized as the principal vector of" syphilis. In the "heteronormative neoliberal societies" of the late twentieth century, what was deployed to identify the subjects from which to immunize society was AIDS, which the US Center for Disease Control (CDC) initially named the "4H disease," from the initial letter of the four social groups mostly affected by the disease: "homosexuals, Haitians, hemophiliacs, and heroin users. Later, hookers were added to the list."

Not much unlike Agamben and following Foucault, Preciado also highlights how epidemics have always been "great laboratories of social innovation." The reclusion of lepers in leper colonies during the Middle Ages and the Renaissance favored the consolidation of that sovereign power—juridical and necropolitical—that condemned the lepers to a kind of "social death" and sentenced other enemies of the sovereign "to physical death." Starting with the seventeenth century though, the "strict segmentation of the city and confinement of each body in every home" during plague epidemics unfolded, on the entire society, a new form of control typical of what Foucault has taught us to call "disciplinary power."[17] This deeply modified the societal fabric. The same could take place currently, according to Preciado. The Covid-19 pandemic might in fact exasperate biopolitical dispositifs of immunitary control that are already present within our societies—border closures for migrants, the construction of walls to ward them off and camps to close them in—to the point of having the borders in need of immunization come to identify with the perimeters of the single homes, with the surfaces of the single bodies. This could lead to completion of a process that has actually started a while back and that leads to the fabrication of a new biopolitical subject: no longer an individual but rather an "un-dividual," a flow of retraceable and controllable data. Preciado writes,

> The subjects of the neoliberal technical-patriarchal societies that Covid-19 is in the midst of creating do not have skin; they are untouchable; they do not have hands. They do not exchange physical goods, nor do they pay with money. They are digital consumers equipped with credit cards. They do not have lips or tongues. They do not speak directly; they leave a voicemail. They do not gather together and they do not collectivize. They are radically un-dividual. They do not have faces; they have masks. In order to exist, their organic bodies are hidden behind an indefinite series of semio-technical mediations, an array of cybernetic prostheses that work like digital masks: email addresses, Facebook, Instagram, Zoom, and Skype accounts. They are not physical agents but rather tele-producers; they are codes, pixels, bank accounts, doors without names, addresses to which Amazon can send its orders.

With respect to this new subject, Preciado too emphasizes its loss of the physical dimension. Referring to some of his earlier essays,[18] Preciado turns to Hugh Hefner, the founder of the magazine *Playboy*, whom he describes as "one of the richest men on earth [who] spent nearly forty years lounging around at home, dressed in pajamas, a bathrobe, and slippers, drinking Pepsis and eating Butterfingers," working on a circular rotating bed that was "connected to a telephone, a radio, a stereo, and a videocamera."[19] Preciado considers Hefner as the prototype of the new "horizontal worker"—the worker who works remotely—produced by the "war" against Covid-19: hyperconnected yet isolated, confined to a domestic space that is simultaneously a center for teleproduction, teleconsumption, and cyber surveillance. We have all become Hugh Hefner, then. As I mentioned earlier, I myself am even in greater shape and more tanned than ever before! For some, this perspective is certainly alluring. One should be careful though, as it also risks being misleading.

Bodies Inclined on the Playboy

In truth, Hefner did have a body—one that was reclined on a rotating bed and that, as Preciado notes, belonged to a white, wealthy, and heterosexual male, whose sustenance in terms of biological life was made possible by the care of others. Hefner had servants who went shopping for him, cleaned after him and changed his bed sheets, washed his robe, his pajamas, and his underwear (assuming he wore some); and his beautiful villa was full of "bunnies" to satisfy his sexual needs. Some rich men whom the health emergency has forced to work from home may perhaps identify with him, while others might be sensitive to the fantasy of such an identification. Yet most women (even wealthy women) who work remotely as well as some other persons of male gender or other genders know very well that the incorporeal avatar of distance work has an opposite side to it: food shopping (even when one places orders online), meals to prepare, housework to take care of, elderly parents—possibly unable, like mine, to order online—to care for, children to tend to and teach in the process of assisting educators who do what they can through online teaching, which nevertheless is not enough. It is not the eclipse of corporality. It is not the rediscovery of the vulnerability of oneself and others via abstention from contacts. It is not the replacement of the male-based imaginary with a feminist imaginary. Even the advertising image of Italians who stay at home and, while working remotely, dematerialize (while simultaneously still taking care of themselves) is basically modeled on a man (and, to a lesser extent, a woman) who is healthy and wealthy, whose primary needs are taken care of through the work done for him (and her) by the body of others.[20] In truth, even during the strictest lockdown, the bodies of the infants, the elderly, the persons who have been seriously disabled or ill have been tended to by relatives and helpers; partnering bodies have continued to touch and love one another. Moreover, many (too many) bodies have not had the luxury of any online meeting avatars. This has been the case for the bodies of doctors and nurses, which have continued being exposed to contact with infected others; and it has also been the case for many other bodies (of pharmacists, cashiers in supermarkets, workers in food production, medical, and information industries), which have continued running the risk of contagion so that essential services could remain available or which were simply forced to work by dishonest employers who certified as essential activities those which were in fact not such (this is, at least, what at times has happened in Italy). If we truly wish to get rid of the male imaginary of an unrelated subject, we must also abandon the idea that the world in which we have lived during the lockdown mode is a world without bodies. Many bodies have continued circulating; many bodies have continued touching one another; and many activities of care have continued in the most traditional ways. These activities have been carried out neither by bodies erected on pedestals, like Agamben's, nor by reclined bodies, like the horizontal online workers described by Preciado, but rather by bodies inclined over other bodies, to return to Cavarero's language, which Cavarero barely uses, though, in the interview on Covid-19.[21] We should also not forget the bodies that have neither a job nor a home; the migrant bodies in transit, in the Mediterranean, toward the European dream (or mirage); the bodies confined in various prisons and detention centers. Many of the bodies amassed in cells or on boats could not maintain distance. Italians have been shocked by the public yet generic mourning that, at the peak of the emergency, replaced the celebration of single funerals. Yet we should not forget that in the main cemetery in Milan, lot no. 87 has been allotted to bodies that no one has claimed. Some have inclined themselves over these unknown bodies in order to grant them at least a burial.

From birth to death and, in truth, even before and after, not "man" but, rather, the human being is a flow of corporeal relations, which are not limited to human relationships. As evidenced by Rosi Braidotti and Donna Haraway among others, human life is interconnected with nonhuman life and with the existence of the whole planet.[22] For decades, the climate crisis has made us aware of this. The zoonotic origin of SARS-CoV-2 is the tragic confirmation thereof. The vulnerability of the subject/body is not simply an ontological condition, though; it is also and primarily a political condition. Those who have read David Quammen's *Spillover* or have even just watched *Pandemic* on Netflix know that, for years, the scientific community had been aware of the risk of a new pandemic with pulmonary pathology.[23] If Italian hospitals were not ready to protect their employees with adequate medical equipment; if family doctors completely lacked such similar devices; if intensive care units were neither sufficient in numbers nor sufficiently equipped with respirators, this has not been a coincidence. Rather, the logic of profit and saving has prevailed over the logic of prevention. It is not difficult to find the reason either for the climate crisis that devastates the planet and, with it, our lives and our bodies or for the intersection of our vital environment with ecological niches of wildlife species—such reason is called capitalism. Likewise, it is not difficult to find the reason why our bodies have found themselves so exposed to the virus, why our nursing homes for the elderly and our hospitals have become, from sites of care, hotspots for the contagion—such a reason is called neoliberal management of the health system. The ontological vulnerability of our bodies has been exasperated by a *vulnus*, by a wound that is entirely political: bioeconomic and biopolitical. As Judith Butler has emphasized very aptly, naked life is not life outside politics, as Agamben would have it; rather, it is life that has been deprived of all forms of protection by politics.[24] Vindicating such protection, reclaiming it for everyone can become the starting point to imagine, as Preciado does at the end of his article, the establishment of "a parliament not defined in terms of the politics of identity or nationality: a parliament of (vulnerable) bodies living on planet Earth," a new, non-immunitary community of care encompassing "all living creatures."[25] With my abstention from singing the national anthem, I cannot but share this appeal—a new Internationale!

Appendix: The Rectum in Parliament

Epidemics accelerate political processes already in progress. Beyond that, however, they also highlight social inequalities and hierarchies, that is, those biopolitical and bioeconomic lines of demarcation, whether material or imaginary, which Foucault had already acknowledged. Moreover, they underline the shifting of such borders within history. With reference to Esposito and Martins in addition to Foucault, Preciado emphasizes the extent to which the Covid-19 pandemic has given literal meaning to an immunitary trend that was already present, and indeed for some time, within our societies.

In the 1987 essay "Is the Rectum a Grave?" Leo Bersani noted how the AIDS pandemic made literal the threat that anal penetration among males represents for the imaginary of heterosexual men.[26] In this sense, for Bersani, the rectum is the grave of the male sovereign subject; it is what reminds such a subject of his own vulnerability by confronting him with the unbearable possibility of getting pleasure out of a passive position deemed acceptable only for women.[27] During the first phase of reopening from the lockdown in Italy, when it was established that one could visit relatives and family members but not friends and acquaintances, the category of family members was made to include also partners in lesbian and gay couples that had been civilly united. In comparison with what had happened in the 1980s, I was struck by this fact. It is as if, in the passage from one pandemic to the next, the liberation of gay men from the stigma of being the plague spreaders has been traded for their sacrifice of being the representatives for the experimentation of lifestyles different from the nuclear family.[28] In situations in which the bodies are far from eclipsed, this fact too has established a hierarchy of bodies and their relationships: some bodies may be encountered, but others may not. It does not matter that still too often LGBTQ+ persons are rejected by their families; it does not matter that they find support in communities of friends rather than their families; nor does it matter that the Italian civil law denies family status to couples that have been civilly united.[29] In Italy, one of the outcomes of Covid-19 has also been the reassessment of the superiority of the family model over any other affective community. This is shocking also in relation to the fact that, for the entire duration of the lockdown, women's associations and antiviolence centers have pointed out the increase in situations of domestic violence due to segregation. There was even a moment when abused women were told that they could/should continue spending time, among relatives and family members, with their abusive husbands and partners. Those among such women who were waiting for the affection of a friend—a friend perhaps capable of providing them with some strength, of persuading them to press charges for the abuses—had to wait longer. These matters too will have to be addressed in the interspecies planetary parliament.

Translated from Italian by Silvia Benso

Notes

1. Michel Foucault, *The Order of Things: An Archaeology of the Human Sciences* (New York: Random House, 1970).

2. Michel Foucault, *Discipline and Punish: The Birth of the Prison*, trans. Alan Sheridan (New York: Random House, 1978) and *The History of Sexuality 1: The Will to Knowledge*, trans. Robert Hurley (New York: Random House, 1978).

3. Michel Foucault, *Security, Territory, Population: Lectures at the Collège de France 1977–1978*, trans. Graham Burchell (New York: Palgrave Macmillan, 2009) and *The Birth of Biopolitics: Lectures at the Collège de France 1978–1979*, trans. Graham Burchell (New York: Palgrave Macmillan, 2010).

4. Bonnie Honig, "In the Street a Serenade," *Politics/Letters Live*, March 14, 2020. http://politicsslashletters.org/uncategorized/in-the-streets-a-serenade/. See also Adriana Cavarero, *For More than One Voice: Toward a Philosophy of Vocal Expression*, trans. Paul A. Kottman (Stanford, CA: Stanford University Press, 2005).

5. Cavarero and other philosophers—including myself—were interviewed for the article by Giulia Siviero, "Il futuro dei corpi: Cosa pensano i filosofi e le filosofe del nostro nuovo rapporto con la pelle e col toccarsi, e di quello che ci aspetta," *il Post*, May 10, 2020. https://www.ilpost.it/2020/05/10/il-futuro-dei-corpi/. Here one can read: "Distance does not allow us to smell the bodily odors of the other, and vision too is somehow mortified. The mask takes away the vision of the other. You cannot see the face of the other, the 'face-to-face' is missing, to use Levinas' expression. What comes to fore in this situation is the vocal element, which, unlike the gaze, is always and irremediably relational. It does not allow for a detached orientation toward the object because, properly, it has no object. It vibrates in the air and hits the other's ear even without a specific intention. Sight is an active sensory mode: I direct my gaze where I want to. The voice instead penetrates, hearing is passive, it receives from everywhere. The voice is also a trace though; it is unique, it lets one feel one's embodied uniqueness and lets one hear the singular voice of the other." This interview started me thinking about some of the themes I am addressing in

this chapter.

6. Siviero, "Il futuro dei corpi."

7. Giorgio Agamben, "L'invenzione di un'epidemia," February 26, 2020. https://www.quodlibet.it/giorgio-agamben-l-invenzione-di-un-epidemia. Some of these reflections appear in English translation, together with replies and thoughts from various other intellectuals, at https://www.journal-psychoanalysis.eu/coronavirus-and-philosophers/.

8. Giorgio Agamben, "Distanziamento sociale," April 6, 2020. https://www.quodlibet.it/giorgio-agamben-distanziamento-sociale.

9. Giorgio Agamben, "Biosicurezza e politica," May 11, 2020. https://www.quodlibet.it/giorgio-agamben-biosicurezza.

10. Giorgio Agamben, "Contagio," March 11, 2020. https://www.quodlibet.it/giorgio-agamben-contagio.

11. Giorgio Agamben, "Chiarimenti," March 17, 2020. https://www.quodlibet.it/giorgio-agamben-chiarimenti; and "Riflessioni sulla peste," March 27, 2020. https://www.quodlibet.it/giorgio-agamben-riflessioni-sulla-peste.

12. Foucault, *History of Sexuality 1*, 6.

13. Cavarero was instead among the promoters of the petition *Basta con gli agguati* (Stop to the ambushes), which was published on the Italian daily newspaper *Il manifesto* at the end of April 2020. https://ilmanifesto.it/appello-basta-con-gli-agguati/. The stated intention of the document is a defense of the way in which the Italian government handled the pandemic from journalistic or politicized and instrumental attacks. However, when one reads the text of the petition, one may have the unpleasant impression of a call to suspend all critique during the state of emergency.

14. Susan Sontag, *Illness as Metaphor and AIDS and Its Metaphors* (New York: Farrar, Straus & Giroux, 2005).

15. See Paul. B. Preciado, "The Losers Conspiracy," *Artforum*, March 26, 2020. https://www.artforum.com/slant/paul-b-preciado-on-life-after-covid-19-82586. Preciado writes,

> During the sickness, I was unable to assess what was happening from a political and economic point of view because the fever and the discomfort took hold of my vital energy. No one can be philosophical with an exploding head. Bursting with the lyricism and anxiety accumulated over a week of being sick, afraid and uncertain, the letter to my ex was not only a poetic and desperate declaration of love, it was above all a shameful document for the one who had signed it. But if things could no longer change, if those who were far apart could never touch each other again, what was the significance of being ridiculous in this way? What was the significance of now telling the person you love that you loved them, all while knowing that in all likelihood she had already forgotten you or replaced you, if you would never be able

to see her again in any case? The new state of things, in its sculptural immobility, conferred a new degree of *what the fuck*, even in its own ridiculousness.

16. Paul. B. Preciado, "Learning from the Virus," *Artforum*, May/June 2020. https://www.artforum.com/print/202005/paul-b-preciado-82823. The quotations in this paragraph are from this text. For Preciado's references to Esposito and Martins, see Roberto Esposito, *Immunitas: The Protection and Negation of Life*, trans. Zakiya Hanafi (Cambridge: Polity Press, 2011) and Emily Martins, *Flexible Bodies: Tracking Immunity in American Culture from the Days of Polio to the Age of AIDS* (Boston: Beacon Press, 1995).

17. The reclusion of lepers is described by Foucault first in Michel Foucault, *History of Madness*, trans. Jonathan Murphy (New York: Routledge, 2006), and then compared with the disciplinary management of the plagued city in Foucault, *Discipline and Punish* and *Security, Territory, Population*.

18. Beatriz Preciado, *Testo Junkie: Sex, Drugs and Biopolitics in the Pharmacopornographic Era*, trans. Bruce Benderson (New York: The Feminist Press at CUNY, 2013); Beatriz Preciado, *Pornotopia: An Essay on Playboy's Architecture and Biopolitics* (New York: Zone Books, 2014). In these books, Foucault's notion of biopolitics is updated through the concept of pharmacopornographic regime, which in the journal article is explained as follows:

> In other writings, I've used the term *pharmacopornographic* for this type of management and production of the body as well as to describe the political technologies that produce sexual subjectivity within this new configuration of power and knowledge. We are no longer regulated solely by their passage through disciplinary institutions (school, factory, barracks, hospital, etc.) but by a set of biomolecular technologies that enter into the body by way of microprostheses and technologies of digital surveillance subtler and more insidious than anything Gilles Deleuze envisioned in his famous prognostications about the society of control. In the domain of sexuality, the pharmacological modification of consciousness and behavior, the mass consumption of antidepressants and anxiolytics, and the globalization of the contraceptive pill, as well as antiretroviral therapies, preventative AIDS therapies, and Viagra, are some of the indicators of biotechnological management, which in turn synergizes with new modes of semio-technical management that have arisen with the surveillance state and the global expansion of the network into every facet of life. I use the term *pornographic* because these management techniques function no longer through the repression and prohibition of sexuality, but through the incitement of consumption and the constant production of a regulated and quantifiable pleasure. The more we consume and the better our health, the better we are

controlled.

19. Hefner's house was the Playboy Mansion—first the original gothic manor in Chicago and then its Los Angeles successor.

20. On the crucial function of exploitation of the work of social reproduction of women and colonized and racialized subjects for the functioning of capitalism, see the fundamental works by Silvia Federici, *Caliban and the Witch: Women, the Body and Primitive Accumulation* (New York: Autonomedia, 2004) and *Revolution at Point Zero: Housework, Reproduction, and Feminist Struggle* (Oakland, CA: PM Press 2012).

21. The reference is here to Adriana Cavarero, *Inclinations: A Critique of Rectitude*, trans. Amanda Minervini and Adam Sitze (Stanford, CA: Stanford University Press, 2016). In the interview mentioned above, Cavarero claims that "the one who cares is inclined on the other, on the weaker. Currently though, this type of caring, caring through touch, through inclination, is prohibited because we know that if we touch the other, we may transmit the virus."

22. See Rosi Braidotti, *The Posthuman* (Cambridge, UK: Polity Press, 2013) and Donna J. Haraway, *Staying with the Trouble: Making Kin in the Chtulucene* (Durham: Duke University Press, 2016).

23. David Quammen, *Spillover: Animal Infections and the Next Human Pandemic* (New York: W. W. Norton & Company, 2012).

24. Judith Butler and Gayatri Chakravorty Spivack, *Who Sings the Nation State? Language, Politics, Belonging* (American Fork, UT: Seagull Books, 2007).

25. Paul B. Preciado, "Learning from the Virus." Even though Preciado does not mention it, the image of the parliament recalls the "parliament of things" evoked by Bruno Latour, *We Have Never Been Modern*, trans. Catherine Porter (Cambridge: Harvard University Press, 1993), where, among other things, the analysis of the AIDS pandemic is crucial. A little while later, Preciado instigates, with tones similar to Agamben's, to "set in motion new forms of antagonism," boycott isolation together with connectivity, turn off phones, and log off the internet. In my view, these are the most arguable lines of his essay. To my mind, the lockdown has been a painful yet necessary measure; boycotting it would have been irresponsible. Also, how can one establish the planetary parliament unless one is connected and even multiplies connections?

26. Leo Bersani, "Is the Rectum a Grave?" *October* 43 (1987); now in Leo Bersani, *Is the Rectum a Grave? And Other Essays* (Chicago: University of Chicago Press, 2010).

27. Preciado too has reflected on the political meaning of anal sex on the basis not of Bersani's but rather of Guy Hocquenghem's thought; see Preciado's essay, "Terror Anal," which constitutes the preface to the Spanish translation of Guy Hocquenghem, *El deseo homosexual. Con Terror anal de Beatriz Preciado* (Barcelona: Melusina, 2009). The English translation of Hocquenghem's book does not contain such a preface. See Guy Hocquenghem, *Homosexual Desire*, trans. Daniella Dangoor (Durham: Duke University Press, 1993).

28. We should recall that the AIDS pandemic has never come to an end.

Whereas in rich countries it is currently possible to control the HIV infection through antiretroviral therapies and even protect oneself through a pre-exposure prophylaxis, in the African continent the access to these medications remains a privilege of the few and the majority goes on dying of AIDS.

29. In Italy, civil unions of same-sex couples are legally recognized through the May 20, 2016, Law Number 76—a law named "Law Cirinnà" because of the last name of its promoter, Senator Monica Cirinnà. This law precludes homosexual couples from accessing marriage and the ability to adopt, which the Italian law still reserves exclusively to heterosexual couples. According to the text of the law, couples that have been joined in civil unions constitute not a family but, rather, a "specific social formation."

Four

Metaphor as Illness?
Life, War, and a Linguistic *Pharmakon*

Alberto Martinengo

"Our Little Army in White Outfits"

In the afternoon of March 28, 2020, a small group of about thirty medical and paramedical personnel flew from Albania to Italy, specifically to Brescia, one of the hotspots of the Covid-19 pandemic in Italy. At the airport in Tirana, the Albanian prime minister, Edi Rama, delivered a farewell speech that became widely popular in the media. On that same day, in Italy, about 6,000 new cases of Covid-19 were recorded among a population of about sixty million people. These numbers were comparable to the previous week, when 6,500 new cases marked the highest daily peak. Still on March 28, the total number of deaths in Italy reached 10,000. Just a couple of weeks later, in mid-April, Italy finally reached its long-lasting *plateau* phase of about 110,000 active cases reported being hospitalized in health structures. It was not until around May 4, almost a whole month later, that there was a significant decrease in the number of infected people, now totaling under 100,000 active cases.

Rama's farewell message strongly affected the public in both countries, Albania and Italy, for various reasons. Rama, who is fluent in Italian, chose to give his speech in both languages. He recalled the recent history of relationships between the two countries and made reference to the emigration of tens of thousands of Albanian citizens to Italy since 1991, following the fall of the communist regime. Currently, in Italy, the community of Albanian origin counts almost half a million people and is second only to the community of Romanian origin. "Our home is there too," Rama said, "ever since Italy and our Italian brothers and sisters saved us, hosted us, and welcomed us in their houses, when Albania was hit by immense sufferings." And he continued: "We are neither wealthy nor forgetful, [therefore] we cannot afford not to show Italy that Albanians and Albania never abandon a friend who is experiencing hard times."[1]

The decision of the Albanian government caught the attention of the Italian media neither because of the nature nor because of the entity of the aids. Albania was neither the first nor the last to send material support to Italy during the months of the health emergency. China sent 300 people, Cuba 50, the United States 60, and Russia—with a form of aid that provoked major discussions because of the paramilitary nature of the dispatched contingent—sent about 130. What aroused great interest was rather the narrative charge of the Albanian mission. Rama's discourse spoke of a reversal of roles in terms of "the helper" and "the helped." It also passed through a rhetorical embellishment of the 1990s migratory events, which were in truth accompanied by a widespread occurrence of ethnically based episodes of discrimination against the people who had arrived from Albania as clandestine. Wisely, Rama did not mention any of this. Some kind of forgiveness in the form of oblivion was offered by those who, in previous times, had been victims and now could return the help that they had received. Hence, the resorting to obvious domestic metaphors of home and family, which are particularly interesting because of their reversal of nationalistic slogans often repeated in various languages such as "Go home," in English and "*Aiutiamoli a casa loro* [Let's help them in their homeland]" in Italian. It is as if Rama had said: "Now it is we who can help you in your own home, in Italy."

In the few minutes of Rama's speech, what dominated the picture was, however, a different metaphorical imagery. Rama's words deserve therefore to be reproduced somewhat at length.

> I know that for some, here in Albania, it may seem odd that thirty doctors and nurses, our little army in white outfits, [leave] today to join the front lines in Italy. I know that thirty doctors and nurses will not [revert] the balance between the lethal power of the invisible enemy and the white-outfitted forces that are fighting on the front lines on the other side of the sea . . . We

are fighting the same invisible enemy. The human and logistic resources of our war are not unlimited. Yet today we cannot keep our reservists on hold waiting for them to be called while in Italy, where Albanians too, wounded by the enemy, are treated in military hospitals, there is a humongous need for help. It is true that all are locked up within their own borders and even very rich countries have turned their back to others. Yet perhaps precisely because we are neither wealthy nor forgetful, we cannot afford to not show Italy that Albanians and Albania never abandon a friend who is experiencing hard times. This is a war where no one can win alone and you, my dear courageous participants in this mission for life, you are leaving for a war that is also ours. Today, we are all Italians. And Italy must and will win this war for us too, and for Europe, and for the whole world. May God bless you all.

"Domestic" exceptions already mentioned aside, the metaphor of the disease as war occupies Rama's speech from beginning to end. We cannot simply say that such a metaphor supports or strengthens his discourse. Rather, it recurs in almost every sentence. Thus, it is at the core of the speech, and it is even its very content. Added to this is the introduction of nontrivial images emphasizing warlike rhetoric. As an example, the medical personnel ready to leave for Italy is qualified with the term "reservist." Nor is there an absence of reversals between the literal and the metaphorical levels. While the lack of beds in Italian hospitals forced the authorities to set up temporary structures normally used by the army—field hospitals—Rama's discourse uses this circumstance further to feed the military metaphor and speaks of people sent to the *lines* or, even, to the *fire lines*. Their anticontamination outfits and their plexiglass face shields are represented as some kind of a new *battle uniform* where the classical military brown-green is deflected toward the sterile white of hospital coats.

In those weeks, similar declarations of war were very frequent among the political authorities of almost all countries. If Rama's discourse deserves analysis because of its creative use of the framework, a few words are worth being said also regarding the announcement made to the French nation by its president, Emmanuel Macron, on March 16, therewith decreeing the most severe stage of the lockdown. Whereas Rama's intervention exemplifies well a short discourse entirely steeped in metaphorics, Macron's speech is the evident case of a more extended discourse—about twenty minutes long—characterized by being rather direct, prescriptive, and very little rhetorical. A remarkable exception, however, takes place in the five central minutes, when the metaphors appear as a refrain to mark perhaps the most delicate stage: here too, the stage devoted to the duties of the hospital workers.

If, since the start of his speech, Macron presents the norms regarding the "confinement of the population" by qualifying them as "exceptional" and "temporary" decisions," which France "never had to adopt . . . during times of peace," the image of war remains subterraneous until the middle of the discourse, when it begins appearing explicitly: "We are at war, in a health war, of course. We fight neither against an army nor against another nation, yet the enemy is here, invisible, elusive, advancing. This requires our general mobilization. We are at war. All government and parliament action must now be focused on fighting the epidemic, day and night. Nothing can distract us from this."[2] "We are at war" is a formula that occurs at least six times in this section of Macron's speech, and it marks its essential parts. Not even Macron's message, with its upbeat rhythm, grounded on the reiteration of the image of war, is surprising. Technically, it is a beautiful speech at the level of effectiveness; yet it does not impress at the level of rhetorical originality. Nor can we be surprised by the pervasiveness of the warlike metaphors that the Sars-CoV-2 pandemic produced in the first months of 2020 in the media and public discourse, well beyond the communication choices of politics. What receives concretization here is the construction of a dictionary of key words and expressions—some kind of an archive of metaphors that are employed mostly unawares and that, during the progression of the pandemic, end up becoming canonical.

Disease and Metaphor

ORIGINS AND STRUCTURE OF THE WARLIKE METAPHOR

Within Western cultures, the canon of *disease as metaphor* has a more than millenary history. Warlike metaphorics is perhaps the most remarkable—besides being the most complex—part of such cultural history. At first, one could think that the case is very similar to what Hans Blumenberg, in his 1960 *Paradigms for a Metaphorology*, qualifies as an absolute metaphor, that is, an expression that resists all attempts at translation into other languages.[3] Mythical materials, in which Blumenberg's absolute metaphors are rooted, offer very eloquent testimonies of this. One could think, for example, of the opening scene of Homer's *Iliad*. Upon learning of the offense that his priest Chryses has received from Agamemnon in the struggle over Chryseis, Apollo inflicts a pestilence on the Achaeans—an infection that the god starts by "twang[ing] his deadly bow, and hissing fly the feather'd fates below . . . for nine long nights." What spreads the contagion in the Greek camp is neither a magic potion nor a mysterious wind or some other form of deceit. Rather, it is a series of arrows—that is, military devices—that spread their effects during a specified time—almost an incubation time—through a leap in species. As the *Iliad* says, "On mules and dogs the infection first began; And last, the vengeful arrows fix'd in man."[4]

Disease as an act of war, then. It is within a similar framework that, in many ancient and modern languages, processes of lexicalization of metaphorical expressions covering most phenomena tied with the pathological occur. It is impossible to produce a complete listing, which however includes terms such as, first of all, immunitary *defenses*, which takes the place of more precise and less metaphorical scientific notions such as immunitary *system* or *apparatus*. The same list also comprises various pathological phenomena such as *attacks* and *bouts*—first of all, heart attacks, but also episodes of disclosure or outbreak such as panic or asthma attacks. If one considers medical remedies, then one finds therapies that can be characterized as *aggressive* or phenomena of *resistance* to medications, whose efficaciousness is reduced because of pathogen *agents* undergoing transformation.

This complex network of references and stratifications turns illness, together with love and death, into one of the most metaphorized life experiences. In its general terms, this stratification fits perfectly with the theoretical model of conceptual metaphors discussed by George Lakoff and Mark Johnson. It is true that, in their 1980 *Metaphors We Live By*, the source domain WAR is monopolized by the *target* domain ARGUMENT due to the greater simplicity of the "ARGUMENT IS WAR" metaphor.[5] Yet the framework is the same, even though it is substantially impossible to establish which constitutes the ground metaphor. Elsewhere, Lakoff maps the conceptual metaphor "DISEASE IS WAR" as follows:

Source Domain: war
Target Domain: illness, treatment, medicine

The Disease Is an Enemy
The Body Is a Battleground
Infection Is an Attack by the Disease
Medicine Is a Weapon
Medical Procedures Are Attacks by the Patient

The Immune System Is a Defense
Winning the War Is Being Cured of the Disease
Being Defeated Is Dying.[6]

Changes in Paradigms

The theory of conceptual metaphors cannot account, however, for the historical aspect of the metaphor DISEASE/WAR, and this aspect is equally interesting. Besides its constant presence in Western cultures, one cannot neglect the evolution that characterizes this metaphor and that, at least in the current form and intensity, has a much shorter history. As Scott L. Montgomery clarifies in an important 1991 article, "Codes and Combats in Biomedical Discourse," the figure of war is only one—neither the first nor the last—of the figures of the pathological. The field of metaphors rather undergoes a transformation similar to the changes in paradigms in the medical-scientific sectors. Yet this process happens with a remarkable difference. The acquisition of scientific discoveries that rationalize—that is, make comprehensible and controllable—the sphere of health is not accompanied by an analogous rationalization of the discourses on illness and disease. One could even claim the opposite to be the case: successes in medical sciences bring with them a proliferation of metaphorics often in a direction contrary to the progression of knowledge. As Montgomery writes: "Yet, one discovers, quite quickly as it turns out, that the very opposite is the case. The ways in which we speak of disease today—both technically and non-technically—are no less limited and anxiety-laden than they have ever been. In some ways they seem even more so."[7]

The figure of war is the cornerstone of such a remarkable evolution as is shown, according to Montgomery's reconstruction, in the nineteenth-century lexicon of cancer and, from the 1980s on, in that of AIDS. The case of cancer-related pathologies is the most noteworthy for reasons having to do with the spread of the phenomenon, its lethality, and the quite long processes of research and cure. Montgomery recalls the "immediate" and "natural" metaphorization of first radiotherapies through the figure of "bombing," which contributes to define the specificity of such therapies in comparison to the other dominating therapeutic protocol, namely, surgery. The war metaphor will apply also to chemotherapy, in addition to radiotherapy, on the ground of their shared difference from surgical methods.

From the standpoint of metaphorical phenomena, the extension to a kind of "nuking" different from radiotherapy implies a not insignificant transformation. The source domain is no longer conventional conflict but rather chemical warfare. This case is interesting not only in itself, but also for the contribution that it brings to the functioning of the system DISEASE/WAR. In the case of chemotherapy, the metaphorical transference becomes more unstable, almost to the point of a reversal. The functioning of radiotherapy connects two domains undoubtedly distinct; that is, it is a metaphor in its own right. It is obvious that radiotherapy is not "truly" a war, and its devices are not the same weapons with which one would fight a battle. Things are far less certain when it comes to chemotherapy. Even though with goals, extensions, and instruments that are completely different, chemotherapeutic action is *identical* with—and not simply *similar* to—the actions at the basis of chemical warfare. From this standpoint, the denomination "bacteriological war" is based on some kind of a reversal of the metaphorical process. This reversal constructs *in reality* the opposite of that which occurs *in language* when one metaphorizes medicine through war. Bacteriological warfare is, in sum, some kind of a countermetaphorical alteration of medical practices; it is an antimedication, an antiremedy (a reversed cure, that is, a poison) that shifts from its own field—the medical field—to become a warfare dispositive; at the same time, it turns from salvific to lethal.

Both in its more frequent form, that is, disease as war, and in its reversed form, that is, war as disease, this complex system DISEASE/WAR can be defined as *biomilitarism,* to use Montgomery's categories.[8] Yet, as mentioned earlier, this dispositive is as much widespread within the contemporary experience of pathology as it is characterized historically and culturally. Its fortune starts at a specific moment in the recent history of medicine and is probably destined to exhaust itself. Montgomery himself makes reference to a competing metaphorical paradigm that is gaining progressive space in medical narration, whether ordinary or specialized. It is the metaphor of the informational code, which arises and develops jointly with genetic medicine, ever since Rosalind Franklin's, James Watson's, and Francis Crick's discoveries from the 1950s onward. For Montgomery, the counterpart of biomilitarism is biotechnological or, better, bioinformational metaphorics. From a battlefield, human materiality is turning into a network, a chain of codes or, better, a mixed semantic field that includes and overlaps the two metaphorical sets. The peculiar inversion of roles that we have observed take place in bacteriological warfare is not absent here either. In the case of bioinformational metaphorics, it turns into the figure of the *informational virus*, the computer bug. Software "infecting" an electronic device is the most plastic representation of the reversed metaphorization of an event within the informational field through an event within the field of disease.

As is the case for its end, the origin of the biomilitary metaphor too can be identified. Even though one cannot mark distinct profiles, in both cases we are confronted with a series of overlapping figures, each of which progressively replaces the previous one. This is what happens during the lengthy stage when the warfare metaphor is already deployed—as we have seen in the *Iliad*—yet clearly in a position of minority. Within this situation, what prevails is the religious and moral major metaphor of pathology as *punishment*—a classical figure that remains intact even within modern rationalism. At least two other images accompany it: the figure of an unbalance within a balanced system, which is a distant legacy of the Hippocratic tradition; and, next to this, the metaphorics of reification and personification, which indeed share some features with the warfare metaphor yet find their deeper roots in metaphysical conceptions of an animist or pagan kind.[9] Regardless of the transcendent or natural foundation, what these "prewar" metaphorics share is the idea of an order whose violation implies disease as consequence. Ultimately, this consequence sanctions (or tries to reconstruct) what has been shattered.

The change of paradigm that archives these figures and places the biomilitary metaphor at the center of discourse is provided by the birth of modern microbiology. The turning point consists in the discovery that, whether in physiological or pathological forms, the human body includes within itself other living entities that are nevertheless invisible to the naked eye. Yet, as the biomilitary lexicon has a very long prehistory, likewise microbiological discoveries are situated within a very vast metaphorical horizon, and this favors their diffusion even outside the boundaries of scientific research. Such is the case for the analogy between the human body and the political body—a long-lasting analogy, which finds its climax in the form of the modern state. On this ground, that which damages the human organism—entering it, threatening to enter it, or being somehow already inside it—can be qualified by the same terms used to identify those who, in a group or alone, attack the *health* of the state. Once this fundamental connection is in place—a connection that has epochal relevance—the two metaphors of the state as a body and of the pathogenic agent as an enemy start feeding each other in an unstoppable process of unlimited extension of the metaphorics STATE/BODY. These two influential metaphorics intertwine in some kind of a "system of images," as Montgomery calls it. It is an ensemble of metaphors that, on the one hand, organizes the dominant discourse regarding the pathological[10] and portrays "the virus in the guise of a guerrilla force (leftist?) and the body more or less as a sovereign and legitimate state,"[11] while, on the other hand, it qualifies wars and revolutions as pathological phenomena (or, at times, as cures) affecting the *life* of states.

Demythicizing War Metaphors?

If we wish to use a second-level metaphor, we could say that the two "systems of images" of the state as a body and of the body as a state mirror each other in many ways and end up sustaining and legitimating each other. Establishing which one precedes the other is therefore complicated and, in the end, superfluous. The truly interesting point is, rather, the fact that the mirror through which the two metaphorics mutually sustain each other is, precisely, pathology (or the lack thereof). *Disease as metaphor* supports the analogy between the domains of the body and of the state, allowing for a punctual transcription of one system of images into the other.

This set of connections is analyzed in depth by Susan Sontag, especially in her works on the metaphors of cancer and of AIDS.[12] Reduced to the essential, Sontag's argument consists in denouncing the harmfulness of metaphors in ill people's self-understanding as well as in their social perception and, indeed, their medical relations. Yet her theses are characterized by a deep ambiguity. They are traversed by some sort of an Enlightenment-based illusion that one can speak of pathology in a direct, literal manner without the mediation of metaphors; even, that the metaphorics of pathology must be deconstructed in order to reduce their violent impact. To speak of disease in metaphorical terms, according to Sontag, is a way to perpetuate fears, prejudices, and moral-theological models that stigmatize the sick person in various ways. In other words, metaphors are the covering up of taboo, the consequence of understanding the pathological as an "ill-omened, abominable, repugnant" reality.[13] This is a harness from which one needs to be liberated.[14] War metaphors are the tip of this dispositive of stigmatization. "Nothing is more punitive than to give a disease a meaning—that meaning being invariably a moralistic one."[15] It is certainly true that "ostensibly, the illness is the culprit"; yet, Sontag concludes, actually "it is also the . . . patient who is made culpable."[16] The patient is even condemned to death *tout court*.[17]

With respect to this aspect, Sontag's argument is very ambiguous. The two main theses—(a) the figures of the pathological *can* always be translated and (b) their translation is *necessary* to save the sick person from the related stigma—are clearly weaker than they seem. First, the existence of untranslatable metaphors is one of the most agreed upon evidences in philosophical and linguistic researches from the middle of the twentieth century on, regardless of traditions and schools of thought. From different fronts, Blumenberg's, Lakoff's, and Johnson's conceptual metaphor theories move precisely from the contestation of the principle according to which, within the linguistic and conceptual formalization of experience, one may disregard metaphorization. As for Sontag's second, antimetaphorical thesis, the issue is more complex. Undoubtedly, Sontag's works *Illness as Metaphor* and *AIDS and Its Metaphors* have the merit of having started a wide debate on these themes.[18] Yet after one isolates their basic presupposition—metaphorizing pathology generates a stigma on the sick person—it becomes easy to show their limitations. Are war metaphors, in fact, not precisely the way in which the sphere of the pathological has been brought outside the boundaries of unsayability? Does treating pathology as an enemy not contribute to erase (rather than strengthen) previous theological and moral implications, which considered the sick person a subject worthy of punishment? As the experience of illness is common to all human beings, do war metaphors not strengthen positive moral sentiments, first among which, empathy? The very case of cancer, which is so crucial in Sontag's analysis, seems to embody the example opposite to that substantiating Sontag's claim. Cancer is the experience of an illness that, within different epochs and cultures, undergoes a similar fate of tabooing and unsayability thereby depriving those who experience it, whether as patients or relatives, of minimal spaces of linguistic articulability—articulability that metaphorization alone seems, in the end, capable of offering. Moreover, even when one remains critically vigilant with respect to language, it is difficult to maintain univocally the harmfulness of the war transfiguration, which sick people themselves regard as unavoidable and "spontaneous."[19]

All considerations regarding the Enlightenment-based inspiration at the foundation of her analysis aside, one cannot dismiss the highly relevant consequences of Sontag's analysis at other levels. These implications risk being obscured by her claims regarding metaphorical stigma. Yet, if one isolates them from the rest, their theoretical relevance is unarguable. It is a reversal in viewpoint which, by inverting source domain and target, shifts the attention from the deployment of political metaphors to speak of pathology (war being the main one) to the utilization of health metaphors to describe political phenomena. The basis for this double operation is the same highlighted by Montgomery, namely, the analogy between organic body and the state. Yet, already in her 1978 book, Sontag emphasizes the bidirectionality of the metaphorical transference that takes place through the medium of pathology. Given that, in her perspective, the original fault of war figures consists in their attributing meanings to that which typically makes no sense, that is, illness, this surplus of meanings makes it so that "the disease itself becomes a metaphor. Then, in the name of the disease (that is, using it as a metaphor), that horror is imposed on other things. The disease becomes adjectival. Something is said to be disease-like, meaning that it is disgusting or ugly."²⁰ This is the decisive passage describing the inversion of the two domains. The superabundance of meanings with which the pathological sphere is loaded through metaphors produces a reversal on whose ground one can then speak of something pertaining to the domain of the *polis* in terms of something belonging to the domain of pathology.

It would be better to say though—and Sontag is aware of this—not that the two domains simply undergo an exchange but rather that they blur into each other and become the same domain. This is additional proof— *contra* Sontag—that the metaphor DISEASE/WAR is an absolute metaphor, given its pivotal function between two such different yet fundamental and complex systems of metaphorization. The truly relevant corollary of the systemic complicity between disease and war is, however, another. Even though she does not pursue this, Sontag is very explicit in speaking of an "ideological mobilization" produced by such a reciprocal invasion of fields.²¹ This applies both to the pre-Pasteur stage of medical research and to the time when the discovery of infective organic agents favors the perfecting of the enemy metaphor. In the first instance, the threshold between health and pathology coincides with that between civil order and disorder. In the second, the order of discourse hinges on the notion of the enemy as stranger and thus as infective agent that attacks the life of the organism, whether the state or an individual.

Hence the ideological power potentially enclosed in the microbiological turn. Sontag writes: "Since then, military metaphors have more and more come to infuse all aspects of the description of the medical situation."²² Such is the clamorous instance of Richard Nixon's "war on cancer," started by a political act similar to a war declaration (the 1971 "National Cancer Act") and with the plan of converting part of the structures at Fort Derrick from bacteriological warfare to cancer research. Sontag does not delve into the theoretical significance of Nixon's decision and simply points to it as to the clearest example of the use of the figure DISEASE/WAR to the goal of building consensus. One should acknowledge, though, that Fort Derrick retains a fascinating explanatory power. Even before Nixon, Fort Derrick was some kind of materialization of that metaphoric domain. Born as a small airport in 1929, it housed the first military settlements in 1931, receiving its name after a World War I soldier. During World War II, it expanded its installations and became a site for the development of bacteriological weapons. In the cold war period, the site remained under the military until the 1969 ban against bacteriological warfare, when it took up an increasing vocation toward becoming a medical research center. In the 2000s, after decades of environmental contaminations and suspicious deaths, the site underwent a severe reduction in activities and its destiny seemed to have its course. Yet the health emergency caused by Sars-CoV-2 led the authorities to reopen some labs that had been previously closed.

In short, Fort Derrick is a place that undergoes, as it were, a series of resemantizations that span the spectrum of disease and its metaphorical uses. First, it is a civil place yet named after a soldier. Then, it becomes a military site in all respects. Later, during the cold war—which is a metaphoric conflict in all senses—it is devoted to scientific research with military purposes. Finally, with the ban on the war *through* bacteria and viruses, it turns into a place devoted to the war *against* bacteria and viruses, first with Nixon and lastly with the coronavirus pandemic.

Biometaphorology and Biopolitics

The issues raised by Sontag with respect to the ideological power of metaphors—the idea that illness is a "political metaphor," to use another of her successful expressions—are much wider.[23] Her remarks hit the target when they speak of the rhetorical strengthening that pathology and war ensure each other or, rather, the one *in place of* the other. Sontag claims that the concept of illness is never innocent. By this, she means that the linguistic uses of the pathological always produce consequences outside the originating semantic field, especially when it comes to building consensus and mobilizing people.[24] Yet we cannot stop here; we must move beyond the limits of Sontag's *Illness as Metaphor*. When Sontag talks about the transformation of disease in an adjectival sense, she is not only referring to its metaphorical deployments within the political context; she is also evoking the adjectivations that accompany its proper utilizations. Above all are the adjectives that qualify illnesses by linking them to their alleged ethnic origins. For example, syphilis has always been named a disease coming from elsewhere. Thus, the end of the fifteenth-century epidemic is called "French pox" in English, "*morbus germanicus* (German illness)" in French, "*mal napoletano* (Neapolitan sickness)" in Florence, and "Chinese disease" in Japan.[25] The same can be said of plagues and many other epidemics, with fancy lexical outcomes based on the perception of what, in a specific culture, is considered as foreign. Briefly, a fundamental issue is coessential to diseases, namely, the relation with what is foreign or stranger, whether such alienness is real or fictional.

This theme evades linguistic and philosophical-linguistic analyses, whether they are heirs to or competitors against the discussion initiated by *Illness as Metaphor*. We must therefore search elsewhere for adequate theoretical resources. In order to do so, we need to consider more carefully the nature of the issue, of which Sontag certainly indicates some features. The real point that characterizes the metaphor DISEASE/WAR, in both senses of *disease as metaphor* and *metaphor of the disease*, is that it is a *biopolitical* figure. Along lines that go beyond Sontag's own intentions, all issues pertaining to the system of images of the body and the state find in fact their most fecund collocation within reflections that concern the political use of the conceptual pair life and death.

Albeit moving from presuppositions and goals different from these, Roberto Esposito clearly states as much in his book *Immunitas* when he addresses the difference between biopolitical models and philosophical anthropology. What characterizes biopolitical models in comparison to philosophical anthropology is their assumption of life in its immediate, formal (as it were) feature. This assumption nevertheless requires linguistic figures coming from the semantic field of the body as *medium*. Esposito writes,

> It is as if politics needed to deprive life of any qualitative dimension, to render it "only life," "pure life," or "bare life" in order to relate to it. This is where the decisive importance attributed to the semantics of the body originates. Contrary to a widespread theory tying the immunitary dynamics of modernity to a procedure of gradual marginalization or emptying of the individual and social body, the biopolitical register is actually built around its renewed centrality.[26]

A few lines below, he goes on:

> It is as if life, to preserve itself as such, must be compressed and kept within the confines of the body. This is not because the body, both individual and collective, is not exposed to processes of involution and dissolution: what has more experience with the bite of evil than the body? Rather, it is because this risk is precisely what sets off the mechanism of alarm, and therefore, of defense meant to protect it. It is true, then, as Foucault himself maintained, that the living being begins to enter onto the horizon of visibility of modern knowledge the moment its constitutive relationship with what continually threatens to extinguish it emerges. Sickness and death make up the cone of shadow within which the life sciences carve out their niche.[27]

Biopolitics radicalizes first of all the centrality of the body because "it is in the body and only in the body that life can remain what it is and even grow, be strengthened, and reproduce."[28] What emerges with the body, however, is also the semantics of disease, of the *pharmakon* (in both senses of cure and poison), and of death: "If the organological metaphor is at the heart of political treatises, at the heart of the metaphor lies disease." In other terms, as Esposito concludes, "the point of intersection between political knowledge and medical knowledge is the common problem of preserving the body," that is, the problem of health and disease.[29]

This is a theoretical point that proves relevant in order to join philosophical considerations on metaphorical tropes with reflections of a biopolitical nature. This connection moves from the acknowledgment that the metaphor of the body is "by far the most influential metaphor used in political discourse to represent life in society."[30] Even in Esposito's reconstruction, this influence has some kind of a double dating. On the one hand, as is well known, the metaphoric STATE/BODY goes back well before modernity, it traverses backward through Christianity and, at least in Western culture, can be found even in Greek philosophy. On the other hand and simultaneously, however, this figure evolves and expresses its entire set of meanings only when it encounters the theme of immunization. Briefly, the question of immunity activates it in all its implications. This occurs when this metaphoric system traverses Christianity, in a complex path that goes from Paul's analogy between individual body and community body to the figure of the sovereign's two bodies analyzed by Ernst Kantorowicz.[31] In other words, the immunitary characterization of the metaphor STATE/BODY is the latest stage in a path that originates in the distant past and is, at the same time, the step that reveals the principle—immunization—on whose ground such a figure can function on the basis of the role played in both domains by the themes of the foreign and the contagion.

The relation between biopolitics and its metaphoric background is fundamental because it confirms, albeit in other terms, the function of disease as a second-level metaphor that we mentioned earlier. This is the idea that without the figure of DISEASE/WAR, not even the dispositive STATE/BODY could be activated. Biopolitical dispositives, in fact, function on the ground of "the great figurative device that medical science has developed around the body's need for self-protection." It is some kind of "semantic wave" that moves from the domain of health and sickness "to wash over the entire gamut of social languages."[32] Disease thus becomes the perspective from which the connection between life of the body and life of the state opens up and can be understood.

Outside Esposito's terminology, we could say that the paradoxically immediate-and-mediate paradigm of biopolitics—that is, its way of considering life—is based on the existence of a *medium*, which nevertheless is simultaneously transparent. The functional yet transparent *medium* is precisely the mirror we described earlier and within which body and state mirror each other, point by point: disease as metaphor. Without this complex construct, made of symmetries and transparencies, the biopolitical model would crumble, starting with the connection between *bios* and *polis* that constitutes it. As Esposito himself acknowledges, it is certainly true that in Michel Foucault's perspective, the birth of biopolitics is tied to the care of life as opposed to sovereignty, which is instead exerted through the right to inflict death. Yet through immunitary logic, death does not cease being "the black box of biopolitics," that which enables the politics of *bios* to function.[33] Death as black box or disease as mirror—in two different forms and through two different metaphors, the connection between politics and life is sustained by some kind of a subtraction of the *medium*.

Within this context, the outline Esposito reconstructs is clear. It is the model gathered around Foucault's notion of nosopolitics, which asserts this very modality of government, that is, the presentation of politics *in terms of* its being a health institution. At the level of figures of speech, the presentation of something *in terms of* something else is indeed the most elementary—and hence, most essential—description of the functioning of metaphors, from Aristotle's *Poetics* on. Nosopolitics, however, means not so much that questions of health and sickness are relevant at the public or political level; rather, it means that politics works through allogeneic dispositives, which find their origin within the semantic domain of health and disease. This explains two factors: first, "the process of medicalization that has invested the entire gamut of social interaction over the last two centuries"; and second, the very "hypertrophy of the security apparatuses that are increasingly widespread throughout contemporary societies."[34]

This is the truly decisive element that many analyses of the metaphor DISEASE/WAR are not capable of grasping, whereas it is incorporated in a viewpoint based on the biopolitical debate. A truly critical analysis of the linguistic models through which one speaks of disease must *also* relate such models to other linguistic structures that use the same fundamental figures—in the specific case, STATE/BODY and its immunitary dispositives. If one underestimates this contextualization, one runs the risk of reaching conclusions that render the complexity of the system DISEASE/WAR overly simplified and banal. For example, one simplifies it and merely censors it or wishes for its overcoming. As much as a similar operation may seem reassuring at the level of individual or collective psychology, the ill-fated outcomes of such a procedure are at least two. First, by ending up considering metaphor as a disease of language, one erases the role that metaphorization is shown to play at various levels, from thought to language itself and up to the intersubjective sharing of experiences. Second, through the naïve hypothesis of a targeted erasure of some metaphors, one neglects that figures of speech—and, specifically, the figure of DISEASE/WAR—are fundamental elements of a whole edifice that stands upon them. From this perspective, developing a critical analysis of the lexicon of disease must include a systemic—and, in turn, critical but also historical-reconstructive and even performative—consideration of the model STATE/BODY. The reading keys are multiple and often alternative. Yet it is evident that a cross-reflection of both a biopolitical and a metaphorological nature is among the most fecund, especially when it operates at multiple levels—not only at the semantic and functional linguistic level, but also at the level of ontology; that is, in a Foucaultian sense, at the level of the order of things.

Translated from Italian by Silvia Benso

Notes

1. Edi Rama's full speech is available here: https://youtu.be/A22V4Gh8-0E.
2. The video and the transcription of Emmanuel Macron's speech are available on the *Le Monde* site. https://bit.ly/32CrL9G.
3. Hans Blumenberg, *Paradigms for a Metaphorology*, trans. Robert Savage (Ithaca, NY: Cornell University Press, 2016).
4. Homer, *Iliad*, 55–70. The quotations are from Alexander Pope's translation available online as part of the Gutenberg Project.
5. George Lakoff and Mark Johnson, *Metaphors We Live By* (Chicago: University of Chicago Press, 1980).
6. http://www.lang.osaka-u.ac.jp/~sugimoto/MasterMetaphorList/metaphors/Treating_Illness_Is_Fighting_A_War.html.
7. Scott L. Montgomery, "Codes and Combat in Biomedical Discourse," *Science and Culture* 3, 2 (1991): 346.
8. Montgomery, "Codes and Combat in Biomedical Discourse," 352 ff.
9. See for example M. Dasal, "Metaphorization of Categories of Disease: From a Perspective of Cognitive Linguistics," *Studia Humanistyczne AGH* 17, 3 (2018): 18.
10. Montgomery, "Codes and Combat in Biomedical Discourse," 344.
11. Montgomery, "Codes and Combat in Biomedical Discourse," 349.
12. The two essays, which appeared eleven years apart, are now also available in one single volume; see Susan Sontag, *Illness as Metaphor and AIDS and Its Metaphors* (New York: Picador, 2001).
13. Susan Sontag, *Illness as Metaphor* (New York: Farrar, Straus and Giroux, 1977), 9.
14. Sontag, *Illness as Metaphor*, 4.

15. Sontag, *Illness as Metaphor*, 58.
16. Sontag, *Illness as Metaphor*, 57.
17. Sontag writes, "Metaphors and myths, I was convinced, kill"; see Susan Sontag, *AIDS and Its Metaphors* (New York: Farrar, Straus and Giroux, 1989), 14.
18. A brief sketch summing up the debate can be found for example in Barbara Clow, "Who's afraid of Susan Sontag? Or, the Myths and Metaphors of Cancer Reconsidered," *Social History of Medicine* 14, no. 2 (2001): 293–312. Among the most successful validations of Sontag's analyses one should mention the research carried out in the linguistic field; for one of the most complete, recent works, see for example E. Semino, Z. Demjén, A. Hardie, S. Payne, P. Rayson, *Metaphor, Cancer and the End of Life: A Corpus-Based Study* (London: Routledge, 2017). For an application to other pathologies, especially those of an epidemic kind, see, for example, P. Wallisa and B. Nerlich, "Disease Metaphors in New Epidemics: The UK Media Framing of the 2003 SARS Epidemic," *Social Science & Medicine* 60 (2005): 2629–39.
19. The records of public sharing of cancer diagnoses are many, and their categorization is not one of the goals of this chapter. A critical analysis of this theme should consider not only the linguistic aspects, but also the dispositives of a narrative kind such as pathographies. An example already in this direction, even though it goes beyond cancer-related illnesses, is the book by Anne H. Hawkins, *Reconstructing Illness: Studies in Pathography* (Lafayette: Purdue University Press, 1999). Among the most recent cases of public sharing, it is worth mentioning at least that of John Lewis, who has left an important mark on public sensitivity, and not only in the United States. Lewis, who died in July 2020, had announced the discovery of stage 4 pancreatic cancer in December 2019. The most remarkable feature in his communication is the analogy between struggles for civil rights and the condition of illness. He says, "I have been in some kind of fight—for freedom, equality, basic human rights—for nearly my entire life. I have never faced a fight quite like the one I have now. [. . .] Treatment options are no longer as debilitating as they once were, and that I have a fighting chance. So I have decided to do what I know to do and do what I have always done: I am going to fight it and keep fighting for the Beloved Community"; see https://bit.ly/30Q5UdH.
20. Sontag, *Illness as Metaphor*, 58.
21. Sontag, *AIDS and Its Metaphors*, 11.
22. Sontag, *AIDS and Its Metaphors*, 9.
23. See, for example, Susan Sontag, "Disease as Political Metaphor," *The New York Review of Books*, February 23, 1978, which is one of the texts re-elaborated and gathered in *Illness as Metaphor*.
24. On these aspects, see, for example, the remarks in Dąsal, *Metaphorization of Categories of Disease*, 22–25. The theme is recurrent and has gained renewed centrality also in the emergency situation due to the coronavirus pandemic. At the beginning of the health emergency, in March 2020, the remarks by Anne Applebaum, in which she denounced the allegedly antidemocratic risks of the health measures against the spreading of the virus, caused quite a stir. See Anne Applebaum, "The

People in Charge See an Opportunity," *The Atlantic*, March 23; see also https://bit.ly/31eGlTW. In Italy, a similar path had already been undertaken by Giorgio Agamben in a series of contributions afterwards gathered in a volume. See Giorgio Agamben, *A che punto siamo? L'epidemia come politica* (Macerata: Quodlibet, 2020).

25. Sontag, *AIDS and Its Metaphors*, 47–48.
26. Roberto Esposito, *Immunitas*, trans. Zakiya Hanafi (Malden, MA: Polity Press, 2011), 20–21.
27. Esposito, *Immunitas*, 21.
28. Esposito, *Immunitas*, 127.
29. Esposito, *Immunitas*, 136.
30. Esposito, *Immunitas*, 127.
31. Esposito, *Immunitas*, 79–86.
32. Esposito, *Immunitas*, 167.
33. Esposito, *Immunitas*, 152.
34. Esposito, *Immunitas*, 22.

Part Two
Vulnerability, Care, and Responsibility

Five

"The Lungs That We All Are"

Rethinking Life in the Times of a Pandemic

Olivia Guaraldo

> My point is that illness is *not* a metaphor, and that the most truthful way of regarding illness—and the healthiest way of being ill—is one most purified of, most resistant to, metaphoric thinking.
>
> —Susan Sontag, *Illness as Metaphor*

The Human as Vulnerable

One of the merits of Emmanuel Levinas, the French philosopher of Lithuanian origins, is his posing the question of vulnerability and its ambivalent relation to violence in philosophical terms. His claim is that "the face of the other in its precariousness and defenselessness is for me at once the temptation to kill and the call to peace, the 'Thou shall not kill.'"[1]

In recent years, scholars such as Judith Butler and Adriana Cavarero have devoted an important part of their work to recasting the Levinasian theme of vulnerability from a feminist perspective.[2] The feminist dimension of this reappropriation lies in the fact that these thinkers understand vulnerability literally, in its corporeal, material element. Embodiment, one of the main themes in second- and third-wave feminist scholarship, undergoes here a negative *torsion* and is framed in its most radical dimension, namely, that of a constitutive exposure of all human bodies to the possibility of a wound, *vulnus*—the Latin word for wound, *vulnus*, is the term from which "vulnerability" stems. We will call this conceptual framework "the vulnerability paradigm." The question that these authors provocatively pose is this: What happens when vulnerability becomes the fundamental feature of the living human? In other words, *what if* the philosophical question regarding the *anthropos*, the human being, were to take its bearings not from human beings' most noble and noetic features (man as a "rational animal" is the classic Aristotelian example) but from their carnal elements? The human then becomes a being whose material constitution (skin, flesh) and exposure (its being in relation to others, ever since birth) renders it constitutively "woundable," that is, vulnerable. The suffix *-able* that composes the adjective vulnerable (*-abilis* in Latin) alludes to the fact that the wound (the *vulnus*) is, however, a possibility, not a certainty.

Because the term recalls the *potentiality* of being exposed to violence, it also contains the possibility of the negation of such violence, of its rejection in the name of an ethical choice in favor of *care*. As Cavarero puts it, vulnerability refers to a reciprocal exposure in which we are given over to either the care for or the harm of the other, "as though the absence of wound or care were not even thinkable." And yet this openness to the wound contains also the possibility of care: "Irremediably open to wounding and caring, the vulnerable one exists totally in the tension generated by this alternative."[3] Provocatively, vulnerability calls on both violence and care. We cannot think of the wound without the alternative that opposes it.

If, in Levinasian terms, the relational dimension that structures life (that is, its being originally exposed to the *face* of the other), violence, and *abstention from it* appear together, what emerges as provocative in the feminist reading of the relationship between vulnerability and violence is not just the ethical commandment not to kill but also *care* as an active alternative.

Therefore, the vulnerability paradigm—or what has been called an "ontology of vulnerability"[4]—adopted in recent feminist scholarship, has proposed a radically pacifist rethinking of human coexistence, paradoxically founded on the mutual exposure to violence. The unprecedented global outburst of violence (from 9/11 onwards) that is still called "war," but that is radically different from the traditional forms of interstate wars of the past, has been the occasion to reflect critically on the predominant martial paradigms that shape the Western imaginary. It has also been a chance to advance, with philosophical audacity, a new theoretical framework in which, as Judith Butler puts it, violence is the always scandalous yet unavoidable feature of our interdependence.

As Butler writes, "violence [. . .] delineates a physical vulnerability from which we cannot slip away, which we cannot finally resolve in the name of the subject, but which can provide a way to understand the way in which all of us are already not precisely bounded, not precisely separate, but in our skins, given over, in each other's hands, at each other's mercy. This is a situation we do not choose, that forms the horizon of choice, and it is that which grounds our responsibility."[5]

Life Is Not "Bare" but Precarious

As it has been noted, "everywhere bodies are somehow gendered. Families, communities, and societies are crossed by inequalities that are often taken to be rooted in forms of embodiment; thus it was feminist scholars who perhaps most powerfully in the twentieth century forced a political anthropology of the body."[6] Feminist scholarship has often remarked that the bodily, carnal component of our being is never separate from the cultural, social, and gendered dimension.[7] Along similar lines of argument, feminists claim that life can never be thought of as an abstract, "naked," bare feature that can be universally posited by thought. Since time immemorial, this has instead been the presumption of patriarchal thought—against which, for example, the thought of sexual difference has sought to oppose a more concrete conception of life, the body, and sexuation.[8] There is no "bareness" in life; there are only different ways of framing life, as it were, and feminism proposes not to discard life's material aspect, concentrating instead on the different social and cultural forms that life has taken up in history. This theoretical attitude, of course, has determined a deconstruction of the patriarchal frame within which the body and women have traditionally been inserted, with a mixture of awe and despisal for the generative potential of the feminine body.

Within the vulnerability paradigm, the feminist awareness towards the body, as said before, is cast in its potentially negative dimension, including in it the potentially violent dimension of *vulnus*. This inclusion occurs, of course, in order not to celebrate this negativity but rather to respond to a historically determined political and ethical need. This is the need to overcome the apparent stagnation of our political imagery and its extenuating use of belligerent discourses, metaphors, and myths. Consequently, the vulnerability paradigm understands life in terms of its fragility, dependence, and precariousness.

The global spreading of war and terror after 9/11 has suggested that vulnerability is not only an ontological feature of the living but also a common historical condition, a mournful example of our global interrelatedness. As Judith Butler points out, 9/11 has proven to Americans that they have lost their "first-world privilege." Butler crucially asks: "Is there something to be learned about the geopolitical distribution of corporeal vulnerability from our own brief and devastating exposure to this condition?"[9]

The need to think of the human in terms of vulnerability reflects the need to disqualify a politics based on the opposition between an invulnerable *us* and a totally vulnerable *them*. In order to be sustained and justified, such oppositional politics must posit some lives as grievable and some others as ungrievable. The "us and them" divide and the belligerent paradigm that follows from it and justifies war *always take the form of a denial of one's own vulnerability*.

To recognize oneself as vulnerable, therefore, means both to take into account the vulnerability of others and to recuperate "our collective responsibility for the physical lives of one another" in order to produce a new imagery and, consequently, a nonviolent politics and ethics.[10]

Vulnerability and the Virus

Can we still adopt, in the times of the Covid-19 pandemic, the vulnerability paradigm we have briefly just illustrated?

In the times of Covid-19, our common vulnerability is, as a matter of fact, even more visible, if not completely undeniable. Yet now we are not facing an "us-versus-them" divide. There is no violence involved in the situation, no friend-versus-enemy opposition. In other words, we are not dealing with a violent act against which we must elaborate a nonviolent politics and ethics. Or such is the case at least in principle.

The present experience of the pandemic places us in front of a new occurrence of the term "vulnerability": one that does not immediately recall the *vulnus*, the wound, the ripping off of flesh, bodies torn apart, torture, and massacre. In this new "war" against the virus, we have not seen bloodshed or decapitations but only face masks and ventilators. Is it really even a "war," then?

While recounting his experience in a radio interview, one of the many heroic Italian doctors working unbearable shifts at one of the hospitals simply said: "When I find myself in front of a person attached to a ventilator, I do not think of some 'enemy' to destroy; I concentrate on the patient in need of care."[11] This statement has the merit of illuminating a crucial aspect of the situation we have been living and witnessing during the outburst of the Covid-19 pandemic: we have been experiencing vulnerability without being able to clearly identify an enemy and, consequently, without the ethical need to rethink the friend/enemy divide in pacifist terms. The shared experience of vulnerability—an experience that has never been so undeniably communal as in the Covid-19 circumstances—immediately calls for *care* to be in the picture. As if, one could speculate, this time the alternative between wound and care did not even present itself. Nobody would evoke the possibility of using the virus as a weapon; no one could exclude himself or herself from the possibility of being infected; we all have been (and are) hoping for science to find a cure.

To put it differently, instead of working toward an *externalization* of our own vulnerability on an enemy (like in war), the pandemic experience has made us all, for a moment, if not equal, at least very *similar*. A common condition of vulnerability suddenly overcame us all. In terms of health measures and public health infrastructures, however, we were not ready. The blow hit us suddenly.

Public discourse (in politics and the media alike) has recurred to a lexicon of war and conflict to name and narrate the situation of emergency, proving itself loyal to a martial imagery—as if unable to think of danger, risk, and death outside a belligerent framework. For a meaningful example of this attitude, one could look at the daily bulletins of deaths and new contagions that, every day at 6:00 p.m., were broadcast on Italian television during the months of the lockdown, approximately from the end of February until mid-June 2020: they resembled a military report of casualties in battle.

This overall picture reveals a lot about our cultural relation to violence, war, conflict, the preponderance of their semantic frame, and the pervasiveness of their mythopoietics. To refer, once again, to the Italian cultural and social landscape during the long period of the lockdown, it is worth noting that what was put in place were very severe measures of confinement including the closing of grade schools, day care facilities, universities, shops, restaurants, cinemas, theaters, and gyms; the prohibition of all outdoor activities, including individual ones, if not within 200 meters from one's home; and the restriction of movement, including visits to relatives and friends. A severe lockdown was accompanied by an insistent punitive discourse coming from public authorities. The government thought that in order to obtain effective measures of confinement—to hinder the further spreading of the virus—Italians, who are notoriously reluctant to follow norms, had to be intimidated with legal arguments that could even lead to penal actions against the transgressors. Additionally, the government determined that the approach had to be reinforced through surveillance devices. At the highest peak of the spreading of the virus, in April, especially during Easter time, drones, helicopters, and police patrols surveyed the territory to verify that no picnics or outside gatherings (traditional Easter activities for Italians) would take place. It must be acknowledged that in Italy, contrary to the stereotype adopted even by the Italian government as a base for its own decisions, there has been a responsible willingness to comply with social distancing, self-isolation, and the wearing of masks. Even though, of course, there have been exceptions, the general mood has overall aligned with the rules of the lockdown.

The militarization of society has been, however, appealing to many. Surveillance and control were not only enforced by the police and the *carabinieri*, but they were also willingly embraced by average citizens, who excitingly turned themselves into whistle-blowers, immediately at ease with an atmosphere of "law and order" that had to do less with health precautions and more with quasi-fascist attitudes that, at times, took disquieting overtones.

The Martial Nostalgia

Finally, the securitization of society through surveillance measures and its militarization through a large use of police patrols, personal identification, and fines elicited *also* the imagination of some political and cultural *milieux* of the radical left. According to their analyses, what was taking place was the *panopticon* come true, that is, the realization of a pervasive structure of surveillance and deterring punishment, more disquieting than the one recalled by Michel Foucault regarding the modern prison in *Discipline and Punish*.[12] The pandemic—so this narrative went and still goes—is a deliberately exaggerated menace, augmented by both the media and governments, in order to give more power to the State (and to Capital) to control its citizens.

Interestingly enough, therefore, the discourse that the State produced to regulate the health emergency (based on its familiar lexicon of rules and prohibitions, of norms and punishment, since the State is the "legitimate monopolist of violence") immediately produced a counter-discourse *against* the State, its controlling drive, and its evil intentions. And, of course, this counterdiscourse lamented the acquiescence of the population to government rules, advocating for rebellion.[13] Opposite yet complementary—the one in favor of order, the other against it—both discourses fail to take into account the *novelty* of the pandemic in its impact on our common, yet unacknowledged vulnerability. Both fail to acknowledge that when common vulnerability is at stake, we should at once abandon the martial field and, instead, all work to *care*, as the Italian doctor in the interview mentioned above rightly claimed.

The point I make is not, of course, that one should not criticize the State and its structural reliance on a monopoly of force that renders its acts always dominating, coercive, and sovereign. My point is that, during the peak of the pandemic, the counternarrative against the State and its apparatus has relied on a discourse of such kind, that is, one that discards the materiality of vulnerability and thereby fails to recognize its impact on all lives. In this case, the *critical* attitude has practiced a refusal, a foreclosure toward a new phenomenon and, instead, has preferred more familiar conceptual and political frames (the narrative of power and counterpower) that, in their antagonism, eventually confirmed that nothing new was happening, that what was taking place was just another version, surely more dangerous, of the emergency and security-oriented discourse by the State to control, discipline, and eventually punish its subjects.

It is pointless to recall that, without the militarized discourse of the State, there would be no reason to be antagonistic. While failing to face the novelty of the pandemic from the viewpoint of care, these positions did not see—or they discarded—a novel ethics of care that, on the other hand, was silently developing in homes and neighborhoods. I will address this more specifically at the conclusion of this chapter.

Dematerialized Life

Another significant aspect of the proliferation of discourses based, on the one hand, on the pandemic as war and, on the other, on the State as a tyrant against individual freedoms, is the fact that little (if any) space has been given to suffering, to mourning. What has been thereby impeded has been the acknowledgment of the concrete effects of the pandemic on the individual lives that have been lost. As Hannah Arendt claims, each human being is unique. It is when we fail to perceive this "uniqueness as it appears" that public life runs amok. Similarly, each loss is unique, and equally unique are the people who die, whose lives are never "bare" but full of desires, affects, and relationships. During the peak time of the pandemic, one of the most negative effects of the lockdown was the impossibility to perceive, to feel—and not just to understand—the concreteness of loss. The absence of all forms of mourning—funerals and other public forms of grieving were banned—contributed to *dematerialize* life in its vulnerability and extreme closeness to death. We all lived the strangest of situations: never before in human history had we experienced such a level of commonality in vulnerability. The opportunity to transform this lived experience into knowledge has failed because we did not (could not?) give enough space to suffering. With this, I do not mean a sentimental discourse like the one that often populates the media. Instead, I rather mean a discourse that, for once, could have taken vulnerability seriously and, with it, the necessity of care. This would be a different type of care, of course, one that paradoxically is based not on an intensification of relationality but on its suspension.

During the situation of emergency, we have missed the opportunity to reflect politically on vulnerability and loss and on their crucial role in taking abide from the belligerent lexicon that usually characterizes the emergency discourse.[14] While allowing little space for the telling of individual, incarnated losses, and conceding instead much space to the insistent counting of nameless deaths, expressed only by numbers, we have missed the opportunity to "learn from suffering," according to the ancient Aeschilean motto tò *pathei mathos*.

The materiality of pain—coughing, hard breathing, excessive tiredness, fever, and loss of taste and smell—has been reluctantly narrated, whereas preference has gone to discourses on the abstract aspects of the pandemic, such as contagion curves, percentages, and statistics.

Thereby, as a consequence of this removal of pain and mourning, the pandemic has taken the form of an immaterial, even *deniable* fact. And this has given rise to conspiracy theories of all kinds. According to Italian philosopher Giorgio Agamben, the "so-called pandemic" has caused an "unmotivated emergency" that serves the all-time resurgent sovereign power of the State in its constant aspiration to control and govern lives.[15] According to rougher positions (often expressed by right-wing politicians and public figures), the virus is nothing more than a normal flu that kills only the elderly or the already ill. In a sort of "spontaneous eugenics," these negationist positions reveal the unconscious racism of the average mentality—a mentality that considers it right that only the strong and the healthy survive.[16]

According to other conspiracy theory positions, the virus is alternatively a Chinese machination (either willfully provoked or as a laboratory experiment gone wrong), a hoax created by a world pedophile project to subvert President Trump, and so on.[17]

Critical Theory and the Lungs

All these different positions have something in common (beyond their morally scary tones): they tend to discard the material element of life, its physiology, and, consequently, its pathology. They tend, in other words, to reduce the body and life to their metaphorizations.

As Paul Elie has pointed out by referring to Susan Sontag's critique of the abuse of illness as metaphor, "the ubiquity of virus as metaphor may have left many of us unprepared to recognize and fear the lethal literal viruses circulating among us, and to prepare ourselves and our societies against them."[18]

My disconcert, at this point, does not certainly apply to obscure, right-wing, white supremacist conspiracy theories but rather to the milieu of critical theory, its philosophical response to the new phenomenon of the virus.

During the peak of the pandemic, the refusal to recognize the materiality of illness and death basically had to do, I maintain, with the difficulty of letting go of the twentieth-century philosophical dogma that, in the human world, everything is language. The fact that, suddenly, "virus" was no longer a figure of speech left many unprepared and caught them off guard. It was no longer a matter of metaphors—so willingly used, in recent critical theory, to illuminate social phenomena.

The absurd aspect of what we could call a "metaphoric collapse" is that it regards concepts that, in past years, have been abundantly used by critical theory such as contamination, contagion, hybridization, immunity, and so on. During the pandemic, we have witnessed the literal embodiment of these concepts beyond any possible imagination. They have no longer been metaphors.

What did those concepts mean before the pandemic? They were elegant and effective transfigurations of biological processes into political processes. They were *critical* concepts meant to reveal hidden realities, unacknowledged political processes that lie below the surface. Perhaps these concepts have indeed manifested what they intended to expose and have been effective instruments for comprehending reality—the immunitarian paradigm, bare life, biopolitics, and, by contrast, contamination, hybridization, and so on have appeared as welcomed, new, transformative horizons against the ethnocentrism of Western theory. Currently, the pandemic puts into question not so much the claim that these concepts can work as much as the fact that they can be used metaphorically. Their being, currently, "the real name of the thing"—in the sense in which the German scholar Bruno Snell used to define "archaic thought"—reverses their critical function, turns it upside down.[19] Presently, those words say different things.

Regardless of whatever the philosopher's authoritative voice might wish to sanction, there is a molecular reality that must be heard: there are—literally—pulmonary alveoli struck by the virus that must be oxygenated, slowly and constantly, in order to make breathing still possible. These alveoli are material parts of our bodies; they are carnal portions of sick bodies that need beds, ventilators, and tubes in intensive care units. In the end, the necessity of a lockdown, at least in terms of the political decision of the State, is based on the need to ventilate lungs. In order to ventilate the maximum possible number of lungs (after a significant reduction of intensive care units in previous years, at least in the Italian public health system), in order not to be forced to leave some body without intensive care (which, unfortunately, has nonetheless happened), we must all segregate. The State imposes on us this isolation, through intimidation and threat—as if we would not otherwise understand.

"*Protego ergo obligo* [I protect you hence I force you]" was the motto of modern sovereignty, as forged in Thomas Hobbes' *Leviathan*. Protection in exchange for obedience is the contract modernity has set up in order to legitimize power. There is, of course, the possibility that this contract be carried out in abusive terms, in times of emergency—this possibility is inherent in the very notion of the State. The point, though, is not how much power has been abusively exercised. The point, this time, has had to do with how many ventilators were needed, how much breathing could be facilitated, and how many alveoli could be oxygenated. The point, furthermore, has been possibly to avoid deciding between lives worth living and saving and lives that are sacrificable. The point, finally, has been (and still is) to contrast a "spontaneous eugenics" that would so vividly appeal to the general public and to the refined intellectual.

In the end, there has been a widespread reluctance to acknowledge the materiality of our embodiment, the unavoidable anatomy of our bodies, and the limits it imposes on us. Corporeal materiality—the body that we all are—seems to refuse the metaphors that transfigure it. Some speak of abusive state control over our lives, surveillance society, and so on. Yet we must come to terms that what is now at stake are breathing, pulmonary alveoli, and their "hunger for air." We can no longer—at least for the next few years—speak of the immunitarian paradigm as something to criticize, since immunity (in a nonmetaphorical sense) is what we all are aspiring to. While hybridization and contamination were once welcomed terms in critical theory, now, when they are seen with nonmetaphorical eyes, they are conditions to avoid as biologically dangerous. Yet the critical ear—the ear of certain critical theory—is not disposed to listen to the materiality of the body, as it is accustomed to move exclusively in a world made of language and figures of speech. Accustomed as it is to apply consolidated paradigms of power to social reality, it is very unwilling to let them go, in a sort of melancholic attachment to the familiar.[20] It seems quite strange, but what once was the avant-garde of a critical discourse that sought to destabilize and depotentiate the restructuring of capitalist societies according to neoliberal tenets is now meeting the extreme right and the *conservative* aspiration it expresses: that of minimizing the danger and implicitly advocating the return to normal.

Susan Sontag, as Paul Elie recalls, claimed that illness is *not* a metaphor, and that "the most truthful way of regarding illness—and the healthiest way of being ill—is one most purified of, most resistant to, metaphoric thinking." Moreover, metaphors of illness often "hinder the rational and scientific apprehension that is needed to contain disease and provide care for people."[21]

Abandoning certain overly metaphorized attitudes that have been typical of critical theory can perhaps serve the very urgent task not only of taking care but also of thinking about care.

The Public Space of the Balcony

One could, in fact, add that Draconian measures would not have worked without a minor, local, diffused "public ethics of care."[22] Such an ethics has come not from the State but from communities, families, and neighborhoods that have recognized that, by social distancing and self-isolation, they are "committing to acts of compassion" and that "withdrawal from physical intimacy is a fundamentally altruistic gesture, helping to prevent the spread of infection to those more at risk."[23]

In conclusion, as promised at the beginning of this chapter, let me attempt a different reading of the role of vulnerability during the peak of the pandemic. Besides police patrols and whistle-blowers, other behaviors have taken place—behaviors that some have defined as tacky, sentimental, rhetorically patriotic, and even pathetic. These behaviors, however, allude to *another possible answer* to the health emergency. It is the solidarity-oriented answer that takes vulnerability seriously, as a common condition that needs common action. As said before, this common action has paradoxical features: physically suspended, our interrelatedness continues to be based affectively on a proximity that is undeniable. Not only the acts of willful, self-imposed social distancing are acts of altruism. Not only is the concern for the elderly a sign that the perception of vulnerability as a common feature of the human discards the individualistic dogma of the concern for self-preservation.

There have also been numerous acts of solidarity and proximity expressed in neighborhoods, via creative modes of mutual help, both material and symbolic. In this context, balconies have played a crucial role by becoming public spaces of *distanced proximity*. An emotional commerce has taken place across balconies. People would receive food and medicines from baskets attached to ropes, elderly persons would benefit from the company of neighbors, and musicians and singers would entertain people living in the same building by singing and playing on the balcony. As a visible, exposed, suspended, yet firm public space, the balcony has served as the symbolic denial of domestic isolation during the lockdown. The balcony seems to have surrogated, as it were, in an architectural form the "urge to appear," as Arendt would say, at times of imposed isolation.

A new politics of balconies has taken place during the lockdown. This is just an example, but it vividly stages a different configuration of the common condition of vulnerability—a vulnerability never so materialized, made flesh—into something positive, into a resource, as feminists have been saying for years. Vulnerability is something that allows us to think of our commonalities, of our similarities not only in deadly terms but also in the form of a new *public dimension of care*. We must give space and name to this new public dimension, seeking to establish new connections between vulnerability and care.

Songs from balconies, as Bonnie Honig has pointed out, are a "serenade for democracy."[24] And if a serenade is usually a song for a loved one who is distant—usually on a balcony—likewise our common singing, together but distant, expresses a desire for being near, a longing for touching one another and for talking to one another, a democratic desire that intensifies, as it were, in the times of its suspension. A "yearning for mutuality" is what can be heard in this singing together from balconies, "the mutuality of citizenship without putting each other at risk."[25]

Who would have imagined that our societies, so depoliticized, consumerist, neoliberal, would have discovered—or rediscovered—at the times of its planetary absence, what Arendt calls the fundamental "pleasure in the company of others"?

In every collective event, there flickers an erotic element of sociality. Yet the form it will take is never clear. It can become democratic *generativity* but it can also *degenerate* into authoritarian or totalitarian drives.

It depends on us, on all of us, to find the words that express this desire, to imagine new forms in which it can become pleasure for everyone—and not just for someone who is usually the one who convokes himself in the position of command.

Let me conclude by saying that a serenade for democracy can take many different tones, not necessarily all melodic. What has happened in the United States since the end of May 2020, through the protests and the gatherings of the Black Lives Matter movement that followed George Floyd's death, is a particularly clamorous, perhaps even cacophonous serenade. Yet it attests to the always resurging need for a public space where people can appear and make their voices heard. The Arendtian "urge to appear," an inherent drive that all living beings share and that is grounded on birth, is the inaugural fact of our existence, which coincides with *appearing to someone* and, therefore, *mattering to someone*.[26] Life is a political dimension insofar as it requires a public space in which to appear. In turn, politics becomes a generative dimension when it gives voice to this human, living need.

Notes

1. Emmanuel Lévinas, "Peace and Proximity," in *Basic Philosophical Writings*, ed. Adriaan T. Peperzak, Simon Critchley, and Robert Bernasconi (Bloomington: Indiana University Press, 1996), 167.

2. See especially Judith Butler, *Precarious Life: The Powers of Mourning and Violence* (London: Verso, 2004), Judith Butler, *Giving an Account of Oneself* (New York: Fordham University Press, 2005), and Adriana Cavarero, *Horrorism: Naming Contemporary Violence*, trans. William McCuaig (New York: Columbia University Press, 2009). See also *Judith Butler's Precarious Politics: Critical Encounters*, ed. Terrell Carver and Samuel Chambers (London: Routledge, 2008) and *Differenza e relazione: l'ontologia dell'umano nel pensiero di Judith Butler e Adriana Cavarero*, ed. Lorenzo Bernini and Olivia Guaraldo (Verona: ombre corte, 2009). There has been a recent surge in studies devoted to vulnerability. Among them, see Estelle Ferrarese, *The Politics of Vulnerability* (London: Routledge, 2018); Miri Rozmarin, *Vulnerable Futures, Transformative Pasts: On Vulnerability, Temporality, and Ethics* (Bern: Peter Lang, 2017); and Erin Gilson, *The Ethics of Vulnerability: A Feminist Analysis of Social Life and Practice* (London: Routledge, 2014). Worth mentioning is also "Vulnerability and the Human Condition Initiative," by Martha Fineman at Emory University. https://web.gs.emory.edu/vulnerability/index.html.

3. Cavarero, *Horrorism*, 30.

4. Olivia Guaraldo, *Comunità e vulnerabilità. Per una critica politica della violenza* (Pisa: ETS, 2012), 9. In *Precarious life*, Butler claims that the recognition of a common condition of shared vulnerability has to do with a rethinking of ontology; it involves "an insurrection at the level of ontology, a critical opening up of the questions, What is real? Whose lives are real? How might reality be remade? Those who are unreal have, in a sense, already suffered the violence of derealization. What, then, is the relation between violence and those lives considered as 'unreal'? Does violence effect that unreality? Does violence take place on the condition of that unreality?" The refusal to recognize a common condition of vulnerability is, according to Butler, often deployed to legitimze systemic violence against lives of people deprived of their status of "real persons." Cavarero speaks of an "ontology of linkeage and dependence"; see Cavarero, *Horrorism*, 21.

5. Butler, *Giving an Account of Oneself*, 66.

6. Margaret Lock and Judith Farquhar, *Beyond the Body Proper: Reading the Anthropology of Material Life* (Durham, NC: Duke University Press, 2007), 9.

7. As Rosi Braidotti pointed out, in a seminal intervention in the Italian feminist debate, "we are the same in our feminine corporeality, but the body is not pure nature (sex) but especially culture, that is, a point of intersection among the biological, the social and the symbolic (gender)"; see Rosi Braidotti, "Il paradosso del soggetto 'femminile e femminista.' Prospettive tratte dai recenti dibattiti sulle gender theories [The paradox of the 'feminine/feminist' subject. Perspectives from the recent gender theories debates]," in *La differenza non sia un fiore di serra* [Difference should not be a greenhouse flower], ed. F. D'Arianna (Milan: Franco Angeli, 1991), 23.

8. On the Italian thought of sexual difference, see Milan Women's Bookstore Collective, *Sexual Difference* (Bloomington: Indiana University Press, 1990), whose original Italian version was published in 1987. See also Adriana Cavarero, "The Need for a Sexed Thought," in *Italian Feminist Thought*, ed. P. Bono and S. Kemp (Oxford: Blackwell, 1991) and L. G. M. Zerilli, "Refiguring Rights through the Political Practice of Sexual Difference," *differences* 15, no. 2 (2004): 54–90.

9. Butler, *Precarious Life*, 24.

10. Butler, *Precarious Life*, 30.

11. This sentence was reported by Guido Dotti, a monk of the Comunità di Bose (an ecumenical religious community founded in 1965 at Bose, in the northern Italian region of Piedmont) in a radio conversation with Italian philosopher Felice Cimatti. https://www.raiplayradio.it/audio/2020/04/UOMINI-E-PROFETI--Pasqua-di-solidariet195160-e-compassione--31ff8aa0-8ac8-41db-92cf-2eadc800b3ff.html.

12. Michel Foucault, *Discipline and Punish*, trans. Alan Sheridan (New York: Vintage, 1995).

13. The Wu Ming collective is emblematic of this type of counterdiscourse. See especially their reportage from the beginning of the lockdown. https://www.wumingfoundation.com/giap/tag/diario-virale/.

14. On the relation between vulnerability and loss, see Olivia Guaraldo, *Comunità e vulnerabilità*.

15. http://positionspolitics.org/giorgio-agamben-the-state-of-exception-provoked-by-an-unmotivated-emergency/.

16. Mario Pezzella, "Sarà un 8 settembre?" March 11, 2020. http://www.leparoleelecose.it/?p=39038. In a similar vein, but highlighting the racial aspect of this "unplanned" eugenics, one that confirms the functioning of a "racial contract" in the USA, see Adam Serwer, "The Coronavirus Was an Emergency until Trump Found Out Who Was Dying," May 8, 2020. https://www.theatlantic.com/ideas/archive/2020/05/americas-racial-contract-showing/611389/.

17. https://www.bbc.com/news/av/world-53507579/qanon-coronavirus-and-the-conspiracy-cult.

18. Paul Elie, "(Against) Virus as Metaphor," March 19, 2020. https://www.newyorker.com/news/daily-comment/against-the-coronavirus-as-metaphor.

19. Bruno Snell, "Die Sprache Heraklits," *Hermes* 61, no. 4 (1926): 353–81.

20. For a thorough analysis of the numerous predicaments of critical theory in the humanities, see Rita Felski, *The Limits of Critique* (Chicago: University of Chicago Press, 2015).

21. Susan Sontag, "Illness as Metaphor," *The New York Review of Books*, January 26 (1978). https://www.nybooks.com/articles/1978/01/26/illness-as-metaphor/.

22. Adriana Cavarero, "Preface to the English Edition," in *Surging Democracy: Notes on Hannah Arendt's Political Thought* (Stanford, CA: Stanford University Press, 2021).

23. Joseph Owen, "States of Emergency, Metaphors of Virus and COVID-19," March 31, 2020. https://www.versobooks.com/blogs/4636-states-of-emergency-metaphors-of-virus-and-covid-19.

24. Bonnie Honig, "In the Streets a Serenade," March 14, 2020. http://politicsslashletters.org/uncategorized/in-the-streets-a-serenade/.

25. Honig, "In the Streets."

26. On the relation among politics, the urge to appear, and public happiness, see Olivia Guaraldo, "Public Happiness: Revisiting an Arendtian Hypothesis," *Philosophy Today* 62, no. 2 (2018): 397–418.

Six

Necropolitics, Care, and the Common

Elia Zaru

Theory, Reality, and Critique

"From the beginning, we knew that this war would never happen. After the hot war (the violence of conflict), after the cold war (the balance of terror), here comes the dead war—the unfrozen cold war—which leaves us to grapple with the corpse of war and the necessity of dealing with this decomposing corpse which nobody from the Gulf has managed to revive. [. . .] War has entered into a definitive crisis. It is too late for the (hot) WW III: this has already taken place, distilled down the years into the Cold War. There will be no other. [. . .] This is why the Gulf War will not take place."[1] These famous words by Jean Baudrillard were published in the French journal *Libération* on January 4, 1991. On January 17, after five months of diplomatic and military tensions between the United States and Iraq on the Kuwait issue, Washington and its allies started Operation Desert Storm. The First Gulf War had just begun and, at its end, tens of thousands of Iraqis would be dead. Baudrillard wrote various subsequent pieces devoted to reconfirming what he had said in his first article, namely, that the Gulf War was a "simulated one," that is, the ultimate manifestation of the *simulacra* and the society of the spectacle. Following Baudrillard's statements, the debate escalated. "How far wrong can a thinker go and still lay claim to serious attention?" asked Christopher Norris in a harsh criticism directed not only against Baudrillard but, in general, against what

Baudrillard represented in the 1980s and 1990s—namely, poststructuralist and postmodern theory.[2] On the contrary, those who aimed at defending Baudrillard argued that his argument was far more complex than the reductionist and caricatural image given by his critics.[3]

Despite its circumstantial character, this controversy reveals to us two general points. First, it suggests that there is a differential between the temporality of theory and the temporality of reality. While the latter (especially in our contemporaneity) is subject to a constant acceleration that produces radical changes within a short time, the former needs stability to deepen its matter (obviously, the contemporary precariousness of this stability is not ground to infer the impossibility of theory). Second, this debate invites us to be cautious in front of any attempt to simply "cover" reality with a pre-established dress knitted by theory, for reality could exceed theory (and vice versa).

Something similar to what occurred with Baudrillard happened in the first months of the Covid-19 pandemic, when Giorgio Agamben interpreted the measures implemented by the Italian government in order to contrast the spread of the coronavirus as an exercise of biopolitics' "state of exception."[4] In this case too, the debate escalated quickly. If even possible, Agamben's words were franker than Baudrillard's. Thus, the possibility of a misunderstanding is quite remote.[5] Yet, even in this situation, one can find the two general problems underlined in the "*affaire* Baudrillard," namely, the differential temporality between theory and reality and the difficulty of perfectly covering reality with theory.

Given these problems, any attempt to assess Agamben's position and the critiques he received is doomed to be unsatisfying. In order to avoid the risk of a dead end, it might be helpful to "provincialize" the debate on biopolitics in light of what happened during the most intense months of the Covid-19 crisis. As is well known, with the expression "provincializing Europe" Dipesh Chakrabarty wants to highlight a new perspective in historiography (and, more broadly, in the humanities and social sciences). The postcolonial approach on which Chakrabarty's method is grounded does not simply aim to refuse "Europe" as a whole. Its purpose is to decenter the "imaginary figure"[6] of Europe in order to disclose what has been concealed by such a conceptual framework, that is, the "other-than-Europe" from a "non-European" perspective. Keeping this in mind, it might be useful to reflect, in light of the Covid-19 pandemic, on the "other-than-biopolitics." Is biopolitics as we know it the only conceptual category we can use to analyze what is happening to our societies? Are there alternatives to biopolitics, and, if so, what do they tell us?

Biopolitics or Necropolitics?

During the third week of April 2020, a letter written by an elderly man living in a nursing home went viral in Italy. Even national TV channels read the letter during the news. The man, who was 85 years old, was dying due to the coronavirus, but before his death, he wanted to describe to his family the situation of what he called "a 'golden' prison." He wrote: "In my opinion, there should be no nursing homes, assisted living facilities, and so on"; he added: "my dignity as a human being [*uomo*] has already been killed"; and he concluded: "ahead of the coronavirus, there is another, even more serious matter that kills us: the absence of any minimal respect for others, the total lack of conscience. We, the elderly people, are just numbers."[7] These harsh words became the symbol of what was happening to an entire generation, especially in northern Italy. At that time, the coronavirus had killed more than twenty thousand people, with the vast majority of them being over seventy years old. Nursing homes soon became a problem all over the world, but in northern Italy, the situation was far more dramatic due to the collapse of the National Health Service and the decision of the local governor of Lombardy to transfer elderly people from hospitals to nursing facilities (where, as some investigations have showed, they were abandoned to themselves) in order to have beds and ventilators available for the younger people with more possibilities to recover.

In Italy, there were no perturbing affirmations like the one pronounced by UK prime minister Boris Johnson on losing "the loved ones," or the one by the Texas Republican lieutenant governor Dan Patrick, who said that old people would be willing to risk their health and lives in order to stop the lockdown on the US economy, a claim reiterated by then US president Donald Trump. Nonetheless, the consequences of thirty years of cuts in public spending, including for the National Health Service, produced the same material effect: the necessity of a (sovereign) distinction between "grievable" and "ungrievable" lives.[8] That is, there are some, within our societies, who are not considered "living subjects" anymore, who are not included in that part of the population to which the politics on life (biopolitics) would apply. Is this a new situation, or is the pandemic simply accelerating processes that already existed? In other words, is this the first time we can observe the presence, within a society, of "ungrievable" lives? Of course not; the lives of the *sans papiers*, the undocumented, the migrants, the homeless, and so on are, by definition, ungrievable for they are excluded from the boundaries of citizenship, the institution within which collective mourning is acknowledged. Thus, there is a link that connects the "newest" ungrievable lives (those who, in this pandemic, have been sacrificed on the altar of national balanced budgets or economic profit) with the "old" ones (the migrants, and all those categories excluded from the institution of citizenship). If this is the case, then the "provincialization" of biopolitics leads us to another category that has been used to interpret the power of discarding lives rather than bio-ruling them. That is the category of necropolitics.

With the concept of necropolitics, Achille Mbembe aims at integrating the notions of biopower and biopolitics.[9] According to Foucault's famous definition, biopolitics is understood as the political power exercised over the life of the population as a whole in order to nurture life and avoid death with the goal of maintaining the health of the productive body. In this sense, biopolitics is strictly linked to the production of value in capitalist society: as long as all physical bodies capable of working are healthy and put to work, the accumulation of capital is guaranteed. Necropolitics, on the contrary, is a political power exercised from "outside" the population, that is, outside the boundaries and borders (both theoretical and geographical) of the territory where the population lives. That is, necropolitics is a power exercised outside the space invested by biopolitics. While biopolitics is intended as a "power over life," necropolitics is conceived as a "power over death," and it is exercised precisely by discarding lives, by deciding which lives are worth living and which are not—or, in the case of the current pandemic, which lives are worth saving and which are not. Mbembe writes: "I have put forward the notion of necropolitics, or necropower, to account for the various ways in which, in our contemporary world, weapons are deployed in the interest of maximally destroying persons and creating *death-worlds*, that is, new and unique forms of social existence in which vast populations are subjected to living conditions that confer upon them the status of the *living dead*."[10] The combination of biopolitics and necropolitics is the fundamental feature of "late modern colonial occupation" (which finds its most representative example in the colonial occupation of Palestine) and allows us to conceive of sovereignty as a power over "the capacity to define who matters and who does not, who is disposable and who is not."[11]

According to Mbembe, necropolitics suffuses the "colony," that is, the other, the "outside." At the same time, as the history of Western colonization has shown, necropolitics serves the "inner" purpose of maintaining the functioning of value extraction processes, both at the regional and global levels. The two dimensions are interrelated: the power over death is the counterbalance to the power over life. "Outside necropolitics" is necessary so that "inside biopolitics" can reach its goal of increasing lives and body productivity. The pandemic conjuncture has now seemingly moved the borders of "otherness" from the outside to the inside, from the colonized to the colonizing. That is, necropolitics—the power to define who is disposable and who is not—has become a matter that regards "us" and not only "them." It is "our" elderly and fragile people who have been affected by the sovereign decision on the "cost" of their life, a cost they are obliged to pay in order to "save" the economy from stopping its growth—as in a colonial relation. Necropolitics has not manifested itself in the form of the weapons used by the Israeli military against the Palestinian population or in the way in which the fortress Europe rejects, imprisons, and exploits migrants from all over the world. Its form has instead been that of "spending reviews," austerity, privatization of health systems, and all the economic measures we have seen implemented all over the world in the recent decades of neoliberal capitalism. This necropolitics operates "an unequal redistribution of vulnerability"[12] in which individual strength is the ultimate thing that matters. The societal sphere and its goal of improving collective capabilities is simply ignored when it is not explicitly challenged. After all, as Brazilian president Jair Bolsonaro said in order to defend his position against any quarantine measures, "The virus is here, we're going to confront it. Confront it like a man, not a boy! We're all going to die one day."[13]

Bolsonaro's words represent a maximum expression of the "brutalism"[14] we all live in: toxic masculinity ("confront it like a *man*, not a boy"), machismo (the very idea of "confronting," as in some sort of a battle), social Darwinism ("we're all going to die," so one could simply ignore the fact that there are some who would die earlier and others who would die later, some who would die *from* the coronavirus and others *with* the coronavirus, as in the distinction used for the official count of the death toll in Europe). It seems that the only part that Bolsonaro indeed got right is the first statement: the virus is here, some of us have been and will be more exposed and vulnerable, while others may hope to be more protected. No one of us can declare oneself to be immune. This is a collective issue, and we should search for collective solutions, against neoliberal necropolitics and its individualization.

Biopolitics from Below, Care, and the Common

What is to be done? According to Panagiotis Sotiris, "simply treating measures of public health, such as quarantines or 'social distancing,' as biopolitics somehow misses their potential usefulness. In the absence of a vaccine or successful antiviral treatments, these measures [. . .] can reduce the burden, especially for vulnerable groups."[15] In other words, these biopolitical measures could materially help in saving lives. This means that they could act as a counterbalance to the necropolitics described above. In fact, as Sotiris argued, in the pandemic crisis, "'naked life' would be closer to the pensioner on a waiting list for a respirator or an ICU bed, because of a collapsed health system."[16] Sotiris calls for a "biopolitics from below," a "communist" or a "democratic biopolitics" based on a "democratization of knowledge," in order to move "from discipline to responsibility in regards to others and then ourselves." He writes: "Instead of a permanent individualized fear, which can break down any sense of social cohesion, we move the idea of collective effort, coordination and solidarity within a common struggle." That is to say, the pandemic crisis has shown that a valuable way to resist and oppose necropolitics could lie in a "biopolitics from below." The latter could reconstruct the collective relations on which every society is built and thus could move against neoliberal individualization and the disregard for the "others" on which the very practice of necropolitics is grounded.

According to Sotiris, this idea of a "biopolitics from below" has its roots in Foucault and his relational conception of power practices. Sotiris is not alone in his call for greater attention to what the French philosopher said with respect to biopolitics. Daniele Lorenzini notes that "Foucault's notion of biopolitics, as he developed it in 1976, was not meant to show us just how *evil* this 'modern' form of power is." At stake in Foucault's reflection is the idea of the "historical crossing of a threshold and more specifically of what he calls a society's '*seuil de modernité biologique*' [threshold of biological modernity]."[17] Thus, continues Lorenzini, "it would be wise for us to refuse the 'blackmail' of biopolitics: we do not have to be 'for' or 'against' it but address it as a historical event that still defines, at least in part, the way in which we are governed, the way in which we think about politics and about ourselves."[18] Lorenzini claims that "biopolitics is always a politics of *differential vulnerability*,"[19] but within neoliberal capitalism this differential transforms biopolitics into necropolitics. Thus, the following questions arise: Is there a way to eliminate this differential, and could a "biopolitics from below" help in this task?

The possibility of a different conception of biopolitics also appears in the works of Roberto Esposito, one of the leading scholars of this concept. Esposito observes that biopolitics must not be considered only as a vertical relation in a top-down framework. On the contrary, especially in the pandemic crisis, it should be considered as a horizontal relation between individuals and communities.[20] Furthermore, the idea of a "biopolitics from below" could help us in dismantling the dangerous link Esposito describes between community and immunity[21] by transforming the very idea of "community" into that of the "common." This is possible thanks to what

Esposito defines as the process of a permanent instituting of life.[22] In the pandemic crisis, this process has taken the form of physical distancing as a defense not *from* but rather *for* others. In Elettra Stimilli's words, this has meant "being in common at a distance."[23]

The idea of the "common" assumes a fundamental role in the framework of a "biopolitics from below" especially in our current situation. Regardless of the distinction that such a concept assumes in its different theoretical formulations,[24] in its basic meaning it expresses the idea of a dimension where the individual dimension is intertwined with the collective one, and neither takes precedence over the other. Following Sandro Mezzadra, we can affirm that "the coronavirus is a threat to [. . .] 'the common.' The ongoing epidemic shows the fragility and precarity of such a common (as well as our very lives), together with the need for 'care.'"[25] This is the reason why, as stated by Sandro Chignola, "staying at home has meant taking care of the common; answering—this is the meaning of the term 'responsibility'—to the risk of the multiplication of the contagion." Yet, this could be not enough: "Taking care of the common also means to confront the politics which, by destroying welfare and healthcare, have condemned men and women to death [. . .]. The process of taking care of the common implies that the urbanistic and social politics of recent decades are being questioned."[26] In sum, to take care of the common means "to attack early capital's command on the economic crisis which characterizes the indefinite post- of the pandemic crisis."[27]

The concept of care has a long history (impossible to summarize here), finding its roots in feminist debates and movements. Due to the pervasiveness and architecture of contemporary capitalism, along with the critique of social reproduction and the processes of racialization in societies, the idea of caring assumes a fundamental importance, which the pandemic crisis has exposed. Abigail H. Neely and Patricia J. Lopez state that "at root, care ethics offers a response to neoliberalism's ideological constructs of individualism, self-responsibilization, and 'boot strapping'" for it offers an alternative based on what Maia Green and Victoria Lawson have called an ontological relationality in our lives.[28] This relationality is concealed by neoliberal capitalism. While the latter "posits the limits of responsibility to 'individuals and their families' (as Margaret Thatcher put it), the coronavirus outbreak (and other public health emergencies) make plain the multi-scalar uncaringness of neoliberal policies and the ideologies that underpin them."[29] The reason why a "biopolitics from below" needs the feminist notion of care lies in what the latter reveals about biopolitics itself. The idea of care releases biopolitics from its curse, that is, the tendency to infinite growth on which its power is structured. If biopolitics reaches its maximum target in the wellness of bodies able to produce and consume, then its power manifests itself in a process of continuous development. Every limit, danger, threat, or inability to keep pace with the normal course established for society has to be removed. Part of this removal is also the process of discarding incapable, disabled, or needless bodies, and here is the link with necropolitics. The concept of care does not imply the idea of a continuous performance towards growth. On the contrary, to take care means to establish a safe space where the rule is the "ecological" cohabitation with human (physical, psychological, and so forth) limits, and not their overcoming.

Those who were (and are) on the front line during the Covid-19 outbreak expressed, *mutatis mutandis*, the same concerns with respect to the catastrophic neoliberal approaches to society in terms of care and public health. On March 21, 2020, *The New England Journal of Medicine* published a letter signed by thirteen medical doctors working at the Papa Giovanni XXIII hospital in Bergamo, Italy which, at that time, was the global epicenter of the pandemic, the first in the Western world. Describing what they called "a public health and humanitarian crisis,"[30] they declared that the main, dramatic problem was the way in which the public health and, more in general, the care systems had been developed in the last decades. They write: "Western health care systems have been built around the concept of *patient-centered care*, but an epidemic requires a change of perspective toward a concept of *community-centered care*."[31] Needless to say, the patient-centered care replicates the ideology of individualization and individuals, in which the stratification of inequalities through gender, races, and classes can be more easily concealed, whereas a community-centered care implies the idea of a collective relation, and thus the idea of social responsibility with respect to those inequalities. Moreover, in a patient-centered care, the differential vulnerability mentioned above disappears, for individualization makes every comparison difficult as each individual is treated independently. In a patient-centered care, where every patient is alone, formally each is equal to the others, yet substantially it is easy to operate a distinction between those who are disposable and those who are not.

In light of the traditional notion of "biopolitics," the idea of a "community-centered care" may sound frightening. However, the possibility of a "democratization" of this biopolitics could remove all danger. Far from being an abstract idea, this is already an actual reality thanks to the countless experiences that, from South and North America to Europe, are calling for and performing mutualism, community care, and assistance from below for those who are suffering.[32] These are material examples of what "taking care of the common" means. Furthermore, as stated by Tania Rispoli, "today forms of social reproduction and care from below arise as the common's leading form of expression. These forms imply struggles and strikes against a work which (if possible) has become more unjust and underpaid in times of pandemic."[33]

Neely and Lopez emphasize three levels at which we can observe the Covid-19 crisis. The first is that of the "individual body," which is exposed to a vulnerability that differs in health, race, unequal distribution of carework, and economic capabilities. Then there exists a "social body," which functions through the unequal distribution of such vulnerabilities and, at the same time, conceals them. Finally, there is a "body politic," which, especially in the last neoliberal decades and thanks to individualization processes and cuts in public spending, has structured and institutionalized those vulnerabilities and their differentials. Surely, "the individual body, social body, and body politic are and have always been entangled."[34]

The idea of "common" as something that links together individual and collective, the feminist critique of social reproduction and its practice of "care" as an overcoming and defeating of the oppression attitude, and the idea of life as a relational and instituting process could challenge what Keeanga-Yamahtta Taylor has called "an existential crisis"[35] and could help us restore dignity to all those lives injured by the continuing search for profit.

Notes

I wish to thank Luisa Lorenza Corna and Paolo Missiroli for their comments on the first drafts of this essay and Dave Mesing for his linguistic help.

1. Jean Baudrillard, "The Gulf War Will Not Take Place," in *The Gulf War Did Not Take Place*, trans. Paul Patton (Bloomington: Indiana University Press, 1995), 23–24.

2. Christopher Norris, *Uncritical Theory: Postmodernism, Intellectuals and the Gulf War* (London: Lawrence & Wishart, 1992), 11.

3. See, for example, William Merrin, "Uncritical Criticism? Norris, Baudrillard and the Gulf War," *Economy and Society* 23, no. 4 (1994): 433–58.

4. The Italian version of Giorgio Agamben's writings on the pandemic can be found at https://www.quodlibet.it/una-voce-giorgio-agamben. The first essay (published on February 26, 2020), "The Invention of an Epidemic," has appeared in English in the *European Journal of Psychoanalysis* together with various responses to this text. https://www.journal-psychoanalysis.eu/coronavirus-and-philosophers/.

5. For a fair discussion of Agamben's argument, see Tim Christiaens, "Must Society Be Defended from Agamben?" *Critical Legal Thinking*, March 26, 2020. https://criticallegalthinking.com/2020/03/26/must-society-be-defended-from-agamben/.

6. Dipesh Chakrabarty, *Provincializing Europe* (Princeton: Princeton University Press, 2000), 4.

7. The original version of the letter has been published on the Italian blog *InTerris* and was read during the LA7 newscast on April 23, 2020.

8. I borrow these concepts of "grievable" and "ungrievable" lives from Judith Butler, *Frames of War: When Is Life Grievable?* (London: Verso, 2009).
9. Achielle Mbembe, *Necropolitics*, trans. Steve Corcoran (Durham: Duke University Press, 2019).
10. Mbembe, *Necropolitics*, 92.
11. Mbembe, *Necropolitics*, 80.
12. Achille Mbembe, "Le droit universel à la respiration," *AOC*, April 6, 2020. https://aoc.media/opinion/2020/04/05/le-droit-universel-a-la-respiration/.
13. Reported by the Associated Press, March 29, 2020.
14. Achille Mbembe, *Brutalisme* (Paris, La Découverte, 2020).
15. Panagiotis Sotiris, "Against Agamben: Is a Democratic Biopolitics Possible?" *Critical Legal Thinking*, March 14, 2020. https://criticallegalthinking.com/2020/03/14/against-agamben-is-a-democratic-biopolitics-possible/.
16. Sotiris, "Against Agamben."
17. Daniele Lorenzini, "Biopolitics in the Time of Coronavirus," *Critical Inquiry*, April 2, 2020.
18. Lorenzini, "Biopolitics."
19. Lorenzini, "Biopolitics."
20. Roberto Esposito and Torbjörn Elensky, "Inställningen i Sverige: de bäst anpassade överlever," *Svenska Dagbladet*, April 22, 2020.
21. See Roberto Esposito, *Communitas: The Origin and Destiny of Community*, trans. Timothy Campbell (Stanford: Stanford University Press, 2009) and *Immunitas: The Protection and Negation of Life*, trans. Zakiya Hanafi (Cambridge: Polity Press, 2011).
22. Roberto Esposito, "Vitam instituere," *European Journal of Psychoanalysis*, March 26, 2020.
23. Elettra Stimilli, "Being in Common at a Distance," *TOPIA. Canadian Journal of Cultural Studies*, March 20, 2020.
24. See especially Antonio Negri and Michael Hardt, *Commonwealth* (Cambridge, MA: Harvard University Press, 2009) and Pierre Dardot and Christian Laval, *Commun: Essai sur la revolution au XXIe siècle* (Paris: La Découverte, 2014).
25. Sandro Mezzadra, "Politics of struggles in the time of pandemic," *Verso Blog*, March 17, 2020. https://www.versobooks.com/blogs/4598-politics-of-struggles-in-the-time-of-pandemic.
26. Sandro Chignola, "Ecotecnia e capitale," *Euronomade*, April 26, 2020. http://www.euronomade.info/?p=13288.
27. Chignola, "Ecotecnia."
28. Abigail H. Neely and Patricia J. Lopez, "Care in the Time of Covid-19," *Antipode online*, April 4, 2020. https://antipodeonline.org/2020/04/04/care-in-the-time-of-covid-19/.
29. Neely and Lopez, "Care."
30. M. Nacoti, A. Ciocca, A. Giupponi, P. Brambillasca, F. Lussana, M. Pisano, G. Goisis, D. Bonacina, F. Fazzi, R. Naspro, L. Longhi, M. Cereda, C. Montaguti, "At the Epicenter of the Covid-19 Pandemic and Humanitarian Crises in Italy:

Changing Perspectives on Preparation and Mitigation," *The New England Journal of Medicine*, March 21, 2020.

31. Nacoti, et al., "At the Epicenter of the Covid-19 Pandemic and Humanitarian Crises in Italy."

32. See, for examples, the *Mutual Aid Network* in the U.S., the experiences described in Diego Arahuetes, "Chile: la autogestión de los cuidados en la resistencia," *Marcha*, May 26, 2020 (https://www.marcha.org.ar/chile-la-autogestion-de-los-cuidados-en-la-resistencia/) for an example in South America or, in Europe, the dozens of grass-root networks activated by social movements.

33. Tania Rispoli, "Stati Uniti, politiche divergenti nella crisi del corona virus," *DinamoPress*, April 2, 2020. https://www.dinamopress.it/news/le-divergenti-politiche-degli-stati-uniti-nella-crisi-del-coronavirus/.

34. Neely and Lopez, "Care."

35. Keeanga-Yamahtta Taylor, "Reality Has Endorsed Bernie Sanders," *The New Yorker*, March 30, 2020. https://www.newyorker.com/news/our-columnists/reality-has-endorsed-bernie-sanders.

Seven

Lacking Beings

Luca Illetterati

Life Does Not Exist

The notion of life is polysemic.[1] This polysemy may also be interpreted as the trace of a profound ambiguity that can be found even in its allegedly most rigorous denotation, that is, the scientific meaning. The attempt at retracing the defining characteristics of living beings often results in a series of problems that are not easy to solve. Some beings possess some of the fundamental features of life, yet they are not considered living (crystals, for example, are certainly highly organized structures that are endowed with a process of growth; yet they are not considered living beings). Some other beings are, vice versa, considered living, yet they do not possess any of the characteristics that are deemed fundamental when one speaks of life (viruses, for example, are beings endowed with genes and evolutionary history, yet they are not capable of self-sustenance and self-reproduction).

In December 2013, the magazine *Scientific American* published an article with the title "Why Life Does Not Really Exist."[2] The author's thesis is that life is not something that truly *is*. In order to be able to say that *there is* life, we would in fact have to be able to identify it clearly according to well-defined criteria. Yet given the actual failures of all attempts at such definition during thousands of years of science and philosophical thinking, we do not seem to be in possession of such criteria. The emphatic conclusion of the article is that *life*, therefore, *does not really exist*. The commentary maintains that life does not exist because life is *only a concept*, that is, a term we use to indicate not something that is but rather a model of organization of something that exists, a certain level of complexity of things that are. That we have never arrived at a satisfactory definition of life in its specific difference from that which life is not depends, according to the author of the essay, on the fact that there is not something that we can isolate as the essence of life analogously to the way in which we say, for example, that water is the liquid composed of two hydrogen atoms linked to an atom of oxygen.

The *Scientific American* piece is, in many respects, philosophically naïve regarding notions such as existence, reality, or concept. Nevertheless, it says something interesting in relation to the path I intend to pursue here. By claiming that life cannot be thought of as something that simply *is*—that is, it cannot be identified in substantial terms in the same way in which we identify water by saying it is two atoms of hydrogen and one of oxygen—the article highlights, in the notion of life, at least one feature worthy of emphasis well beyond the intentions of the essay itself. That feature is the impermeability and resistance of life with respect to an ontology of substance. The impermeability and resistance do not reveal, as the author of the above-mentioned article claims, that life does not exist; rather, they show the impossibility of grasping life through an ontology of substance understood as presence; that is, through an essentializing ontology that claims to recognize the substantial element capable of identifying life.

Life exists, and it is real, but not in the same way as a thing, an object, or a substance. In this respect, to understand the being of life implies a way of thinking of reality that is not reduced to an ontology that considers real only that which exists in the form of substance understood as presence.

Between Crystals and Smoke

The being of life is irreducible to substantial presence because life is a process that is always on the verge between crystals and smoke. It is the precipitate of a negotiation between a deterministic order and a stochastic disorder; it is an uninterrupted creation that emerges as "the compromise of a liquid vortex, between the redundancy of the crystal and the complexity of smoke."[3] To be a living being does not mean to be in a specific state. Rather, it involves an incessant dynamic of disorganization and reorganization in which lumps of matter and energy seem to rebel against a natural necessity—as if they were escaping from the need of their own dissolution—that nevertheless constitutes them by transforming disorder into organization and noise into information. Life-being (*essere-vita*)—the being of life, being life, being alive—means being steeped in some sort of struggle of nature against itself, as if life were some kind of an aporia of nature; as if life were the event that leads nature to the extreme limit at which nature discloses some form of unnaturalness or, at least, of resistance against its reduction to a physicalist concept.

This is what emerges from Xavier Bichat's *Recherches physiologique sur la vie et la mort*. In this work, the major French physiologist of the Revolutionary period proposes what is considered to be one of the most powerful definitions of life in the course of Western thinking. Bichat writes that "life consists in the sum of the functions, by which death is resisted."[4] As evident, we are not confronted here with a definition that tells us what life *is*. On the contrary, we are told what life is not, that with respect to which life presents itself as an opposition. If there is something that *is*, something that has the characters of substance and presence, in Bichat's definition, that is, death or, as it were, materiality as dead matter. Death is what is presented as the *normal* condition of being, as the *standard* condition in relation to which life represents a form of *resistance*, an *oppositional action*.

Bichat does not tell us, then, *what* life is. He does not indicate any substance that may be identified with life. Yet he says a lot about the way of being of that which lives. He says that the living being is the labor of a process that is inevitably destined to end. Life is, for Bichat, resistance and struggle to persist in the condition of never being a still substance. In this tension to persevere, which has nothing to do with the will because it does not imply a "beyond" life itself, one realizes that precisely this movement is, simultaneously and in the same respect, that which both makes beings alive and leads them to death.[5] Death is never given according to the logic of certainty, though. The molecules of life are in fact subject to a randomness that is never entirely controllable or governable—unless, that is, they give up their being alive or their being the never completely predictable and programmable movement that belongs to everything that lives. Life unfolds within randomness. Immersed in the most radical and extenuating contingency, within a swirling movement that is inevitably destined to entropic stillness, life—even the most inactive life—succeeds in its being alive only to the extent to which it resists and persists in its activity. Even though destined to failure, nevertheless, life is this stubbornness—tenacious and, at times, even blind to the inexorable grind of time, to the indifferent succession of events. This is out of the conviction—which is embedded in materiality and, therefore, prior to all forms of consciousness—that in that conatus to persevere, in that effort that may appear naturalistically meaningless, there is contained a sense of being. In it, there may even be contained the only sense of being that we can experience.

Action-Being

The living being lives through self-consumption. As is well known, in *On the Soul*, Aristotle claims that "the soul is cause and principle of the living body."[6] This statement does not mean that the soul is the producer that, from the outside, gives form to a body, which would thus be something other from the soul. The living being does not possess the way of being of *technai onta*, the artifacts that receive their meaning based on their producer's design and their user's forms of employment. As Ronald Polansky explains, "because causes and principles are said in many ways—Aristotle recognizes four sorts of causes—he specifies three ways in which the soul is the cause and principle of ensouled bodies: as mover, as end, and as substance (*ousia*), that is, form (415b8–12)."[7] What should be kept in mind here is that the soul is the cause according to all three determinations, that is, as principle or origin, as end, and as essence. It is therefore possible to say that life is its own self-realization at each moment of the process; that is, at each moment, life is the realization of its own essence. Again quoting Aristotle, "That [the soul] is so (cause) as substance is clear; for substance is *the cause of being* in all things, and for living things it is *living* that is being (*einai*), and the cause and source of this [living] is the soul."[8]

For living beings, being is living. For living beings, the essence is not a thing, a *res*, but rather an action, a dynamic. In such action and dynamic, the living being consummates itself in order to continue being a living being; that is, in order to continue being the activity that constitutes it. In this sense, for living beings, being means self-consumption. Living beings do not exist outside the action that constitutes them. The living being is nothing outside the action that it itself institutes and by which, in turn, it is constituted.

Life is action, says Aristotle. That is, in the words he uses in *Politics*, life is *praxis* (doing or acting) and not *poiesis* (making). *Poiesis* is, first and foremost, work or production. As is well known, *poiesis* is a way of making that finds its meaning in an object in which *poiesis* itself as activity comes to an end or dies. *Poiesis* is, for example, the activity of the woodworker who builds a chair, of the architect who plans a house, or of the assembler who puts together the various components of a computer. *Poiesis* is that action that finds its rest in its product, which is simultaneously the completion and the end of the action itself. What happens in *poiesis* is that, as long as there is activity, there is no product, and when, finally, there is a product, there is no longer activity.

An important text regarding the theme we are here addressing is Martin Heidegger's 1929–30 lecture course titled "Fundamental Concepts of

Metaphysics." In it, Heidegger addresses the way of being of living beings while confronting his own failure to think of life as such, that is, life that is not the human being's life. In this text, Heidegger plays on the notions of completion (or fulfillment) and conclusion with reference to the German term *fertig*. In German, *fertig* in fact means, at the same time, *finished*, ended (as in *die Arbeit is fertig*, the work is done) and *ready* (as in *bist du fertig?* are you ready?). It thus indicates that characteristic of poietic action for which such an action stops and ends when the product of this activity comes to completion.[9] *Poiesis* has to do with making something *fertig*, with the being of something that is ready and, therefore, suitable only when the activity of its production is over and finished.

Whereas *poiesis* is the action that finds its meaning in the product that emerges from its ending, *praxis* is instead the action that has its goal within itself, in its unfolding. The action of *praxis* finds its meaning not in an object outside itself, in some goal that lies *beyond* action, but rather in its very happening. *Praxis* does not find rest and satisfaction externally; rather, it is action finding its fulfillment in the action itself. As when one makes music, for example. Or when one plays. Or, moreover, when one does something right.

Life is *praxis* and not *poiesis* in that it does not aim at something outside itself but is rather accomplished within itself, within that movement—always unstable, uncertain, and exposed to risks and adversities—which is living. A life that were to find its meaning and sense of accomplishment in something exterior to itself would be an expropriated, alienated life—a life that lives for something else than itself.[10] Life is *praxis* because it escapes perfect planning, it takes up shape during its very unfolding, in the casualness of various circumstances, adapting to the landscape, developing in constantly unexpected ways within situations that shape life and that life itself shapes.

Briefly, life is *praxis* because the ways of its taking up form and of its resisting are structurally unpredictable. These ways are always newly unexpected responses to contexts, environments, and circumstances that can never be decided ahead of time. That unpredictability is precisely the constitutive aspect of life is what needs to be emphasized here.

Unpredictability reveals, as Hannah Arendt argues, the most originary and radical structure of action, that is, its intrinsic tragicity, the fact that in order to be—that is, to be truly itself—action must accept the contingency of the course by which it is actualized. Action must accept its own possible deformation, its own possibly turning into something else than itself. Action, in fact, modifies itself in the world that it enters. Every time, it assumes its own peculiar configuration, which can never be completely replicated. It takes up its own unrepeatable profile, its own specific consistency that is necessarily tied to situations, time, and contingency. If it does not transfer itself into the world, that is, if it does not accept the challenge to become itself world, action is nothing and becomes stuck in nothingness, taking up, at most, the density of a sleepy neuronal quiver. Action is always a mixture of more or less clear intentions and more or less shady outcomes, more or less coherent thoughts and more or less bloody and violent forces, more or less neat ideas and more or less sticky and putrid mud.

Impurities, Conflicts, and Contradictions

In "Zinc," the third section of his book *The Periodic Table*, Primo Levi writes:

> The course notes contained a detail which at first reading had escaped me, namely, that the so tender and delicate zinc, so yielding to acid which gulps it down in a single mouthful, behaves, however, in a very different fashion when it is very pure: then it obstinately resists the attack. One could draw from this two conflicting philosophical conclusions: the praise of purity, which protects from evil like a coat of mail; the praise of impurity, which gives rise to changes, in other words, to life. I discarded the first, disgustingly moralistic, and I lingered to consider the second, which I found more congenial.[11]

Life is not about purities. Where everything is pure, everything is foreseeable and, in some way, already decided. Where there is no mixture, medley, or crossbreeding of substances, every effect is already contained in its premises; every gesture is, as a matter of fact, already anticipated as for its unfolding and realization from the preconditions from which it arises. On the contrary, life—and with it, freedom, which is the extreme articulation of life—needs the action of some difference, struggle, contrast, the erotic intersection of elements, the possibility that, upon their meeting, two substances may become a third that is completely irreducible to the two from which the third nevertheless comes.

In the absence of conflict, everything is like everything else, and thus everything is like nothing. Life exists only within a spurious space. Only within conflict, only *thanks to*—and not despite—suffering, that is, only within the labor and fatigue implied by conflict, is there life.

Life-being (*essere-vita*) means thus that one is always and necessarily exposed, that one is always consigned and delivered to the threatening, harsh, and not rarely abrupt experiences of the world, of reality, and of time. There is no life prior to this delivery. Life *is* this very being delivered. Because it is delivered to some other than itself, life is always within a necessary and ineludible danger—not an accidental danger, which may simply happen, but rather a danger that constitutes life for what it is. As it always comes unexpected—if danger were sought after and defied, then we would be faced with a case of pitiful and horrid arrogance—danger puts the ordinary on hold, interrupts habits, breaks down the automatisms of gesture and gaze. Danger—and the effects it provokes: fear, gasping and almost paralyzed breath, muscles acting reflexively—brings existence back to itself; it confronts existence with being constantly situated within the world that it inhabits, with being constantly the "here and now" of life, and with being the very form of time.

Life is this impulse, this tension, this anxiety. Life is this persistent response to an ancestral need that is constitutive of life's form of being because life is, first of all, lack; and because it is lack, life is yearning and desire.

Eros

When, in Plato's *Symposium*, it is his turn to speak to advance his encomium of Eros, before proceeding with his speech, Socrates asks Agathon a question. Agathon is the one in whose honor the party is gathered; he has spoken just prior to Socrates in the sequence of discourses Plato has wisely orchestrated, and, in some way, he brings together in his own the sense of all preceding speeches. "Is Love (*Eros*) the love of something or is he the love of nothing?" Socrates asks Agathon; and also, "Does Love desire that thing which he is the love of, or not?"[12]

By agreeing to such a sketch of an argument that Socrates advances, Agathon declares straight away the vanity of his own speech; that is, he discloses the emptiness of that elegant and polished discourse that, synthesizing all previous discourses, attributed to Eros all possible positive qualities. If Eros is the desire of something that it does not possess, as Agathon now admits, it is evident that Eros cannot be, at the same time, characterized by that in whose direction it turns. What Agathon—and, with him, all those whose speeches Agathon somehow gathers within his encomium—has not understood or has not been able to see is Eros' essentially desiring structure; that is, his being, in his most ancestral core, desire, tension toward that which Eros does not possess, and longing that corresponds to a feeling of lack. Not understanding this, Agathon does also not understand that life, from its simplest to its most complex structures, is precisely such a *conatus*—the turn toward some other in order to realize oneself—that is desire.

Eros, that is, desire, is a *daimon* and, like all *daimons*, is "something in between (*metaxù*) mortal and immortal."[13] A *daimon* is an intermediary between the mortal and the god. It is that which finds its place in the distance that separates the mortal from the god and, by being situated *in* such a distance, in such a *limit*, it is also that which enables some form of communication and contact between the extremes whose difference it marks. A *daimon*, to use Plato's words, is the one that "fills the space between" and, in this sense, functions as mediation between two worlds.[14] As it is neither mortal nor immortal, but rather places itself in the distance that separates the two dimensions, it is neither of them and therefore participates in them both. Desire is the experience of such a limit.

The way of being of that which lives in desire cannot be reduced to either of the two dimensions between which it finds its place. It partakes of both without being reducible to either one alone. It lives in balance, in the interstitial space between itself and the other from itself, in a position that is always liminal between one's own and that of the stranger. In this sense, desire has a *contradictory* character that cannot be pacified without its radical distortion or nullification. As Derrida writes, the status of the *daimon*—and, we add, that of the desiring nature—appears as that "of a being that no logic can confine within a noncontradictory definition."[15] As a matter of fact, as structurally marked by lack and poverty, Eros is never fulfilled. Yet this being unfulfilled does not amount to being nothing. The desiring nature—that is, the way of being of the living—can be itself, can be desire only within the experience of lack. Consequently, it can *be*, it can *exist* only to the extent that it is lacking. Thus, it finds its condition of possibility in lack and not in the removal thereof. Once again using Diotima's words, Eros shares in the nature of his mother, Penìa, and therefore "want is his constant companion"[16]; he lives in the condition of need; need is a constituent of his nature and structures his way of being. Yet Eros also shares in the nature of his father, Poros, and therefore he is a hunter, desires learning, is continuously stretched toward overcoming need, which nevertheless constitutes him so intimately.[17]

The Activity of Lacking

Desire is, simultaneously, both the *experience of lack* and the *movement* produced by such an experience.

The living being, as a desiring nature, is a way of being whose constitutive form of being is need. To say that need is constitutive of the living is to say that a living being that is alien to the condition of need would no longer be living. Any living being in fact needs, in order to sustain and support itself as living, to destroy and reconstruct its constitutive "materials" through metabolic activities that, basically, consist in assimilation, transformation, and elimination. In their deepest structure, all these activities can be understood as forms of the articulation of need. We could say that being the activity of lacking or a lacking being—*die Tätigkeit des Mangels*, in Hegel's particularly effective expression—is what differentiates the living from the realm of pure inorganic materiality. As it does not imply any mutation that is self-initiated, inorganic materiality is completely unfit, due to its very constitution, to be affected actively by something such as lack.[18]

To claim that, in its way of being, the living is marked by need does not mean to say that the living needs the other from itself in order to be able finally to be itself, as if there were something that it needed to acquire in order to come to completion. To say that the living is constitutively marked by lack does not at all mean that the living fulfills itself as living only once it has filled such lack. The living is "a system that, at each moment, is unity in its fullness,"[19] that is, it is fully itself while being in lack and in need, and not once they have been eliminated. In this perspective, as far as life is concerned, lack is not the manifestation of a defect that must be fixed in order to allow life to exist in its fulfilled form; nor is lack the realization that some piece is missing thereby preventing the well-functioning of the system. As lack is constitutive of life's way of being and, therefore, is intrinsic in life, the fact that there is lack is integral to life's fulfilled or complete form.

If, following Aristotle, we consider *complete* that being that lacks nothing of what is required by its ownmost constitution, and if we accept that life is *constitutively* the activity of lack, then what life cannot lack in order to be life is, precisely, lack. Without the activity of lacking, life itself would not be.[20] The need and lack that belong to life cannot be understood, therefore, as defective moments or breaks whose overcoming would restore life to some prior positivity or future fulfillment. What life is, its abilities, its peculiarities, and, therefore, its *perfection*, is not something other from the negativity that manifests itself in the need and lack interwoven with life's way of being; on the contrary, such negativity is one and the same as life.

Supporting Contradiction

This is, according to Hegel, what renders the living being a *subject*. That is, the fact that the living is not simply a lacking being as much as it is the ability of *sensing* and *living* lack within itself. The living is a subject insofar as it is the ability to perceive and live its own state of indigence and, hence, its own contradiction and painful laceration as decisive moments of its ontological constitution. Hegel writes, "The *subject* is a term such as this, which is able to contain and *support* its own contradiction; it is this which constitutes its *infinitude*."[21]

It is evident that the infinity that is here attributed to the way of being of the subject is not to be understood as the possibility, on the side of the subject, to overcome the concrete forms of lack and need that constitute it or, said otherwise, to situate itself beyond its necessarily desiring—and as such, finite—nature. The infinity of the subject—the infinity of which the subject is an expression—discloses itself as the subject's ability to transcend itself in the very act in which, in desire, it perceives itself as finite.

Here we reach a crucial point. Desire is that which enables us to think the aporia—the truth—of the living finite. It is that which enables us to realize that the living finite is such only insofar as it experiences, within desire and lack, itself and the other from itself; or, better said, it experiences the inseparable relation between itself and the other, the tension that, from itself, pushes it toward the other. In this way, desire is, as it were, the condition of possibility of the world. This is so not because the desiring activity as such institutes or constructs the world; rather, in the sense that the world is always the relation and concatenation of a form of being that experiences and inhabits the world.

Desire is the mark that belongs and characterizes the finite that experiences itself. That is, it is the character of the finite that senses its limitation and, in sensing it, is already somehow situated beyond it. It is the mark of the finite that, in its aporetic structure, is also always infinite because, in the activity of lacking, in sensing itself through the lack of itself, and in opening up, through lack, to the other from itself, it is never simply a finite being. In this movement, the finite is always already self-activation, being outside of itself, and being what it is through attrition and resistance toward the other from itself. Desire is what renders the self-sensing finite an immanent transcendence; that is, a movement of overcoming that does not produce any beyond; a tending always and incessantly beyond itself not in the direction of an infinity in which lack is overcome or annihilated, but rather in the direction of an infinity where, precisely through lack and the need lack produces, the finite experiences its own being what it is.

The Privilege of Pain

Because it is marked by lack and need, the being of the living is the being of a body that senses. In the living, this body is always a *Leib*, a living body, and not a *Körper*. Being a sensing body means perceiving oneself as immersed and steeped in necessary pain. "To feel pain is the privilege of sentient nature," Hegel writes in *The Science of Logic*.[22]

There is something perturbing, something repelling and even repugnant in the idea that pain is a privilege. Thinking of pain as privilege seems to reveal no compassion for the agonizing scream of the slaughtered animal, for the wounded bird crying its existence, for the desperate and absolute gaze of the one who is exhausted.

In these lives and in our feeling perturbed, there is no confutation, though. There is no existing being, no atom of life, no substance that is capable of sensing without pain—unless one longs for an anesthetized and congealed life, for a life subjected to those processes of purification and sterilization that produce nothing except simulacra of existence. An example of this can be seen in the *mannequined lives* which Don DeLillo narrates in *Zero K*. These lives are certainly safe, for the most part insensitive to pain, sustained and protected by technological devices that guide their actions and prevent any possibility of slashes or contagion. Wishing to eliminate the contradiction and the negative that constitute them, these lives inevitably translate into the annihilation of life itself, into the reduction of sentient bodies to aseptic mannequins, which are perfect in their inviolability precisely because they are incapable of sensing.[23]

Something Missing

In the *Childhood of Jesus*, J. M. Coetzee describes a society in many respects immunized against pain and suffering. It is a sort of land of salvation, a perfectly organized place where all gestures seem to correspond to a logic of effectiveness and efficiency, where there seems to be no passion and enthusiasm, rage and love, pain and rebellion; where one tries to keep under control everything that might produce unforeseen instabilities, rushed reactions, improvised actions. Life is here bloodless, according to Simòn, the protagonist (together with the young David), who has arrived in this land from an unspecified elsewhere, for some unspecified necessity, and who cannot accept this way of living life. He notes: "Everyone I meet is so decent, so kindly, so well-intentioned. No one swears or gets angry. No one gets drunk. No one even raises his voice. You live on a diet of bread and water and bean paste and you claim to be filled. How can that be, humanly speaking? Are you lying, even to yourselves?"[24]

Simòn cannot take it, as revealed when he claims: "We are angry, this child and I [. . .]. We are hungry all the time. You tell me our hunger is something outlandish that we have brought with us, that it doesn't belong here, that we must starve it into submission. When we have annihilated our hunger, you say, we will have proved we can adapt, and we can then be happy forever after. But I don't want to starve the dog of hunger."[25]

The reference to the dog seems to be the reference to a dimension of animality that this new life intends to suppress. Yet to suppress such a dimension, according to Simòn, means to suppress life itself. This new world intends to suppress lack and the pain that is connected to it. In suppressing lack and pain—hunger—though, what it suppresses, according to Simòn, is life. The woman whom Simòn desires tries to make him understand why his way of being, his claim to life, is inadequate. She tells him: "To my ear that is an old way of thinking. In the old way of thinking, no matter how much you may have, there is always something missing. [. . .] This endless dissatisfaction, this yearning for the something-more that is missing, is a way of thinking we are well rid of, in my opinion. *Nothing is missing.*"[26]

A life that lacks nothing, where nothing is missing, is not life, though. Lack—and hence, need, yearning, tension, desire, pain—is not, for life, the manifestation of a defect that should be fixed so that life may exist in its fulfilled form. Life—its splendor as well as its misery; its opening to joy as well as its sliding into the black hole of nothingness—is nothing except the activity of such a lack.

Conatus in existentia perseverandi (strive to persevere in being), yearning to exist: escape from stillness, the energetic state of stationary unbalance, and therefore the dread of chemical neutrality, the ferocious fight against the laws of physics. Such is the powerful fragility of life; such is the almost impossible condition in which something like life-being exists.

Life, or at least the life we experience, is not suitable for the gods. Or, to be radical, perhaps no life suits them. The one who lacks nothing does not live. The one who does not die, who does not sense the dread of emptiness, of loss, of anxiety, does not and cannot know what life is; does not and cannot know what a smile, the pain of mourning, the joy of an encounter are.

In order to live, even a god must suffer.

Translated from Italian by Silvia Benso

Notes

1. A significant part of this chapter had initially been written as a set of remarks on the works of Arcangelo Sassolino (https://www.arcangelosassolino.it). I am convinced that, as paradoxical as this may seem because of the industrial and

machinistic dimension that his works embody, the topic of Sassolino's entire artistic production, the theme of his devices, performances, and artifacts is precisely the condition of the living.

2. The article can be accessed at https://blogs.scientificamerican.com/brainwaves/why-life-does-not-really-exist/#.

3. Henri Atlan, *Entre le cristal et la fumée: Essai sur l'organisation du vivant* (Paris: Seuil, 1979); Italian translation by R. Coltellacci and R. Corona, *Tra il cristallo e il fumo. Saggio sull'organizzazione del vivente* (Florence: Hopefulmonster, 1986), 7.

4. Xavier Bichat, *Physiological Researches on Life and Death*, trans. Gold (London: 1815), 21. The original French version was published in 1801.

5. On the relation between the notions of life and of the will, see Davide Tarizzo, *Life: A Modern Invention*, trans. Mark W. Epstein (Minneapolis: University of Minnesota Press, 2017), 129, where Tarizzo writes: "According to Kant, the will only obeys itself, this being the deepest meaning of the 'categorical imperative.' Likewise, according to Darwin, life only obeys itself, this being the deepest meaning of 'natural selection.'"

6. Aristotle, *On the Soul* 415b7–8.

7. See Ronald Polansky, *Aristotle's* De anima (New York: Cambridge University Press, 2007), 208.

8. Aristotle, *On the Soul* 415b12–14.

9. See Martin Heidegger, *The Fundamental Concepts of Metaphysics*, trans. W. McNeill and N. Walker (Bloomington: Indiana University Press, 1996), 220.

10. On the topic of alienation, see Rahel Jaeggi, *Alienation* (New York: Columbia University Press, 2014).

11. Primo Levi, *The Periodic Table*, trans. Raymond Rosenthal (New York: Schocken Books, 1984), 36–37.

12. Plato, *Symposium* 199e–200a.

13. Plato, *Symposium* 202e.

14. Plato, *Symposium* 202e.

15. Jacques Derrida, "Plato's Pharmacy," in *Dissemination*, trans. B. Johnson (London: Athlone Press, 1981), 117.

16. Plato, *Symposium* 203d. The Greek text reads *endeia synoikos*, that is, "at home with need," always in need.

17. Plato, *Symposium* 203d–e.

18. Hegel uses the expression *Tätigkeit des Mangels*, activity of lacking or lacking being, when determining the structure of the impulse, or *Trieb*, that belongs to the living being. See G. W. F. Hegel, *Zum Mechanismus, Chemismus, Organismus und Erkennen*, in *Gesammelte Werke*, Bd. 12 (Hamburg: Meiner, 1985), 259–98, and in particular 280. With respect to this text and its relevance both theoretically and in relation to the development of Hegel's thought, see my remarks to the Italian edition in G. W. F. Hegel, *Sul meccanismo, il chimismo, l'organismo e il conoscere*, ed., trans., and with an introduction by Luca Illetterati (Trent: Verifiche, 1996), 54.

19. Humberto R. Maturana and Francisco J. Varela, *Autopoiesis and Cognition: The Realization of the Living* (Dordrecht: Kluwer, 1980), 87.

20. When explaining the various meanings that "necessary" may have and in order to clarify the first of such meanings, Aristotle says that "'Necessary' means that without which, as a concomitant condition, life is impossible"; see Aristotle, *Metaphysics* 1015a20. As nourishment and breathing constitute the articulation of a lack, one could say that what is necessary is lack itself.

21. G. W. F. Hegel, *Philosophy of Nature*, trans. M. J. Petry (London: Allen, 1970), 141.

22. G. W. F. Hegel, *The Science of Logic*, trans. George Di Giovanni (Cambridge: Cambridge University Press, 2010), 106.

23. See Don DeLillo, *Zero K A Novel* (New York: Scribner, 2016), 146.

24. J. M. Coetzee, *The Childhood of Jesus* (New York: Penguin, 2013), 30.

25. Coetzee, 30.

26. Coetzee, 63.

Eight

Vulnerable Existences

Caterina Resta

Life and Death

The twentieth century, inaugurated by Friedrich Nietzsche's announcement of the death of God and the advent of the Overman, has inflicted unprecedented wounds on the dominating humanism, thereby forcing to the relinquishment of all dreams of glory, once and forever. This change took place on the battlefields of World War One and Two where human beings, reduced to "human material" similar to other war materials, became usable, replaceable, pieces among others in the huge war machine and its lethal as well as senseless mechanisms that are anonymous even in death. It is undoubtedly at Auschwitz though that humankind reaches its extreme limit: that of bare life radically exposed to annihilation up to the point of becoming ashes. The twentieth century consumed its material and symbolic massacres not without paradoxes, pursuing the utopian, ultrahumanistic dream of the "new human being" that quickly turned into the totalitarian nightmares of Nazi fascism and communism. Even though with not irrelevant ideological differences, both Nazism and communism are nourished with a similar aspiration to shape the Overman. For this reason, they both engage in a fight for life in order to assert the superiority of their own model of humanity and impose it at the global level.

What is the ground on which, in the 1900s, this strife for the creation of the new human being has played itself out—a strife with no respite, an absolute war that is, each time, final and *conclusive*? What were the stakes for such a century, as Nietzsche had already grasped with extraordinary clairvoyance? In one of his most fascinating books titled *The Century*, Alain Badiou writes: "The main ontological question that dominates the first years of the twentieth century is: What is life? [. . .] What is the true life—what is it to truly live—with a life adequate to the organic intensity of living? This question traverses the century, and it is intimately linked to the question of the new man [sic], as prefigured by Nietzsche's overman. The thinking of life interrogates the force of the will-to-live. What is it to live in accordance with a will-to-live?"[1]

When life is made to coincide with the will to power, inevitably there seems to be no escape to its reversal into the opposite, that is, death. We should not be surprised by this peculiar paradox. The century that wishes to assert life to the bitter end, that pursues the highest *intensity* of life, and that fights an endless fight for life ends up sowing death everywhere; everywhere does it offer the cruel and seductive show—as if it were a festival—of a great massacre, a slaughterhouse, death towering everywhere on the foreground of the stage of the first half of the twentieth century. This paradox is not the outcome of a perversion or heterogenesis of goals. On the contrary, it is the other, lethal side of the same coin—a form of life that, longing for the highest degree of intensity, must always go beyond itself, until the *end*, until it necessarily "fulfills" itself in its (apparent) opposite that is death. Hence, "a sort of reversal between life and death, *as if death were nothing but the instrument of life.*"[2]

The stakes of the century, those that characterize it through war, have been the assertion of a *politics of life*. They have been the attempt at answering the question that Nietzsche, more radically and before anyone else, had left unanswered at the threshold of the twentieth century. That is the question: What kind of animal is the human being? What *can* human beings become if they do not disavow life and its power? It is only by taking up the power of life as both subject and object of its own task that can politics measure up to the century.

Yet, and from an ontological standpoint, taking up the presupposition of the indefinite affirmation of an overpowering life can translate into nothing else except the *horror* and *terror* of a *politics of death*. This reveals the essential intertwining that indissolubly connect life and death; it shows how the one inevitably turns into the other, how the one carries with itself also the other. Not only is death not the simple opposite of life; it is also its vehicle. Likewise, life—the *intensive* and *absolute* assertion of life—becomes the vehicle of death, which is spread everywhere. The one always "travels" with the other. This is what, on the wave of the First World War that has just started, Sigmund Freud realizes at the conclusion of his 1915 essay *Thoughts for the Times on War and Death*: "*Si vis vitam, para mortem*. If you want to endure life, prepare yourself for death.³" We must acknowledge the *finite* character of existence; we must recognize that we are mortal, and our existences are precarious and vulnerable.

The New Plague

In some pages of *Discipline and Punish* that nowadays speak to us again in a particularly eloquent manner, Michel Foucault recalls how, when confronted with two major epidemic curses such as leprosy and plague, power adopts two different procedures of containment. Lepers are marginalized *outside* the town, and they are exiled, secluded, and enclosed in a rigorously *separate* space in order to avoid contact and contagion—thus, they constitute the paradigmatic model of *exclusion*, of a form of power that pursues absolute purity and immunity. With respect to plagues, however, power devises a different strategy, thereby displaying, perhaps for the first time in an incredibly transparent manner, its own *disciplinary* character at work—that is, the dream of a society incessantly controlled and ordered. In the case of plague, power articulates itself: it divides, distributes, and differentiates no longer along the lines of a binary opposition (outside/inside, sick/healthy, and so on) but rather along differentiations that are individualized (case by case, one by one) and spatial (house by house, neighborhood by neighborhood), thereby multiplying its sensors and its modalities of constant surveillance. Power records, becomes *analytic* and *capillary*, intensifies its abilities for control, traces divisions and areas that need to be circumscribed, produces minute regulations, issues ordinances, controls all movements, penetrates in the most intimate aspects of existence, applies to everyone's behaviors, and enters the details of everyone's forms of life, of what characterizes and qualifies such lives. Power exercises itself with no interruptions and becomes omnipresent, omnipervasive, and omniscient. It observes, transcribes, authorizes, bans, rules, and controls day and night like a humongous panopticon.

It is worth quoting at length some passages from the description Foucault offers of this complex dispositive based on an ordinance from the end of the seventeenth century. What it says sounds incredibly timely and current for us.

> First, a strict spatial partitioning: the closing of the town and its outlying districts, a prohibition to leave the town on pain of death, the killing of all stray animals; the division of the town into distinct quarters, each governed by an intendent. Each street is placed under the authority of a syndic, who keeps it under

surveillance; if he leaves the street, he will be condemned to death. On the appointed day, everyone is ordered to stay indoors: it is forbidden to leave on pain of death. The syndic himself comes to lock the door of each house from the outside; he takes the key with him and hands it over to the intendent of the quarter; the intendent keeps it until the end of the quarantine. Each family will have made its own provisions; but, for bread and wine, small wooden canals are set up between the street and the interior of the houses, thus allowing each person to receive his ration without communicating with the suppliers and other residents; meat, fish and herbs will be hoisted up into the houses with pulleys and baskets. If it is absolutely necessary to leave the house, it will be done in turn, avoiding any meeting. Only the intendants, syndics and guards will move about the streets [. . .]. It is a segmented, immobile, frozen space. Each individual is fixed in his place. And, if he moves, he does so at the risk of life, contagion, or punishment.

Inspection functions ceaselessly. The gaze is alert everywhere: [. . .] guards at the town hall and in every quarter to ensure the prompt obedience of the people and the most absolute authority of the magistrates [. . .]. At each of the town gates there will be an observation post; at the end of each street sentinels. Every day, the intendent visits the quarter in his charge, inquires whether the syndics have carried out their tasks, whether the inhabitants have anything to complain of; they "observe their actions." Every day, too, the syndic goes into the street for which he is responsible; stops before each house: gets all the inhabitants to appear at the windows [. . .]; he calls each of them by name [. . .]; if someone does not appear at the window, the syndic must ask why: "In this way he will find out easily enough whether dead or sick are being concealed." Everyone locked up in his cage, everyone at his window, answering to his name and showing himself when asked—it is the great review of the living and the dead.

This surveillance is based on a system of permanent registration [. . .]. At the beginning of the "lock up," the role of each of the inhabitants present in the town is laid down, one by one; this document bears "the name, age, sex of everyone, notwithstanding his condition": a copy is sent to the intendant of the quarter, another to the office of the town hall, another to enable the syndic to make his daily roll call. [. . .]

This enclosed, segmented space, observed at every point, in which the individuals are inserted in a fixed place, in which the slightest movements are supervised, in which all events are recorded, in which an uninterrupted work of writing links the center and periphery, in which power is exercised without division, according to a continuous hierarchical figure, in which each individual is constantly located, examined and distributed among the living beings, the sick and the dead—all this constitutes a compact model of the disciplinary mechanism.[4]

As Foucault suggests to sum it up, the plague takes up the symbolic meaning of the disorder, of a social contagion with everything that is disorderly, and as such it has to be confronted, through a political-medical power that responds to the imperative of *discipline*. For this reason, such a power adopts techniques of surveillance and control that are constant and ubiquitous. It is the general trial of those *dispositifs* of power which have been governing us for a long time and which the current coronavirus pandemic has simply made more visible and tangible.

The beginning of the twenty-first century will most likely be remembered because of a new and different pestilence—the one caused by an unknown virus, the coronavirus, which, in a very short time, has spread all over the globe, endangering the life of all peoples on the planet. This is perhaps the most accurate mirror image of globalization and its catastrophic side. It constitutes the unavoidable scenario where we situate ourselves in the effort to answer the same question, once again: What is life? Or, better: How should we rethink life in light of such an epochal event that has radically upended our existences? Beyond the daily counting of the infected and the dead, what can this invisible, insidious enemy tell us—this enemy that continues to rage subjecting us to unimaginable restrictions of our freedom, radically transforming our perception of space and time and breaking apart all forms of social relationships? What truth does it reveal with respect to ourselves? With respect to our life, which is forced to confront itself daily with death? How do we coexist with a virus that isolates us in an unbearable solitude and makes all forms of human coexistence and contact threatening? How do we respond to the challenges that this virus has launched at us except than by acknowledging that we are exposed and vulnerable bodies?

Even more meaningless than any war, the coronavirus pandemic—this *natural* calamity in front of which we have verified our complete fragility and powerlessness—has disclosed the insufficiency and limits of science and technology, has brought us back to the times of the great plagues and has forced us to resort to ancient, basic remedies such as isolation and quarantine.

Bare Life

We are vulnerable coexistences, exposed and without defenses. This is the truth of the human that the coronavirus pandemic imposes to our thinking while we shiver in the face of a contagion coming from an invisible and ungraspable alterity such as that of a virus that takes our breath away.[5] Does vulnerability then name the *essence* of the human? The answer is negative. On the contrary, vulnerability decrees the end and the impossibility of a metaphysical dream that has been cultivated for long. It exhibits the illusory and even ghostly character of an ontological arrogance that, for millennia, has claimed not only to be able to assign human beings an essence that could be *fixed* once and forever but also that such an essence could be identified exclusively with *logos*, with rationality. Thereby, this ontology removes the meaning of being a body that, in order to live, must breathe and is susceptible to suffering, to pain, and even to succumbing up to the point of death; it forgets that *being in the world* means, first and foremost, *to live*.

Being vulnerable does not define an essence but, simply, the condition of our existence, our being exposed to an outside over which we cannot have power, which we cannot possess, and which even prevents self-appropriation. Only if we think of the humanness of the human in terms of infinite vulnerability and exposure can we perhaps start thinking of what is "properly" human, namely, the radical inappropriability that constitutes us thereby deposing and disavowing the autonomous and sovereign subject entirely master of itself, the illusory mirage of forms of power and mastery that especially modernity has elevated onto a pedestal and idolized. Already at the beginning of the previous century, such a specter of omnipotence started receiving some first, inevitable blows and, on the battlefields of World War One and, even more tragically, in the death camps of the Nazi period, it revealed the defenseless powerlessness of a "passivity more passive than all passivity" (according to Levinas' expression) that is naked exposure without protections.

What is proper to human beings would therefore consist in a paradoxical property, namely, their being "improper" or "not within the proper" [*improprio*], that is, their being exposed—defenseless, without shelter or protection—with respect not to this or that danger but, rather, with respect to the loss of their own humanity. It is only with respect to humans that we can, in fact, speak of being dehumanized [*disumano*] or inhuman [*inumano*]. By these terms we mean the possibility, which is *exclusively human* and, for that reason, still entirely human, of not being able to testify for oneself. Decaying from the human or being dehumanized is not at all to be understood as loss of humanity or trespassing into sheer animality but rather as a possibility of the human—as even the most appropriate possibility, the one belonging to the human the most [*la più propria*] even though as the most disappropriating. To define the human as defenseless exposure and vulnerability means to accept the idea that not only there is no human essence or nature that are established once and for all but also that the humanity of the human must be testified, attested, defended, conquered, even invented time after time. The humanity of the human is a task, a risk, a struggle, a resistance, something that may even be lost yet never erased forever; it may be denied to us, yet it can never be entirely taken away from us. It must be acknowledged to us and we must never stop fighting for it.

This is what the epochal event of a global virus demands that, once again, we think of. Not only has the global virus subverted our lives and dictated new rules of coexistence that *de facto* impede such a coexistence; the virus also peremptorily calls us to relinquish all illusory mastery, all ghosts of powerfulness. In front of the superpower of the virus that threatens us with death, the sovereign is not the one who decrees the state of exception. It is the virus that carries the *corona*, the crown. The one who decrees the state of exception is, in turn, ruled by the virus and by those knowledge-powers—first of all, medicine—that try to challenge the virus and fight over its crown, to which politics itself has to bow.

Being vulnerable goes well beyond being exposed to the contagion and the disease; it also implies, as we have said, running the constant risk of being reduced to bare life, on the verge of slipping into the dehumanized [*dis-umano*].[6] Subjected to *political* decisions that time after time establish the boundaries of the human and its exclusion, the human being has no ontological consistency and can only avail itself of an ethical resistance—human beings exist on the edge of their abyss. They are nothing except the movement of resistance at this threshold. It happened to the Jews in the Nazi extermination camps, which were filled also with gypsies and homosexuals; it happens now to the "wasted lives" of the migrants,[7] swallowed up by the waters of the Mediterranean Sea; it may happen any day to those who do not receive adequate cures or are left to die of starvation because their life is worth less that the life of others. It happens every time that biopolitical boundaries are set in place between lives worth being protected and lives that are not worth living.

Yet, we must ask ourselves, as Judith Butler has repeatedly done in several occasions while criticizing the depoliticized use of the concept of "bare life" through which human beings would be reduced to bare zoological life:

> Are they mere life or bare life? Are we to say that those who are excluded are simply unreal, disappeared, or that they have no being at all—shall they be cast off, theoretically, as the socially dead and the merely spectral? [. . .] Do such formulations describe a state of having been made destitute by existing political arrangements, or is that destitution unwittingly ratified by a theory that adopts the perspective of those who regulate and police the sphere of appearance itself? [. . .] If we claim that the destitute are outside of the sphere of politics—reduced to depoliticized forms of being—then we implicitly accept as right the dominant ways of establishing the limits of the political.[8]

Power *naturalizes*; that is, it produces a "natural" life that has absolutely nothing natural about it insofar as, on the contrary, it is "a life steeped in power," as Butler remarks.[9] To speak of "bare life" is thus merely the outcome of a *depoliticization* and an artificial *renaturalization*. It is therefore necessary to remind ourselves that "those who find themselves in positions of radical exposure to violence, without basic political protections by forms of law, are not for that reason outside the political [. . .]. Even the life stripped of rights is still within the sphere of the political."[10] *Human* life, in its being simply human, *is never bare*; it is not bare regardless and despite all attempts at divesting it of its multiple forms, which are always also *particular* and *unique*.

In a very moving essay significantly titled "Violence, Mourning, Politics" and written the day after the Twin Towers attack on September 11, 2001, Butler identifies the recognition of shared vulnerability, interdependency, and exposure to being in contact with the other not only as the primary condition of our coexistence but also as the presupposition necessary for an alternative politics capable of wiping out, once and for all, the ghost of the autonomous and sovereign self. Such a self is at the root of the frenzy for power by singular individuals as well as nation-states. At a time when the United States celebrates a collective mourning for its dead, Butler, thinking of those who are denied such mourning in the emergence of global violence, provocatively asks: "Whose lives count as lives? [. . .] What *makes for a grievable life?*"[11] Almost as if reaffirming Antigone's vindication,[12] according to which not even the worst enemy can be denied the burial and grief that accompany any loss insofar as these activities mark one's belonging to humankind, Butler too asserts the need to recognize the shared vulnerability "that one cannot will away without ceasing to be human."[13]

Against the logics of exclusion and erasure, Butler reiterates the need to consider the fact that *all* lives are worthy of commemoration, grief, and sorrow; all lives are worthy of mourning, which is never individual or private but always also collective and public as it is mourning that strengthens, in the most extreme manner, the tie connecting us in the grief for a loss that gathers us. That *all* lives are worthy of grieving testifies that we are all exposed to violence and death. Mourning and loss name the paradox of an insuppressible relationship, which is each time unique, particular, and, at the same time, universal and which is grounded on our mortality, on our vulnerability, and on the imperative that no life ought to be lost forever. Each life has the right to survive, at least through grieving and memory.

This grief—which discloses that we depend on others, that our lives are interwoven with relationships, and that we do not exist outside of such connections that constitute us—shows that vulnerability, grieving the loss, and mourning for the other even to the point of anticipating the other's death are precisely the ultimate ground of our coexistence. As Butler writes, "many people think that grief is privatizing, that it returns us to a solitary situation and is, in that sense, depoliticizing. But I think it furnishes a sense of political community of a complex order, and it does this first of all by bringing to the fore the relational ties that have implications for theorizing fundamental dependency and ethical responsibility."[14] The grief and mourning for the loss of the other are not simply private feelings; they take up a *political* significance insofar as they attest the social bond that ties our existences and the shared vulnerability that mutually exposes the ones to the others. As Butler still writes, "mindfulness of this vulnerability can become the basis of claims for non-military political solutions, just as denial of this vulnerability through a fantasy of mastery (an institutionalized fantasy of mastery) can fuel the instruments of war. We cannot, however, will away this vulnerability. We must attend to it, even abide by it, as we begin to think about what politics might be implied by staying with the thought of corporeal vulnerability itself, a situation in which we can be vanquished or lose others."[15]

Living Well Together

In his *Politics*, Aristotle claims that the goal of the *polis*—and therefore of politics—is not simply coexisting, living together, but rather *eu suzen*, living *well* together.[16] Unlike other communities of living beings such as flocks, herds, and packs, human beings' living together does not consist in merely being the-ones-*with*-the-others. Martin Heidegger and, more recently, Jean-Luc Nancy have claimed that, at the ontological level, being-with signifies the originary character of the social bond, the fact that human existence is always *co*-existence, being-together, and coinhabiting a shared world.[17] Yet this claim is not sufficient to qualify the *political* vocation of co-existing human beings, who are not merely *coexisting* but also aspire to exist *well* together in that public space that is the town, city, or village. Human beings, in fact, always *inhabit* a world and live in a space whose boundaries ought to always be thresholds of transit and passage. Politics should have no other goal, no other finality than this, namely, to find the rules for the common good and dictate the laws of this civil coexistence. It should fulfil this need, namely, to ensure that the good of the one does not prevail on the good of all.

Yet this is the most difficult task to accomplish. The *polis* has always been torn by conflict; it has always seen, almost fatefully, the prevalence of one part or party, be it the majority, that prevaricates over another within a clash of forces. It has always been prey of tensions and conflicts of opposed forces, antagonisms, and power games. The *good*, which ought to be the good of all, ends up becoming the good of some to the detriment of others. How can we live *well* together, then? Is it possible?

What we have said so far seems to suggest that such a living together well could occur only through a reversal, only if we could find another foundation for the political, only when we are able to recognize a new ground not in the will to power and force, but in fragility and weakness and in the vulnerability that mutually exposes the ones to others. No one ought to be excluded from such a new ground, on which it would be possible to build a *polis* that is liveable for all. As long as the polis is ruled by mere power relations, as long as politics is conceived of as power arrogance, as long as even one single human being on earth is banned from the polis, living together well will also be precluded. As suggested by Butler, it is only in the vulnerability that we share, that we suffer, that exposes us to violence, loss, and even death; it is only in this unbearable fragility that makes us tremble with pain as well as with joy that we can recognize that which we have in common and can be shared. This is the only antidote against violence, which is always lying in wait wherever there are existences that are exposed. This is the only premise for and, perhaps, the only promise of a living together *well*.

Solely the defenseless nakedness of vulnerable existences can be recognized not only as the sole universal principle of *inclusion* but also as the sole presupposition enabling us to coexist in peace the ones with the others and caring the ones for the others, for some more than for others. Vulnerability, in fact, is not the same for everyone, and it is distributed differently among human beings: there are some who are on the verge of succumbing, entirely exposed to violence, and others who are, on the contrary, protected even to an excess. Preserving the life of those who are more vulnerable ought to be the premise, the first imperative of a politics of vulnerability, the only one that is capable of pursuing the goal of living *well* together. Living well together is neither utopian nor unattainable. Nor is it to be postponed to a future always beyond realization. On the contrary, it can be accomplished at every moment—albeit never in a conclusive form—every time a life is saved, a wound is healed, an injustice is mended, a forgiveness is granted, a grief is shared, a loss is mourned—even though it is the loss of an unnamed stranger.

Perhaps not all bad things come to harm us. I do not share the illusion of those who, optimistically, think that nothing will ever be the same as before once the pandemic due to this virus that takes away our breath is over. Nevertheless, I do hope that, at least to some, the thought will occur regarding how vulnerable our existences are and how this catastrophe has forced us to rethink the foundations of our lives. We should not forget this, so we can try to find and even invent, or at least start to imagine, forms of life and coexistence that are radically different.

Translated from Italian by Silvia Benso

Notes

1. Alain Badiou, *The Century*, trans. Alberto Toscano (Malden, MA: Polity Press, 2007), 13–14.
2. Badiou, *The Century*, 16. Translator's note: italicized by Resta.
3. Sigmund Freud, "Thoughts for the Times on War and Death," in *On the History of the Psycho-Analytic Movement Papers on Metapsychology and Other Works*, vol. XIV (1914–16), trans. James Strachey (London: Hogarth Press, 1957), 300. It is not a coincidence that during the war years, Freud comes to shake psychoanalytic theory radically with the introduction of the death drive. In 1920, Freud will produce his famous *Beyond the Pleasure Principle*.
4. Michel Foucault, *Discipline and Punish: The Birth of Prison*, trans. Alan Sheridan (New York: Random House, 1995), 185–97.
5. The theme of breath—the vital element par excellence—and the new threat coming from it even in terms of death by suffocation has been aptly emphasized by Donatella Di Cesare, *Immunodemocracy: Capitalist Asphyxia*, trans. David Broder (South Pasadena, CA: Semiotext(e), 2021).

6. In some pages of her 1951 work on totalitarianism that have by now become famous, Arendt spoke of "the abstract nakedness of being nothing but human"; see Hannah Arendt, "The Decline of the Nation-State and the End of the Rights of Man," in *The Origins of Totalitarianism* (New York: Harcourt, Brace & World, 1973), 297. On the concept of "bare life," see Giorgio Agamben, *Homo Sacer: Sovereign Power and Bare Life*, trans. Daniel Heller-Roazen (Stanford: Stanford University Press, 1998).

7. Zygmunt Bauman, *Wasted Lives: Modernity and Its Outcasts* (Cambridge, UK: Polity Press, 2004).

8. Judith Butler, "Bodies in Alliance and the Politics of the Street," in *Notes toward a Performative Theory of Assembly* (Cambridge, MA: Harvard University Press, 2015), 78. It is not by chance that Butler prefers to use the expression "precarious life"; see especially Judith Butler, *Precarious Life: The Powers of Mourning and Violence* (London-New York: Verso, 2004); "Introduction: Precarious Life, Grievable Life," in *Frames of War: When Is Life Grievable?* (London-New York: Verso, 2009), 1–32; and *Dispossession: The Performative in the Political: Conversations with Athena Athanasiou* (Cambridge, UK: Polity Press, 2013).

9. Judith Butler and Gayatri Chakravorty Spivak, *Who Sings the Nation-State? Language, Politics, Belonging* (London-New York: Seagull Books, 2007), 9.

10. Butler, "Bodies in Alliance," 79–80.

11. Butler, "Violence, Mourning, Politics," 20.

12. See Judith Butler, *Antigone's Claim: Kinship between Life and Death* (New York: Columbia University Press, 2000).

13. Butler, "Preface," in *Precarious Life*, xiv.

14. Butler, "Violence, Mourning, Politics," 22.

15. Butler, "Violence, Mourning, Politics," 29.

16. Aristotle, *Politics* 1280b40.

17. See Martin Heidegger, *Being and Time*, trans. Joan Stambaugh (Albany: State University of New York Press, 2010) and Jean-Luc Nancy, *The Inoperative Community*, trans. Peter Connor (Minneapolis: University of Minnesota Press, 1991).

Nine

Life and Useless Suffering

Responsibility for Others and Impossible Theodicy

Rita Fulco

Why are we significantly struck only by the suffering of those who are closest to us? What is the difference between human beings who can feel compassion and even suffer for those who are not their neighbors and whose faces are totally unknown and other human beings who are instead unmoved by the pain of strangers or who, somewhat frequently, even feel relieved in thinking that bad luck has fallen on a stranger rather themselves? The most immediate answer, of a psychological nature, is that both indifference and superficial attention to the suffering of strangers are, after all, healthy responses on the side of the self, which thereby protects its own *right to be* and defends itself from the huge burden of the overabundant presence of pain within life.

Are things really this way, though? Does removing strangers' suffering from one's attention really preserve one's right to be? Furthermore, is there really a substantial difference between neighbors and strangers? My claim is that it is not just psychological matters that are at stake in these questions; rather, they also include elements that have directly to do with ontology, both of the human being and of suffering. And, therefore, they concern the meaning of life, at both the individual and the collective levels.

This is actually the thesis that I wish to advance in this chapter: what is *at stake* in attending to suffering is the very humanity of the human.

In other words, the way in which the suffering of strangers (even more than the suffering of neighbors) is perceived, judged, and assumed reveals something essential about the being of humans and their lives in the world.

Useless Suffering and Impossible Theodicy

In its different degrees and occurrences, the mental phenomenology of pain is easily recognizable. When the suffering that one experiences exceeds a certain level, one's consciousness undergoes a radical *stiffening* of its faculties, reaching such a state of prostration that thinking becomes increasingly exhausting, if not downright impossible. In other words, past a given threshold, which varies with the individual, suffering affects consciousness in such a way as to alter deeply its ability to perceive and judge. As Levinas argues, "Suffering is, of course, a datum in consciousness, a certain 'psychological content,' similar to the lived experience of color, sound, contact, or any other sensation. But in this very 'content' it is an in-spite-of consciousness, the unassumable. The unassumable and 'unassumability.' "[1] The harshness of pain is refractory; it somewhat impedes the reception of stimuli that come from the external world.

Actually, suffering changes the modes of perception of the world. It changes the way we relate to others and disrupts the way we relate to ourselves, making us not infrequently unable to gather external stimuli into a meaningful whole. As Levinas writes, "It is as if suffering were not just a datum, refractory to the synthesis of the Kantian 'I think'—which is capable of reuniting and embracing the most heterogeneous and disparate data into order and meaning in its a priori forms—but the way in which the refusal, opposing the assemblage of data into a meaningful whole, rejects it; [it is] at once what disturbs order and this disturbance itself."[2] Whether physical or mental, the experience of suffering makes one lose one's grasp on the world and makes the world lose its grasp on the self. An inaccessible monad, exhausted by coping with pain and by carrying it while enduring it, the self is stiffened in an effort that is intolerable because it has no end except the end of the very effort to endure. Being released from the grip of pain may take up the comforting appearance of healing, of the disappearance of anguish, as well as the petrifying face of death. Both the remainder and the end of time are presaged in the end of suffering.

As long as suffering is there though, the self is *riveted* to its own stifling present. "The humanity of those who suffer is overwhelmed by the evil that rends it, otherwise than by non-freedom: violently and cruelly, more irremissibly than the negation that dominates or paralyzes the act in non-freedom."³ Suffering rivets the individual to a *not*, to a *negative*, whose power is manifested by the production of more negativity. All that is perceived is perceived as part of suffering, up to the point where it can no longer be even distinguished from it. It is a self-irradiating of the negative, which, like a black hole, swallows everything up into pure negation, into pure suffering: "What counts in the non-freedom or the submission of suffering is the concreteness of the *not*, looming as an evil more negative than any apophantic not. This negativity of evil is probably the source or kernel of all apophantic negation. The *not* of evil, a negativity extending as far as to the realm of un-meaning."⁴

Suffering is thus the revelation of an absolute evil, of a negative that cannot be considered, especially by those who are immersed in pain, as the opposite of a positive. Those who are immersed in such suffering can only feel its absurdity, as they only perceive their being riveted to it. It is no coincidence that, because of the *material* riveting it involves as it affects body and mind down to their deepest recesses, physical suffering is considered the paradigm of evil. "While in moral pain one can preserve an attitude of dignity and compunction [. . .], physical suffering in all its degrees entails the impossibility of detaching oneself from the instant of existence. It is the very irremissibility of being. The content of suffering merges with the impossibility of detaching oneself from suffering [. . .]. In suffering there is an absence of all refuge."⁵ Such a mode of pain manifestation can in fact be referred not only to physical suffering but also to any suffering that exceeds the threshold leading from mere *malaise* (*malessere*) to *pain of being* (*male di essere*), that is, to one's being riveted to one's own life as evil and suffering. The intensity of spiritual, emotional, or moral suffering can in fact lead to despair in the same violent and radical way as physical suffering does. In Levinas' words, "All evil relates back to suffering. It is the impasse of life and of being—their absurdity—in which pain does not just somehow innocently happen to 'color' consciousness with affectivity. The evil of pain, the deleterious per se, is the outburst and deepest expression, so to speak, of absurdity."⁶

It is time itself that then becomes pure absence of a refuge. The mental absence of time, which is reduced to stifling present, condemns those who are in the grips of suffering to an intolerable torment to which they cannot put an end. This suffering, whether it is the pain of being riveted to a psychic condition or to an intolerable physical suffering, can only be tragically useless, vain, and absurd. As Levinas puts it, "Thus the least one can say about suffering is that, in its own phenomenality, intrinsically, it is useless: 'for nothing.' Doubtless this depth of meaninglessness that the analysis seems to suggest is confirmed by empirical situations of pain, in which pain remains undiluted, so to speak, and isolates itself in consciousness, or absorbs the rest of consciousness."[7]

Pain is inescapable, and no theodicy, no comforting or compensatory "redemptive" conception can vindicate or give meaning to the uselessness of suffering. When confronted with pain, the subject—supremely active—finds itself marked by an irremediable powerlessness, which prevents it from opposing—even just on a theoretical level—such uselessness. Such powerlessness heralds the potential occurrence of irremediable suffering, of the total darkness of the mind or of death and thereby opens up a horizon of *passivity* for the subject who is prevented from planning a future. Once again, in Levinas' words, "There is in the suffering [. . .] this reversal of the subject's activity into passivity. This is not just in the instant of suffering where, backed against being, I still grasp it and am still the subject of suffering, but in the crying and sobbing toward which suffering is inverted."[8]

It is then in suffering itself, even earlier than in the presence of death, that the reversal of activity into irremediable passivity occurs. It happens as soon as one is seized by the nightmare of the ineluctable, by the announcement of the irremediable and of the final, and one feels riveted to the inescapable. In suffering, in pain, the sovereign subject finds itself in the grips of ultimate ineluctability, whose tragic imminence on humans is shown by suffering and pain: "Suffering, in its woe, in its in-spite-of-consciousness, is passivity. In this case apprehension, a taking into the consciousness, is no longer, strictly speaking, a 'taking,' no longer the performance of an act of consciousness, but, in adversity, a submission—and even a submission to submission, since the 'content' that suffering consciousness is conscious of is precisely this same adversity of suffering—its woe."[9] Suffering is, therefore, the harbinger of an even more radical suffering, an *ontological* suffering, and the suffering of *unassumable passivity*. "Subjecting oneself to subjection" means a double surrender: consciousness surrenders to its content of suffering, and the body surrenders to the grip that clenches it.

Against any potential assumption of suffering within a context of meaning, Levinas therefore emphasizes the uselessness of suffering. Only through such a statement of uselessness can the horror of suffering be possibly retained, especially in relation to those who are pained, reduced to dumbness, to drowning, and to withdrawing from the world. Nothing can justify suffering as suffering.

On the contrary, Western culture has tried instead the way of justification—even with respect to the most intolerable suffering—through a form of theodicy that aims at *thwarting* the senselessness and outrage that accompany any natural disaster, incurable diseases, mental pain, or the massacres of innocents. Levinas writes, "Western humanity has nonetheless sought the meaning of this outrage by appealing to a meaning that would be peculiar to a metaphysical order and an ethics that are not visible in the immediate lessons of moral consciousness. [. . .] This is pain henceforth meaningful, subordinated in one way or another to the metaphysical finality glimpsed by faith or belief in progress. Beliefs presupposed by theodicy!"[10] In this way, suffering would retrieve some meaning, at least within a superior order or within the larger picture. A reward at the end of times or a slow progression of the human mind would decree the usefulness of suffering within the economy of goodness, even if it is in the long run.

Yet theodicy meets its conclusive defeat with the Shoah, according to Levinas. The *disproportion* of such suffering could only ratify the end of *any* theodicy and proclaim, once and for all, the uselessness of suffering, in all its forms. In the face of the Shoah, any attempt at justifying suffering, at making it *useful*, is immoral, in Levinas' opinion: "For an ethical sensibility [. . .] the justification of the neighbor's pain is certainly the source of all immorality. [. . .] The philosophical problem, then, that is posed by the useless pain that appears in its fundamental malignancy through the events of the twentieth century, concerns the meaning that religiosity, but also the human morality of goodness, can continue to have after the end of theodicy."[11]

Ultimately, then, a sort of reversal occurs. Rather than receiving its meaning from religion or morality, suffering invalidates forever their ability, in the face of suffering, to give meaning to the world and events, especially to the event of suffering itself. Far from providing answers, religiosity and morality are questioned by the uselessness of suffering, by its excess, which may go so far as to turn into the meaninglessness of an unexpected end or of death—being this the last and conclusive riveting, the always possible end of suffering, which is bound to ratify its uselessness in the never-again that seals off the relationship with the dead.

"A Heart That Could Beat Right across the World": Responsibility for Others

Exemplary with respect to the questions I raised at the beginning of this chapter is, to my mind, the meeting between Simone De Beauvoir and Simone Weil, which De Beauvoir herself narrates in her *Memoires d'une jeune fille rangée*. De Beauvoir writes,

> A great famine had broken out in China, and I was told that when she [Simone Weil] heard the news she wept: these tears

compelled my respect much more than her gifts as a philosopher. I envied her for having a heart that could beat right across the world. I managed to get near her one day. I don't know how the conversation got started; she declared in no uncertain tones that only one thing mattered in the world today: the Revolution which would feed all the starving people of the earth. I retorted, no less peremptorily, that the problem was not to make men happy, but to find the reason for their existence. She looked me up and down: "It's easy to see you've never gone hungry," she snapped. Our relationship did not go any further. I realized that she had classified me as "a high-minded little bourgeois."[12]

Probably, De Beauvoir is not wrong regarding the judgment that Weil passes on her: "a high-minded little bourgeois." Yet Weil's answer, as a matter of fact, brings the attention back not so much to De Beauvoir as a person as to the questions I raised at the beginning.

What does "It's easy to see you've never gone hungry" actually mean? Does it mean, perhaps, that unless one has already personally experienced firsthand a given type of suffering, one cannot understand it when it affects others? Is this, then, the reason why indifference to other people's suffering is so widespread within human relationships?

Speaking of *transference*, Levinas seems at first to endorse such an assumption as he too, not by coincidence, refers to suffering caused by *hunger*. It is precisely the other person's hunger that, in his opinion, prevents one from feeling content with one's own satisfied hunger. The hunger of others, whether neighbors or strangers, reminds those who are well fed that the hungry cannot feed themselves on the smell of roasting meat or on their trust in providence. As Levinas writes, "The hunger of another awakens men from their well-fed slumber and their self-sufficiency. We cannot wonder enough over the transference, which goes from the memory of my own hunger to suffering and compassion for the hunger of the other man. This is a transference in which an untransferable responsibility is expressed."[13] So it would seem that, according to Levinas, some memory of one's experience of suffering is required in order to understand other people's suffering and take it over. This is an unexpected statement by the thinker of *pre-original* responsibility, which would exist "despite myself," as he states on several occasions.[14]

Elsewhere, Levinas actually goes far beyond the concept of *transference*, for instance when he speaks of the great religious traditions that, apart from any potential transference, regard *feeding* neighbors and strangers as a divine commandment. As he notes, "Monotheism; feeding the men—here is the sacred task embraced by Messer Gaster, the first master of arts in the world, despite the humbleness of the place that Rabelais gives him, after all."[15] Far from being entirely focused on faith or the worship of God, commandments also deal with human basic needs, the fulfillment of which is raised to the rank of a divine law.[16] Since its beginning, Hebrew law has been intended to create a hiatus between *one's own* biological needs, *one's own* right to be, and *responsibility* for others. The time it takes for a *mitzvah* to be performed should provide a *hiatus* in the spontaneity of action, which, in the case of hunger, would lead one to grab food without any care for the needs of others, especially if those others are strangers. In those who accept such practice, the pause that such a rite establishes creates a movement "against nature," that is, a progressive release from that natural condition that makes humans wolves to other humans, ready to tear one another to pieces.

Though Weil herself seems to point to transference as a way to understand and take care of the suffering of others, she actually emphasizes, in more than one place, that the commandment to take care of other people's hunger is shared not only by the three major monotheistic religions, but indeed by all religious traditions. In *The Need for Roots*,[17] human hunger is actually taken as the paradigm for all other human needs, to which one is obligated to respond. She writes,

> On this point, the human conscience has never varied. Thousands of years ago, the Egyptians believed that no soul could justify itself after death unless it could say: "I have never let any one suffer from hunger." All Christians know they are liable to hear Christ himself say to them one day: "I was an hungered, and ye gave me meat." Every one looks on progress as being, in the first place, a transition to a state of human society in which people will not suffer from hunger.[18]

Simone Weil actually believes that no individual can be considered innocent if, having enough food and finding oneself confronted with a hungry human, such a person does not share it. As she writes, "So it is an eternal obligation towards the human being not to let him suffer from hunger when one has the chance of coming to his assistance. This obligation being the most obvious of all, it can serve as a model on which to draw up the list of eternal duties towards each human being."[19]

By analogy, we could therefore state that both Levinas and Weil claim that, in fact, human beings' being-in-the-world has always already been a form of suffering for some unsated hunger, whether biological, emotional, or spiritual. Being subject to needs, therefore, makes human beings inherently *vulnerable* beings, and such vulnerability, which is imparted by need, reminds those who pay enough attention to this of the constitutive interdependence that is one of the distinctive traits of life.

As explained by Levinas, such interdependence should turn into inalienable responsibility for neighbors and strangers alike. In other words, the suffering of others would reveal a *pre-original* responsibility, one that is taken on even before other people express their suffering and despite any resistance of the ego, which would like to keep the boundaries of the *proprium* closed and protected. Levinas writes, "This gaze that supplicates and demands, that can supplicate only because it demands, deprived of everything because entitled to everything, and which one recognizes in giving [. . .]—this gaze is precisely the epiphany of the face as a face. The nakedness of the face is destituteness. To recognize the Other is to recognize a hunger. To recognize the Other is to give. But it is to give to the master, to the lord, to him whom one approaches as 'You' in a dimension of height."[20]

It is the lack of awareness of this dimension of universal responsibility that Weil blames on De Beauvoir. Weil blames De Beauvoir for what De Beauvoir gives Weil credit for, that is, not having "a heart that could beat right across the world." Yet such a judgment does not belong to the order of morality. Being unable to care for the suffering of strangers is the indication of one's forgetfulness of that pre-original responsibility that suffering demands in order not to turn into totally useless suffering—an illegible symbol, an undecipherable alphabet, which can no longer truthfully speak of life in the world and of the humanity of the human. This does not mean that caring for suffering would lessen its relevance. Woe on those who give any redeeming meaning to the suffering of neighbors and strangers! Such a redemptive operation can be accomplished—and only with great caution—when one has to do with *one's own* suffering and, even then, perhaps only *a posteriori*, once the suffering has lessened. If this were not the case, one would slip into sterile dolorism or, as already mentioned, into an intolerable theodicy.

It is actually one's caring for suffering, however, especially for the suffering of strangers, that can help in understanding its deep connection with the humanity of humankind. Being vulnerable, being exposed to wounds is actually the original mark of being in the world. Confronted with such a revelation, as Weil clearly explains, the first response is to flee, to recoil. She writes, "Thought revolts from contemplating affliction, to the same degree that living flesh recoils from death. A stag advancing voluntarily step by step to offer itself to the teeth of a pack of hounds is about as probable as an act of attention directed towards a real affliction, which is close at hand, on the part of a mind which is free to avoid it."[21]

The deepest reason for such a flight response has therefore to do with the revelation of *vulnerability* as the most typical feature of the human.[22] One flees such revelation as long as one can until, for instance, a pandemic—that is, an event that, at least in principle, sweeps away differences between neighbors and strangers since all human beings, no one excepted, are exposed to the infection—confronts us with such vulnerability: with *our own* vulnerability as well as with the vulnerability of neighbors and strangers. The result is—as has happened with Sars-CoV-2—a deep questioning of those categories that used to work as sound mechanisms of self-protection and removal in the occasion of other situations of suffering and death that, since time immemorial, have presented themselves as ghosts. The West has always been living with such ghosts while trying to protect itself from them through *immunitary* politics focused on the all-out protection of some lives to the detriment of others. This protection has been sought through biopolitical measures that, more often than not, as has already happened in the past, turn into thanatopolitical practices, at least for some of the human beings who are subjected to them. Such has been the case for the migrants, left to die in the Mediterranean Sea or at the threshold of walled borders that spring up everywhere around the world—the result of a wicked mixture of sovereign power and governmental practices, between affirmative biopolitics and thanatopolitics.[23]

Confronted with the global outbreak of the Covid-19 infection, it is quite disturbing to think of the walls of separation that have been built exactly in order to establish with certainty the difference between neighbors and strangers.

> Firstly, the Israeli "wall of separation," which is also called the "Security Fence," but which Palestinians have dubbed the "wall of shame" or "apartheid" [. . .]. This fence serves to "shut out" (*ex-claudere*) Palestinians, but it also has the function of locking them up inside their territory, transforming the Gaza Strip into an open-air prison. [. . .] But the whole European continent, which abolished the frontiers between different States of the European Union, is now surrounded by new walls, which are strategically placed on the borders in defense of migration flows, which are perceived as an "invasion." Europe is turning into a besieged fortress, which multiplies its levees and its defensive barriers.[24]

Of course, one should think of other walls too, which are geared, legally and physically, toward establishing legal forms of exclusion and defense from quite a different sort of infections: "The American 'Great Wall' or, better, 'Border Fence,' as the US administration prefers to call it, is a sort of *cordon sanitaire*, which protects the healthy body of wealthy North America from the dangerous contagion of Latin America's miseries."[25]

None of such walls has managed to protect anyone from Covid-19 though, which has uphinged the immunitary defenses of the whole humankind and, with it, the deeply immunitary-based politics that inspires many states around the world.[26] On the one hand, Covid-19 has exasperated such immunitary politics while, on the other hand, it has showed its at times preposterous side due to the paradox of those massive yet useless walls, thwarted by the invisible virus's ability to penetrate.

Despite all the individual and collective attempts at diverting the attention from the misfortune, the pandemic has made it clear, apparent, and explicit that human life is *ontologically* exposed to *vulnus*, to being wounded, and such "susceptibility" makes everyone constitutively vulnerable. When faced with such vulnerability, the difference between neighbors and strangers disappears. The political world should let itself be deeply and seriously questioned by such vulnerability. Actually, vulnerability might become the point of contact between *life* and *institutions*, a matter that Italian philosophers have tried to rethink in new ways during the last few years.[27] As a matter of fact, *vulnerability* relates to a *life* that is never *purely* biological but is always a "form of life," and it cannot be taken over without rethinking the connection between biopolitics and institutions.

Institutions that will be capable of coping with human vulnerability will be those that will be able to respond to differences, including economic and social differences, neither by building more walls of separation nor by "marketing" communism, which appears as the last utopia advanced by the global network (in the form of the mechanical and, not infrequently, anonymous sharing of all kinds of information and dematerialized objects).[28] The task will be, instead, that of hearing, in vulnerability, the appeal to a form of—individual and collective—responsibility capable of reuniting life and institutions in an unprecedented relationship, while fighting any institutional obstinacy, behind which bureaucratic tyranny invariably lurks.

Considering vulnerability as ontologically inherent in the human, as suggested by Judith Butler, does not rule out its political potential especially, may I add, in connection with the relation between life and institutions. In fact, vulnerability ultimately highlights the primeval, inescapable *interdependence* of human beings. As Butler puts it, "To say that any of us are vulnerable beings is to mark our radical dependency not only on others, but on a sustaining and sustainable world. This has implications for understanding who we are as emotionally and sexually passionate beings, as bound up with others from the start, but also as beings who seek to persist, and whose persistence can be imperiled or sustained depending on whether social, economic, and political structures offer sufficient support for a livable life."[29]

In the end, no matter how obsolete or trite this may seem, I argue that the suffering of neighbors and strangers can find no other response—that is, no response that is serious, sensible, and never flaunted—except responsibility, both at the individual and institutional levels. Answering *to* and *for* the others' suffering—a suffering that remains "useless" anyway—is the ethical and political task that, now as ever, needs to be pursued.

Notes

1. Emmanuel Levinas, "Useless Suffering," in *Entre Nous: On Thinking-of-the-Other*, trans. Michael B. Smith and Barbara Harshav (New York: Columbia University Press, 1998), 91. Levinas' philosophy is the subject I explored in my book, *Essere insieme in un luogo. Etica, politica e diritto nel pensiero di Emmanuel Levinas* (Milan-Udine: Mimesis, 2013), to which I refer for insights into some of the themes (subjectivity, passivity, responsibility) addressed in this chapter.

2. Levinas, "Useless Suffering," 91.

3. Levinas, "Useless Suffering," 92.

4. Levinas, "Useless Suffering," 92. About the centrality of the *not* and the *negative* as elements that can give an essential *Stimmung* to relationships, especially in the political sphere, see the fundamental reflections by Roberto Esposito, *Politics and Negation: For an Affirmative Philosophy*, trans. Zakiya Hanafi (Cambridge: Polity Press, 2019). I analyzed the question of the negative in connection with pain and violence in "La irreductibilidad de lo negativo. Notas sobre la violencia a partir de Simone Weil," in *La mágica fuerza de lo negativo. Diótima* (Madrid: Horas y Horas, 2009), 189–223.

5. Emmanuel Levinas, *Time and the Other*, trans. Richard A. Cohen (Pittsburgh: Duquesne University Press, 1987), 69.

6. Levinas, "Useless Suffering," 92.

7. Levinas, "Useless Suffering," 93.

8. Levinas, *Time and the Other*, 72.

9. Levinas, "Useless Suffering," 92. As to the subject's passivity when confronted with pain and especially death with respect to Levinas and Heidegger, see the important reflections by Caterina Resta, "L'impossibile. Il potere e la morte tra Heidegger e Levinas," *Giornale di Metafisica* 2 (2017): 623–37.

10. Levinas, "Useless Suffering," 95–96. The mystery of suffering and evil is at the core of the Jewish-Christian tradition, previously disputed by Job's questions.

However, in Christianity, through the Passion of Christ, suffering, even in its most extreme forms, takes on a *redeeming* connotation that finds no matches in the Hebrew tradition. That is precisely what theodicy has been feeding on for centuries.

11. Levinas, "Useless Suffering," 98–99.

12. Simone De Beauvoir, *Memoirs of a Dutiful Daughter*, trans. James Kirkup (New York: Harper & Row, 1974), 236.

13. Emmanuel Levinas, *God, Death and Time*, trans. Bettina Bergo (Stanford, CA: Stanford University Press, 2000), 171. I have reflected on the importance of hunger within Levinas' philosophical journey in "Un altro inizio per la filosofia. Levinas e la fame dell'altro," *Giornale di Metafisica* 2 (2018): 598–607.

14. Fine-tuning Levinas' thought, Gérard Bensussan believes that "the immanent or 'materialistic' response to other people's hunger is not induced by transference [. . .] but by the fact that fundamental unfamiliarity turns into responsibility through an a-symmetrisation that disrupts any internalised or lived experience"; see Gérard Bensussan, "'Les hommes se cherchent . . .'. Politique de l'identité et politique de l'etrangèr," in *Éthique et expérience. Levinas politique* (Strasbourg: La Phocide, 2008), 83.

15. Emmanuel Levinas, *Carnets de captivité et autres inédits Œuvres 1* (1940–1945), ed. Robert Calin and Catherine Chalier (Paris: Grasset & Fasquelle/IMEC, 2009), 339.

16. This entwining between the human and the divine makes the association between monotheism and the character of Messer Gaster less paradoxical. Even while in captivity, Levinas had already focused his attention on Rabelais' *Gargantua and Pantagruel*, often quoted in *Carnets de captivité*. See François Rabelais, *Gargantua and Pantagruel*, trans. and edited with an introduction and notes by M. A. Screech (London: Penguin, 2006).

17. Simone Weil, *The Need for Roots: Prelude to a Declaration of Duties towards Mankind*, trans. Arthur Wills, with a preface by T. S. Eliot (London-New York: Routledge, 2002).

18. Weil, *The Need for Roots*, 5.

19. Weil, *The Need for Roots*.

20. Emmanuel Levinas, *Totality and Infinity: An Essay on Exteriority*, trans. Alphonso Lingis (The Hague: Nijhoff, 1979), 75.

21. Simone Weil, "Human Personality," in *An Anthology*, ed. Siân Miles (London: Penguin, 2005), 85.

22. I delve on this matter in Rita Fulco, *Soggettività e potere. Ontologia della vulnerabilità in Simone Weil* (Macerata: Quodlibet, 2020). Quite interesting are the reflections by Arthur Bradley, who, with a historical-philosophical as well as a theoretical approach, chronicles the concept of "unbearable life" in Arthur Bradley, *Unbearable Life: A Genealogy of Political Erasure* (New York: Columbia University Press, 2019).

23. As to the always possible wicked drifting of biopolitics into thanatopolitics, see the enlightening reflections in Roberto Esposito, *Bios: Biopolitics and Philosophy* (Minneapolis: Minnesota University Press, 2008). As to the issue of migrants, see

the important, far-ranging book by Donatella Di Cesare, *Resident Foreigners: A Philosophy of Migration* (Cambridge: Polity Press, 2020).

24. Caterina Resta, "Walled Borders: Beyond the Barriers of Immunity of the Nation-States," in *Debating and Defining Borders: Philosophical and Theoretical Perspectives*, ed. Anthony Cooper and Søren Tinning (New York: Routledge, 2020), 208. Since the 1990s, the topics of *hospitality* and *strangers* have been the focus of Caterina Resta's reflections; in particular, see Caterina Resta, *L'evento dell'altro. Etica e politica in Jacques Derrida* (Turin: Bollati Boringhieri, 2003) and *L'estraneo. Ostilità e ospitalità nel pensiero del Novecento* (Genoa: il melangolo, 2008).

25. Resta, "Walled Borders: Beyond the Barriers of Immunity of the Nation-States," 207. As to the philosophical and political issues raised by the "politics of walls," see Wendy Brown, *Walled States, Waning Sovereignty* (New York: Zone Books, 2010).

26. On this issue, see the decisive volume by Roberto Esposito, *Immunitas: The Protection and Negation of Life*, trans. Zakiya Hanafi (Cambridge: Polity Press, 2011). An important use of the concept of *immunitas* is the one brought about by the exceptional situation caused by the Covid-19 pandemics; see Tim Christiaens and Stijn De Cauwer, "The Biopolitics of Immunity in Times of COVID-19: An Interview with Roberto Esposito" (2020). https://antipodeonline.org/2020/06/16/interview-with-roberto-esposito/?fbclid=IwAR16BcM07RjGaOOpmJkL3qn8JSBn2UsqXx8FB7dVhBK9WL-lP8FSUyuuzz8. This renewed interest is to be contrasted with Han's critical appraisal of the immunitary paradigm; see Byung-Chul Han, *The Burnout Society* (Stanford, CA: Stanford University Press, 2015). On this issue, see also Robert Wyllie, "Roberto Esposito: Philosopher of Community and Immunity?" (2020). https://churchlifejournal.nd.edu/articles/roberto-esposito-philosopher-of-community-and-immunity/.

27. I am referring to Roberto Esposito, *Instituting Thought: Three Paradigms of Political Ontology*, trans. Mark Epstein (Cambridge, UK: Polity Press, 2021) as well as to the further developments of such topics Esposito addresses in another of his books, which I believe to be decisive for its clear-cut stance on life, namely, *Istituzioni* (Bologna: il Mulino, 2021). Important views on the matter of institutions can be found in *Almanacco di Filosofia e Politica 2. Istituzione. Filosofia, politica, storia*, ed. Mattia Di Pierro, Francesco Marchesi, and Elia Zaru (Macerata: Quodlibet, 2020), and in the monographic issue *Il problema dell'istituzione. Prospettive ontologiche, antropologiche e giuridico-politiche*, ed. Enrica Lisciani Petrini and Massimo Adinolfi, *Discipline Filosofiche* 2 (2019). For an overview of some of the key issues deployed by Italian philosophers, see *Contemporary Italian Philosophy: Crossing the Borders of Ethics, Politics, and Religion*, ed. Silvia Benso and Brian Schroeder (Albany: SUNY Press, 2007); the monographic issue *Italian Philosophy from Abroad*, ed. Silvia Benso and Antonio Calcagno, *Trópos: Rivista di Ermeneutica e Critica Filosofica* 22 (2019); *Differenze italiane. Politica e filosofia: mappe e sconfinamenti*, ed. Dario Gentili and Elettra Stimilli (Rome: DeriveApprodi, 2015); *Effetto Italian Thought*, ed. Enrica Lisciani Petrini and Giusi Strummiello (Macerata: Quodlibet, 2017).

28. See Byung-Chul Han, *Psychopolitics: Neoliberalism and New Technologies of Power*, trans. Erik Butler (London: Verso, 2017).

29. Judith Butler, "Bodily Vulnerability: Coalitional Politics," in Judith Butler, *Notes toward a Performative Theory of Assembly* (Cambridge: Harvard University Press, 2015), 150. An interesting development of such reflections can also be found in Judith Butler, *The Force of Non-violence: An Ethico-Political Bind* (London: Verso, 2020).

Part Three

Rethinking Life

Ten

Greek Zèn

Living Starting from the Origin

Alessandra Cislaghi

> Life is the mystery of every being,
> it is so admirable that we can always love it.
> —Marguerite Yourcenar, *Alexis*

Primum Vivere

Primum vivere, deinde philosophari: first, to live, and then, to philosophize. This old adage has entered common usage with an oppositional value, as if it placed the urgency of vital needs (*vivere*) prior to the pleasures of thinking (*philosophari*), which are deemed perhaps even useless. Yet there is no apparent opposition in this expression (if there were, philosophy would appear as an added and inessential ornament, which means nonvital). There is, instead, the realization of a given succession: one is born, one enters life, and then, as a living human being, one becomes capable of thinking, of developing a passion for wisdom. The cogency of life does not postpone, does not subordinate the desire for the love of knowing. On the contrary, it seems that once one starts to live, one philosophizes. This succession indicates an unfolding and an explication. The adverb *deinde* (then) has a demonstrative, descriptive, and concluding value.

The Latin verb *philosophari*, to philosophize, strikes one's attention because of its deponent, middle form. It is a verb that has deposed, has put down the active form and presents itself as passive while nevertheless expressing an active meaning. Thus, the Latin grammar confronts us with an action that belongs to the subject while traversing and expressing such a subject. I am a philosopher insofar as I am traversed by the love of wisdom, which places me in front of myself as one who is capable of thinking because I am a living human being, a being who has been born to life. The verb *nascor*, to be born, also has a deponent form. The subject is in fact a living being not as self-produced but rather as brought into life, as woven with life. The two Latin verbal forms—*philosophari* and *nascor*—express the condition of the one who is present to the world by having found oneself placed in it. No one is issued a request to consent to one's being brought to life. Analogously, no one certifies us for the exercise of philosophizing. Life and our passion for life traverse and constitute us. Through the middle form of the deponent verb, this starting point indicates the form of the living human being. From this perspective, living subjects begin from a passivity that antecedes them absolutely.

The verb *vivere*, to live, on the contrary, in Latin maintains the definiteness of the regular active form, as is also the case for the verb to begin, *incipere*: I begin (*incipio*) to live to the extent that I take up passivity and turn what is given into a creation. The Greek model, in turn, asserts the ability to philosophize as an active gesture, thereby expressing its status and transitiveness: *philosopheo*, literally, I love to know. It is thus the Latin language that introduces an interpretation of the meaning of philosophizing as a secondary moment. Yet the famous Cartesian deduction—*cogito, ergo sum*, I think, therefore I am—which is formulated in Latin during the modern times, reverses the ancient saying for which life precedes thinking. It may be that the break revealed by modernity manifests itself perhaps already in this expression, which inverts the old precedence of life to philosophy and discloses an activity prior to passion and its assumption. If I think ahead of recognizing myself as a living being, it could also be that I can exist without life. In its own way, feeble postmodernity attests to such a consumption of the vital energy of the subject, which, as sheer data, has become so pixelated and computable that it can now do without its biological dimension.

Descartes has also produced, however, a more extended version of his lapidary deduction, which has then been handed down to the history of ideas in its epistemological (*cogito*) and, subsequently, ontological (*sum*) reductions. Descartes, in fact, writes, "[I am] a thing that thinks; that is, a thing that doubts, affirms, denies, understands a few things, ignores many others, loves, hates, wills, refuses, and that also imagines and senses."[1] I am one who thinks, that is, one who lives as a human being. The extended formulation supports the deponent interpretation we have seen at work in the Latin *nascor* and *philosophari*: I am a desiring being, a lover (*philosopher*) insofar as I am living (*vivo*). I live; therefore, I philosophize. Since I partake in living, I love to know what living is.

The Names of Life

In Plato's dialogue *Phaedo*, Socrates too raises the question of what life is—life that cannot be logically contradicted by its alleged opposite, namely, death. The dialectics of contraries or oppositions does not affect the power of life, which dominates as an absolute term. The body perishes, whereas personal life—*psyche*—remains immune from death because "whatever the soul (*psyche*) occupies, it brings life to it."[2] Everyone's vitality is intrinsic in life, which, in its self-affirmation, does not tolerate anything that negates it. When *psyche* is present in the body, it refreshes such a body, animates it, infuses life through it, and supports its nature. The body that breathes is alive.

Psyche is the living principle and origin (*principio*) of the body, that which makes the body alive. Life that makes *psyche* immune to death, that is, extraneous to the concept of annihilation, is surging, springing life (*zoe*). Surging life is within the first principle and, for that very reason, it is diametrically opposite to absolute nothingness. This denomination of the notion of life—a denomination that is the most fecund and highest—appears repeatedly in the texts of the main ancient authors (such as Plato, Aristotle, and Plotinus) and is attested in the Gospels as a way to signify the life of the origin and first principle. Likewise, Neo-Testament Greek continues to use *psyche* when it names personal life.

The Gospels present a paradox, namely, that the one who wants to save his or her *psyche* will lose it, whereas the one who loses it will find it and will keep it alive.[3] The will to indefinite self-preservation achieves the opposite result. At first, this situation may appear hopeless, similar to the tragic predestination that has always tormented Greek reflection. For the Greek tradition, Sophocles' Oedipus actualizes the destiny he is intent on escaping, as if his quest entailed a death sentence. Narcissus too is subjected to the same prophecy as he would live were he not to know himself.[4] The condemnation to death on the ground of one's quest for life seems to hold true also by way of a proxy. For example, Eurydice is lost because of the gaze of Orpheus, who wants to save her. Ancient myths preserve within themselves this fear of the cognitive gaze, which, once it fixes itself on something, decrees death, final eclipse, and loss without return. The positive news, the glad tidings—the *evangelium*—announced with the advent of Christianity introduces the negation of such destinal consequentiality. That is, Christianity introduces the idea that the loss of oneself amounts not to death, but rather to the affirmation of life. The Greek fear of a discovery that brings death is substituted with the paradox of a loss that vivifies, that brings life. What manifests itself is thus the possibility of living without the tragedy of ending. *Psyche*-life taps into *zoe*-life and discloses itself as a possibility not only for the first principle or origin but also for the living human being.

In its being rooted in originary *zoe*, *psyche* expresses human life. The metaphysician Plotinus is convinced of this. He writes: "To ask how those forms of life come to be There is simply asking how that heaven came to be; it is asking whence comes life, whence the All-Life [*zoe*], whence the All-Soul [*psyche*], whence collective Intellect: and the answer is that There no indigence or impotence can exist but all must be teeming, seething, with life [*zoe*]."[5] According to Plotinus, the universe exists in relation to its model; if the world is full of life, the case is even more so for its first principle or origin. The metaphysical argumentation coordinates the investigation on the origin of living things with the investigation on the first principle so that one can retrace, at the level of lived experience, the specificity of the first constituent, which is full of life and the maker of life. On the basis of the principle and origin—an inexhaustible spring, budding with life—one can then look, by similarity, at the blooming of nature and the existing things. Physical qualities mirror the characterizing features of the first principle. Analogously, the origin—as the unique spring from which a kind of tide flows—ensures that its same quality, its same properties, match with those that one can detect in life: "Sweetness with fragrance, wine-quality and the savors of everything that may be tasted, all colors seen, everything known to touch, all that ear may hear, all melodies, every rhythm," writes Plotinus.[6]

If, thanks to Aristotle's notes, we go back to the Presocratics, we learn that the most ancient of our ancient predecessors explained life as *psyche* in terms of heat, and they understood the word to live, *zèn* (*zao*), as coming from a verb (*zeo*) that meant to "boil, seethe, foam."[7] Plotinus is perhaps mindful of this when he depicts the "great seething" of originary life. Well before Martin Heidegger, philosophers' etymologies were quite daring. Specifically, they display the power of an idea, namely, the idea that associates heat, fire, and vital ardor with the splendid intensity of the origin and principle.⁸ Metaphors aside, fire, energy, and spirit (*pneuma*), which once again indicates the breath of life, are part of the same perceptive experience.

Concerning the absolute and supersensible principle, the Greek metaphysical tradition affirms what the Gospel narration reveals within the human experience, that is, the discovery of a personal life (*psyche*) that is correlated with originary life (*zoe*). The life having to do with the principle that posits such a life becomes shared life; it becomes life that is partaken and is even understood in its ineradicable and inexhaustible spring. Such a life, which is the source of living, is always itself, never changes, and lasts forever.⁹

Life as *zoe* is the unprecedented. It is not mere biological vitality, but rather absolute qualification, life-life, superlative, inextinguishable, vivifying, and generative. Zoe is the power that makes beings alive; it makes them live, be living. It belongs also to the god as the first principle that Aristotle investigates. "Life [*zoe*] belongs to God . . . We hold, then, that God is a living being [*zoon*]," Aristotle writes.¹⁰ The way of living in which the god dwells forever and which the human beings enjoy now and then is surprisingly wonderful. The activity that is conceivable as divine is pleasure; and pleasant are, for the human beings, the state of wakefulness, the ability to perceive and know in the immediacy of presence. The one who enjoys such a pleasure at its highest degree benefits from the most pleasant and capable power of vision. Such a one lives in or inhabits *theoria*. Thus, the activity that human beings experience from time to time can be thought of, once such an activity is intensified, as the life of the first principle or origin. Vital energy, as the activity that qualifies the first principle, characterizes also the living human beings, even though in a temporal manner. Aristotle reaches this comprehension in his *Politics* when he says that "*anthropos* is the only living thing [*zoon*] that is furnished with the faculty of speech [*logos*]."¹¹ Living-*zoon* is the human being that knowingly avails him or herself of life-*zoe*.

In the subsequent history of words, the terms we have been considering take up different destinations, as is the case for the prefix *zoo-* (or suffix *-zoo*), which, in modern languages, qualify the animal (zoological) sphere with no consideration either for the concept of life that innervates *physis* as a whole or for life in its originating feature.¹² Yet it is interesting to note that the way to say life considered in its surging inexhaustibility can be the same as the way to indicate the life that pulsates in nonhuman living beings. A similar destiny happens to the prefix *bio-* (and suffix *-bio*), which name life with respect to natural germination as well as in its individualized subsistence (as in biological; biographic), therefore referring, on the one hand, to scientific knowledge and organic functions and, on the other, to the narration of one's personal existence. The "obscure" Heraclitus has preserved for us the first image of *bios*, namely, the bow: "The name of the bow [*biós*] is life [*bíos*], but its work is death."[13] The word immediately delineates the reality of the bow/life and the intrinsic opposition that appears within the temporal horizon; and the term also refers us to the arc of individual existence, to the way of living and the means needed to support oneself, and to everydayness. Thus, the word allows us to say the ethical and political experience, the actions that take place in the relationships with others.

Lexical extravagancies in semantic developments progressively muddy terms. Thus, even with respect to the suffix -*psyco*, the meanings of the words that make use of it no longer concern the ability to breathe as indicated in ancient etymology. These lexical variations and their original *etymos* may help when investigating the thinkability of life because the possibility they reveal of naming life in many ways—*psyche*, *zoe*, *bios*—discloses the multiplicity of the ways of partaking in living. By expressing the function and energy of breath, by indicating vitality, *psyche* also means creativity; thereby, it relates to the meaning of *zoe* as the spring, the source that makes one live, and the life that, through individuation, becomes narratable as *bios* while anchored in *physis*. Living is breathing, is partaking in *zoe* in the dimension of self-individuation. One's personality, one's living pulsing, and one's story are interrelated. *Bios* (in Latin, *vita quam vivimus*, the life that we live) defines determined life, life that has a beginning and an end, and refers to *zoe*, that is, to the essence of what is vital (again in Latin, *vita qua vivimus*, life by which we live or are alive). The potentialities of living take place at multiple, interconnected dimensions—physical, historical, and metaphysical.

Surging Life and Life That Is Borne

The way of living worthy of a human being's choice is happiness (*eudaimonia*). This is what Aristotle, at least, is convinced of. For him, happiness is the highest good, that to which nothing else can be added. As sheer living (*zèn*) is also common to plants and, with respect to nutrition and sensation, also to all animals, Aristotle aims at investigating the kind of life that is specifically human. The analysis leads him to the discovery that "the proper function [*ergon*] of the human being [*anthropos*] is an activity [*energheia*] of the soul in conformity with a rational principle [*logos*]."[14] If this is the case, the specifically human acting is a living (*zèn*) that consists of the activity of the *psyche* and of practices that are carried out with *logos*. Aristotle's conclusion is that the human good is the activity of the *psyche* according to its best and most complete abilities and a complete life (*bios*). For a life to be happy, it is not sufficient to have either a space that is limited in time, a condition of sleeping inactivity, or the exercise of power over other lives. As Aristotle claims, "what is by nature proper to each thing will be at once the best and the most pleasant for it. In other words, a life [*bios*] guided by intelligence [*nous*] is the best and most pleasant for the human being [*anthropos*], inasmuch as intelligence, above else, is the human being. Consequently, this kind of life is the happiest."[15]

The Greek-Latin legacy has highlighted the fecundity of life in its biopolitical and psycho-logical dimensions. Yet this focalization has neglected the power of *zoe* to the point of relegating it to the mythical-religious background. We need, therefore, to retrieve the theological horizon in order to glimpse the meaning of *zoe* as infinite, inexhaustible, and surging or originating (*sorgiva*) life. According to John, the most theological among the evangelists, life (*zoe*) was in the beginning (in the *arche*), which was *logos* that was by God.[16] When we read this terminological sequence side by side with Aristotle's texts, we note that it too offers a configuration of living in its originary givenness that makes itself visible to human beings.[17] In its *incipit*, John's Prologue connects *logos*, God, and life, here named *zoe*. The life that one will have in the name of Jesus, the Son of God, is also called *zoe*. As John writes, the *zoe* that was in the beginning was light of the *anthropoi*, of the human beings. What was in the beginning, in that connection by God, was life. Moreover, in a way that is entirely novel when compared to Greek *theoria*, the *logos* of the beginning is said to become flesh.[18] The first principle can become the subject of contemplation in the prismatic splendor of the Incarnation.

The Son offers, and is capable of taking back, his own *psyche* because he lives of *zoe*, of life that is more abundant than anything, beyond measure, overflowing, and excessive.[19] The life that can be lost is *psyche*; the life that can be gained and in which one can remain in a fecund manner is *zoe*. What begins to be disclosed here is the idea that one may be able to assume being alive in such a way as to turn it into a life that does not self-annihilate, unlike what happens in the case when life identifies univocally with *psyche*. A novel possibility of being alive in an overflowing manner becomes manifest here together with the need to cultivate a life that is so lively that it cannot end.[20]

The theme of an everlasting life unfolds through the use of a very peculiar verb, namely, *zoopoieo*, which means to render alive, give life, vivify, and, in its intransitive form, germinate.[21] The attribute of life-*zoe* is *aionios*, usually translated as "everlasting, eternal." It refers to continuing (everlasting) endurance, and, therefore, it strengthens the idea of a life that is truly such, that is, that lasts.[22] The New Testament announcement concerns the happy possibility that one may always have life according to the law of the spirit of life, which liberates life and which makes life (*zoopoiei*).[23]

Christian iconography maintains the image of the spring [*sorgente*] in the Son's generating parent, Mary, who is mother of God and hence *Zoodochos Peghe*, Life-giving Spring. There is a leap in life that is re-asserted cyclically also by biological spring [*primavera*].[24] To the God of the biblical tradition who is celebrated as the Living One and therefore as the God of the living, Christian theology adds the notion of one's intimate familiarity, of one's shared nature with such a God.

Within contemporary phenomenology, Michel Henry is a master in stating philosophically the condition of incarnation of the living human being. Henry writes:

> Because I who live did not bring myself into life myself (nor into the Self I am, nor into my flesh, being given to myself only in flesh), this living being, this Self, and this flesh do not arrive in themselves except in the proceeding of absolute Life, which arrives in itself in its Word, and experiences itself in this Word, which experiences itself in it, in the reciprocal phenomenological interiority of their common Spirit. Thus in contrast to the formal God of monotheism, the Trinitarian God of Christianity is the real God who lives in each living Self, without which no living being would be alive, and to which every living being bears witness in its very condition as living.[25]

Within the human adventure, which, ever since birth, traverses the entire course of one's life, the living subject strives to give birth to itself. Such a subject discovers that, in order to succeed, it needs a second birth. The second birth will no longer be biological. Rather, it will be accomplished through the choice of wanting to be the living self that one has found oneself having since the beginning. One needs therefore to recreate, to regenerate oneself while one is, actually, already living at the individual level; this is necessary in order to have life forever, according to the explanation of *zoe aionion*, of everlasting life that, in John's account, is given to the wise man who, at nighttime, asks the Teacher, Jesus Christ, about this.[26] This self-generation, which is second in relation to the givenness of biological birth, can be understood at the ontological level. The connection with life in its constitutive originarity explains the anteriority of the conscious self. John's Jesus shifts the order of the historical calculation of time to the generative nontemporality of the Absolute and, in this light, the assertion that "before Abraham was born, I am!" takes up meaning.[27]

Human life is chosen a second time. Human life is given as a gift and, by assenting to it, it is taken up and enjoyed as a "Yes!" to absolute life. "You must be born again . . . you must be born of the Spirit (*pneuma*)"—this seems entirely consequential, if originary life precedes and constitutes biological life.[28] This birth from breath, this being born of spirit, is "a thing of the earth" that one needs to experience in order to become oneself and generate oneself to a life that is recognized as not merely biological factuality. Moreover, the human need for a procreation from above ("You must be born of the Spirit") unfolds the relationship between Spirit as creative power and breath as vital blow. Whereas *psyche* is the power of respiration and, therefore, vital principle of the body, *pneuma*—breath, Spirit, vitality that proceeds from itself—reveals the dimension of constitutive, properly generative life.

The interpretation of life is therefore intensified as one moves from the consideration of *psyche* to the idea of *zoe* to end up with an understanding of the power of the link with the overflowing, inexhaustible, and inextinguishable life and of the experience of such an intense vitality that overcomes contraries and oppositions such as life and death, soul and body. From abysmal distances, there echoes an Edenic invitation to multiply life in the midst of the creeping doubt of a destiny of death. In the light of *zoe*, however, the invitation to live life in a multiplying fashion cannot concern mere procreation and the continuation of the species; rather, it regards the intensity of individual life, which implies a birth to oneself in order to become alive and live in such a way as not to die.

The nighttime dialogue mentioned above between Nicodemus and the Teacher from Nazareth, Jesus, can be read with reference to another famous dialogue, that is, the Platonic conversation of Socrates with the prophetess Diotima. Diotima illustrates the various possibilities of being generative—from biological reproduction up to the creativity of *psyche*, fecund with its own thoughts and works, within "the region of life that is worth living by a human being."[29]

Living does not appear as independent from personal will. In some way, one is born by discovering that one wants to be born. Within modernity, Kierkegaard is the one who understands the fact of wanting one's own very self, of wanting to be oneself as the climax of an existential itinerary that leads from despair to the confidence of being able to live fully. By discovering, in all transparency, that one's very self is posed by some other, the living subject finds the self that makes its own self be and therefore lives on the basis of such a grateful and certain recognition. Kierkegaard claims that this self is "the theological self, the self directly before God . . . what an infinite accent falls on the self by having God as the criterion!" and thus "the self in being itself and in willing to be itself rests transparently in God."[30]

Living Nature

Not only do we feel alive; we also want to know that we are alive. For a long time though, this has appeared as either a tragedy or a fall (a decay). The eponymous heroes of such a form of knowledge have been Oedipus and Adam. Things did not turn out well for either of them, and for Adam, this took a radical turn. The natural immediacy in which the first Adam found himself is described as a garden. The very thinkability of the notion of living refers to the concept of nature, to *viriditas*, greenness, that is, the power to become green, to bloom, to bear fruit, so that "vital" comes to indicate that which is capable of development at all levels.[31]

The notion of *physis* as a peculiar condition of the living thing and of that which has its own principle of development within itself is mutuated from Aristotle and also implies the idea of order, of state. On the basis of such an idea, Christian theology has illustrated a series of various states of nature, that is, of different natural conditions that are possible: (0) pure nature, (1) whole or intact nature, (2) fallen or decayed nature, (3) saved nature, and (4) glorious nature.

It thus appears that nature can be said in many ways and is multiplied in its possibilities of being. The zero point is a pure mental exercise; it is the exercise that defines "naked life." Such a state would in fact presuppose the creation of a human being that is not destined to the supernatural and, therefore, it is in a condition of no internal development, without vitality, with no further dimension (*ulteriorità*). The whole or intact state considers nature in its very rich wholeness, that is, endowed with all those features that pertain to human beings according to their wishes. This condition of life does not exclude becoming; on the contrary, it implies becoming yet without obstacles or conflicts. Thomas Aquinas offers an eloquent example of this. In this condition, Aquinas says, the pleasures of the senses would be (would have been) more intense because sensory abilities would be complete, with no limitations.[32]

Fallen nature, that is, nature that has decayed from its good proportionality, is nature as we experience it in history. This nature is necessary for life, and yet it is frail; it can be destructive and be destroyed. Therefore, the theological horizon opens to the hope of a possible salvation that, rather than destining life to its decline, may heal ruptures and eschatologically fulfill the entirety of nature in the fullness of its realizations, which are guaranteed to reach the maximum of their potentialities.

Nature as it is known within historical times is already richly gifted; and yet it is also deprived, so much so that the attribute "decayed" (or fallen) aptly applies to it. Nature has lost some of its possibilities, which are no longer pursuable in their entirety. Becoming, in the modality of decline and death, now appears natural, even though it is contrary to the principle of life. Imagined as Edenic, nature could avail itself of additional givens and gifts (for example, power and knowledge without abuse, development without decay, and transition to higher levels without death). The privation of such gifts is perceived (and resented) as the condition of an essential loss—we should be entitled to them as conditions to be able to live humanly, without self-privation, without violence to other(s). The bountiful nature of the beginning and the even more glorious nature of the *eschaton* express what nature already is, albeit in its limits. For human beings, nature is full of life; it is never naked. The supernatural, perceived as lost or longed for, marks that which is essential in the natural; it ushers in its own self-giving within a dynamics of additionality and ulteriority (*ulteriorità*), and never of reduction.

With respect to this, contemporary Italian thinker Enrico Guglielminetti writes that

> the reduction of good life to naked life is the spoliation not of an accidental part, but of that which is proper to it, that is, an essential accident. In other words, there is no naked life. Life is always clothed. . . . If life is always clothed, then evil manifests itself, first of all, as the positive power of stripping bare, as the attempt at reducing life to naked life. The human being is never without skin; a skinned reality is possible only at the cost of unprecedented suffering. Yet this form of reduction does not succeed; rather than a simple reduction of additions, evil is, instead, the substitution of natural additions with erroneous additions.[33]

Life with additions, according to Guglielminetti's theoretical proposal, recalls the powerful tradition of the doctrine of grace, which posits nature as grace's first and pure expression. Life is full of grace.

Within the aesthetic field, nakedness—which is already adorned with the natural grace of the living—has appeared as a good manifestation of the truth as opposed to the artifice of clothing, which is not an essential addition but rather a falsifying cover-up. In this case, too, nakedness appears as a value to be preserved and not as a reduction that impoverishes. The veil of appearance and of time is stripped away from *nuda veritas*, naked truth, so that its pure beauty may be revealed.[34]

According to the reading provided by Giorgio Agamben, "bare life," or "naked life," should instead be understood along the same lines of the sacred life of the Roman law: that is, as a life dependent on the sovereign power and therefore abominable and disposable, in a state of exception to the law itself.[35] In this sense, the political would be the real addition to the living nature of human beings, in whom no trace of animality should remain. Through Hannah Arendt, Agamben interprets along these lines the passage from Aristotle's *Politics* where the distinction is made between properly human language and voice, which is a characteristic of animal life. The nakedness of the living being appears as something unbecoming also in this distancing from shared animal life. One can certainly agree with Agamben regarding the reduction to "bare life" accomplished, in terms of the definition of personal identity, by biometrics, genetic measurements, or through the accumulation of health, personal, and bank data. This addition of objective elements does not express the living human being. Hospital denudation and the privation of one's own clothing in coercive institutions are expressions of a life that has been robbed of its fullness. A body that has been reduced to the knowable and measurable objectivity of naked life does not have the grace of the living being; it is naked corporeality void of grace, a body that is shamefully exposed and vilified.[36]

Agamben applies this same interpretative key also to the Edenic myth and describes the discovery of nudity as the loss of the garment of grace.[37] If the living human being originally asks for clothing to cover himself up, the naked corporeality of nature is opposed with the garment that is grace. Agamben writes, "If already before sin there was a need to cover up the human body with the veil of grace [*grazia*], then the blissful and innocent paradisiacal nudity was preceded by another nudity, a 'naked corporeality' that sin, by removing the clothes of grace, allows, mercilessly, to appear."[38] In this correspondence, nature amounts to lack and, therefore, to evil. Nature before grace, however, remains inaccessible because—*pace* Agamben—it is inexistent. Theologically, there is in fact no state of mere nature, no natural human being without grace, that is, without the possibility of constant transcendence.

Nature before grace in Agamben's sense would correspond to that stage 0, which is the stage of a hypothetical nature deprived of its possibility for self-transcendence. It would be some kind of robotic Eden, the space of the nonhuman, of the purely bestial, assuming that the animal could be hypothesized as a fixed mechanism. On the contrary, though, no previous condition precedes the theological representation of intact nature—which is the nature of the living human being. Intact nature does not fear the order of biopolitics.[39] The hypothesis of the originary separability of nature and grace, nakedness and clothing, is not part of the context of the biblical myth. There is no nature of which to be ashamed. There is only the living grace that one should magnify.

When one starts from the theological vision, which, in an Aristotelian manner, can be defined as first philosophy, as philosophy of the first principle and origin, living can be considered in its infinite intensity, freed both from reduction to the biological and from exposure to the political existent. Only the activity of the first principle or origin can properly be named zoopoietic. Such an activity makes the living being, vivifies it, and renders it alive.

Translated from Italian by Silvia Benso

Notes

1. René Descartes, *Meditations on First Philosophy*, trans. Donald A. Cress (Indianapolis: Hackett, 1993), 20. In the Latin and French originals respectively, Descartes says: "Ego sum res cogitans, id est dubitans, affirmans, negans, pauca intelligens, multa ignorans, volens, nolens, imaginans etiam et sentiens" (*Meditationes de prima philosophia*, 1641); and "Je suis une chose qui pense, c'est-à-dire qui doute, qui affirme, qui nie, qui connaît peu de choses, qui en ignore beaucoup, qui aime, qui hait [these two qualifications are missing in the Latin version], qui veut, qui ne veut pas, qui imagine aussi, et qui sent" (*Méditations sur la philosophie première*, Paris 1647).

2. Plato, *Phaedo* 105d3–4.

3. Luke 9:24 and 17:33; Matthew 10:39; Mark 8:35.

4. Ovid, *Metamorphoses* III, 348.

5. Plotinus, *Ennead* VI.7.12, 11.18–22. See also *Ennead* I, which is among the last texts written by Plotinus and is entirely devoted to the question of what is the living thing and what is an *anthropos*, that is, a human being.

6. Plotinus, *Ennead* VI.7.12, 11.27–30.

7. Aristotle, *De Anima* 405b26–28.

8. This kind of inquiry appears in Simone Weil's notebooks, in particular in *Bṛhadāraṇyaka Upaniṣad*, I, 5, 21–23, and in Simone Weil, *Oeuvres complètes: Cahiers*, tome IV/2 (Paris: Gallimard, 2002). Weil notes an equivalence between the notion of vital breath and *pneuma*. Heraclitus also considered respiration as igneous breath that provides energy.

9. John 6:68 says "*zoes aioniou* [everlasting life]."
10. Aristotle, *Metaphysics* 1072b25–30.
11. Aristotle, *Politics* 1253a10.s
12. I here understand "*zoopoiesis*" and "*zoopoietic*" in their original sense, unlike the use made of them in biotechnologies and mythographies.
13. Heraclitus, Fragment B 48.
14. Aristotle, *Nicomachean Ethics* 1098a7–8.
15. Aristotle, *Nicomachean Ethics* 1178a 5–8.
16. See the prologue in John 1:1–4.
17. The term *bios* does not appear in John's Gospel. *Psyche* is used a few times to indicate the life that ends with death.
18. John 1:4.
19. John 10:1–21 and 12:25.
20. See François Jullien, *Ressources du christianisme, mais sans y entrer par la foi* (Paris: Ed. de l'Herne, 2018); on the vital breath, see the novel by François Cheng, *L'éternité n'est pas de trop* (Paris: Albin Michel, 2002).
21. See John 5:24, 5:30, and 20:31.
22. John 14:19 has Jesus say: "You will see [*theoreite*] me; because I live [*ego zo*], you also will live [*zesete*]."
23. The language is this time from Paul, Romans 8:2 and 2 Corinthians 3:6.
24. The title *Zootokos*, the one who gives birth to living offspring, was assigned to Mary, the mother of Jesus, in 431 CE during the Council of Ephesus.
25. Michel Henry, *Incarnation: A Philosophy of Flesh*, trans. Karl Hefty (Evanston, IL: Northwestern University Press, 2015), 171 and Michel Henry, *Barbarism*, trans. Scott Davidson (New York: Continuum, 2012), especially chapter 4, "The Sickness of Life."
26. John 3:1–16.
27. John 8:58.
28. John 3:7, 3:8.
29. Plato, *Symposium* 211d.
30. Søren Kierkegaard, *The Sickness unto Death*, in *The Essential Kierkegaard* (Princeton, NJ: Princeton University Press), 363 and 365.
31. *Viriditas* is a nice neologism coined by Hildegard of Bingen. An interesting parallelism among the life of plants, animals, and human beings is made, in the circle of Husserl's students, by Hedwig Conrad-Martius, *Bios und Psyche* (Hamburg: Classen und Goverts, 1949) and Hedwig Conrad-Martius, *Metaphysische Gespräche* (Halle: Max Niemeyer, 1921).
32. Thomas Aquinas, *Summa Theologiae*, Quaestio 98.
33. Enrico Guglielminetti, *Logica dell'aggiunta* (Milan: Mursia, 2020), 81. On the addition of Edenic privileges, see Alessandra Cislaghi, *L'invenzione della grazia* (Milan: Mimesis, 2018), 103ff.
34. See Pierre Hadot, *The Veil of Isis: An Essay on the History of the Idea of Nature*, trans. Michael Chase (Cambridge, MA: Harvard University Press, 2006). Naked truth is originary truth, whereas clothed truth is historical truth; examples

of this are the artistic works inspired by Neoplatonism such as those by Titian and Botticelli.

35. See Giorgio Agamben, *Homo Sacer: Sovereign Power and Bare Life*, trans. Daniel Heller-Roazen (Stanford, CA: Stanford University Press, 1998) and Giorgio Agamben, *Nudities*, trans. David Kishik and Stefan Pedatella (Stanford, CA: Stanford University Press, 2010). On the complex relation between state of nature and common life, between care for life and relation to death, see Roberto Esposito, *Communitas: The Origin and Destiny of Community*, trans. Timothy C. Campbell (Stanford, CA: Stanford University Press, 2009) and Roberto Esposito, *Immunitas: The Protection and Negation of Life*, trans. Zakiya Hanafi (Malden, MA: Polity Press, 2011).

36. It is accidental that we also clothe the dead, when they are not cruelly thrown into mass graves as during wars. It is only some mystics who have wanted to be buried naked in the ground, as in a return to the maternal womb where, however, nakedness is fully protected.

37. Agamben refers to the work by Erik Peterson, "Theologie des Kleides," *Benediktinische Monatsschrift zur Pflegereligiösen und geistigen Lebens* 16 (1934): 347–56. The concept of *bloßes Leben*, naked life, comes from Walter Benjamin, "Zur Kritik der Gewalt," in *Gesammelte Schriften*, ed. Rolf Tiedemann and Hermann Schweppenhäuser (Frankfurt a. M.: Suhrkamp, 1974), vol. II/1, 179–203. This 1921 essay by Benjamin constitutes one of Agamben's main references.

38. Agamben, *Nudities*, 60, translation modified as the English translator inexplicably renders the first occurrence of the term *grazia* (grace) with "glory."

39. See Michel Foucault, *The Birth of Biopolitics: Lectures at the Collège de France, 1978–79*, trans. Graham Burchell (New York: Palgrave Macmillan, 2010) and Roberto Esposito, *Bios: Biopolitics and Philosophy*, trans. Timothy C. Campbell (Minneapolis: Minnesota University Press, 2008).

Eleven

Life and the "Black Swan"

Enrica Lisciani-Petrini

> For we are only the rind and the leaf.
> The great death, that each of us carries inside,
> Is the fruit, everything enfolds it.
>
> —Rainer Maria Rilke, *Das Stundenbuch*

Annus Horribilis

In history books, 2020 will probably be remembered, and rightly so, as "the year of the pandemic." Since the beginning of January, the coronavirus has progressively burst into the entire world in a totally unforeseen modality. It was so unexpected—for its insidious clinical effects and the consequences that have come from it—that, with a suggestive metaphor, some have referred to it as "a black swan."[1] Within a few days, measures were implemented that progressively restricted our daily social practices and confined us within our individual homes, often in isolation. Additionally, on our TV screens, there started to be broadcast figures telling us about the exponential increase in the number of people that had been infected or gotten sick. Furthermore, in Italy, there appeared the images, which will remain indelible, of the long lines of coffins transported by military trucks first toward cremation sites and then to cemeteries—with no spouse, child, relative, or friend able to accompany that last earthly trip of the deceased and bury them.

In those images—markers, at the same time, of a missed burial ceremony and of the reduction of burials to mere destruction of infected bodies—it has been our very humanity (*umanità*) that has been "symbolically" disfigured. The practice of burials is, in fact, the primary characteristic of our species—so much so that it renders it human. As the Neapolitan philosopher Giambattista Vico notes, humanity "started with *humare*," that is, with placing into the ground (*humus*), with burying, the bodies of the dead.[2] The verses of the poem by Italian writer Ugo Foscolo are also a reminder of this very fact. As Foscolo writes in *Dei Sepolcri* (*Of the Graves*), a work that is very well known in Italy, "Under the shadow of the cypress trees, / within the urns wetted by loving tears / can the slumber of death be less profound? / [. . .] Oh! No flower can bloom / over the dead, unless it is enlivened / by human praises and by loving tears. // Since when weddings and tribunals and altars allowed the human beasts to have some mercy / of themselves and of others, the survivors / kept from wild animals and corrupting weather / the pitiful remains that Nature dooms, by unalterable changes, to a new form."[3]

Aristotle condenses the nature of the human being in the fact of being "a political animal," a *zoon politikon*, and, therefore, a social animal (*Politics* I, 2, 1253a). When we keep such a consideration in mind, we have a measure of the devastating impact—at the level of the *human and social essence* characterizing us—that the pandemic event has had on the world since the beginning of this *annus horribilis* (horrible year). It is as if existence has been suddenly pulled back, violently brought back to its minimal terms, and contracted into its extreme points: life and/or death.

This situation has been the occasion for a series of impelling questions, which have bounced back from one side of the planet to the other for days and days and have pushed us to the threshold of the extreme:[4] What happens to existence when it is reduced to its ultimate elements or finds itself confronted with tragedy and death? What constitutes our humanity? Ultimately, *what is life?*

When faced with this kind of questioning, the answers cannot occur at an immediately reactive, narrative, or chronicling level, no matter the perspicacity of the considerations that may be generated. This is because at this level of immediacy, the overall horizon of meaning within which the questions are situated becomes, perhaps unconsciously, lost. It is therefore necessary to delineate a larger perimeter and to plunge into a more radical terrain. In the first instance, one needs to explore the major "subterranean" movements, as Hegel says, which, beneath history, lie at the origin of history, that is, of our vision of the matters at hand; and then, consequently, it is necessary to understand *the sense* of that which now appears to us as "obvious." It is thus appropriate that preliminarily, we take a step back and grasp, even in broad strokes, the long historical-cultural path that has led to the notion of life as we understand it currently. After that, we can return to the sense of existing and its most intimate "folds" that, in normal conditions, often remain unnoticed.

Thinking Life—A Historical-Theoretical Excursus

A Sagittal Look at the Past

First of all, it seems appropriate to recall a fundamental point. In our culture, since the beginning, the notion of life has been divided into two opposed fields. On the one hand, there is *zoe*, "naked life," in its purely animal-material flowing; on the other hand, there is *bios*, life as "formed," that is, gathered in a form that is qualified and qualifies life itself. Significantly, for Plato, real life was the *bios philosophos*, the philosophical life, which is constitutively distant from everyday material matters and is aimed at "true knowledge." Aristotle in turn distinguished among three "life forms": *bios apolaustikos*, the life of pleasure; *bios politikos*, the life of honor; and *bios theoretikos*, the life of thought.[5] As Bergson notes, this partakes of the "Platonist" view according to which reality is viewed at two separate levels, one (*sub specie aeternitatis*, from the standpoint of eternity) that is superior, ideal, transcendent, and eternal; and the other (*sub specie durationis*, from the view point of duration) that is inferior, material, immanent, and temporal.[6] In this view, the former founds and orders the latter. This vision transfers in its entirety to Christianity, for which Jesus' "incorporation" into terrestrial "flesh" takes place within the superior perspective of "saving" flesh to the dimension of Spirit and, therefore, "saving" earthly mortal life by bringing it back to "true Life," which is eternal and spiritual. Such a structure, which aims at retracing, within living matter, preforming "reasons" of a superior order, is adopted by Neoplatonism, which reaches up to the Italian Renaissance with Marsilius Ficinus.

This modality of vision of reality has been, for many centuries, dominant and "major" (and is, in many senses, still operational in some theoretical and theological milieus). Yet ever since the beginning, next to it, there is another view that is opposed to the first, divergent and "minor" when compared to it.[7] Instead of starting from a dualism that cuts reality into two orders, this second modality operates immediately at the level of the *mobile materiality of the real*, which Bergson qualifies as *mouvante*, moving. The conviction is that the production of the forms that progressively shape such an incandescent matter originates *only* from within such matter itself. They are produced not from the heights of a spirit or a logical domain that is legislator and sovereign, but rather from below, from a power that gives to itself, by itself, its own norms (its forms). Here, forms are not given once and forever; they are not eternal and immutable; rather, they are constantly transformable and transformed by *living matter itself*.

In the last three centuries, this view of reality progressively imposes itself in a decisive manner. This happens thanks to the transformations that occur at the historical-theoretical level and lead to a profound revision of the notion of life.

In the eighteenth century, there appears a notion of life that produces an epistemological break possibly without precedents. This notion is completely different from the one that had been conceptualized and accepted up to that point.[8] As we have mentioned, from antiquity and then for centuries, the spiritualistic-theological framework has been dominant; during the sixteenth and seventeenth centuries, this framework is replaced with a quantitative-mechanistic paradigm. Starting in the middle of the eighteenth and, especially, at the beginning of the nineteenth century, a different cognitive approach becomes widespread; this approach is intent on grasping the *qualitative movement* that traverses living organisms and transforms them incessantly.[9] It is the entry into the picture of biology. This is a completely new science if compared, for example, with the mechanistic view, which is incapable of grasping the living being insofar as it encapsulates it within quantitative and classificatory schemas that are closed and eternal (in this sense, they are the materialist counterpart of the theological perspective based on eternity). On the contrary, biology modulates the various forms of knowledge by introducing the *historical factor*, that is, the temporal dimension; thus, it enables the move from fixism to evolutionism. This shift opens the way for a vision of life as an *open, dynamic dimension*, which is regulated not by repetitive, unchangeable structures and by a preformed movement, but rather by uncontrollable forces and unpredictable events. Among these, death is greatest and supreme. This dimension had been removed, marginalized, or sublimated by previous perspectives; now, it instead bursts in with unfathomable power and crushes long-standing theoretical layouts. This takes place to such an extent that, concerning life—that is, concerning that which earlier had been regarded as a spiritual, eternal dimension theologically fixed a priori—Bichat could say that life "is the collection of those forces which resist death."[10] Death places itself firmly within the notion of life as an internal and unsurpassable element that guides life itself, without any possibility that life may be "saved" from death.

THREE "PHILOSOPHERS OF LIFE": BERGSON, SIMMEL, AND JANKÉLÉVITCH

Since the beginning of the nineteenth century, the question of life (*bios*) enters the cultural scenario in the modes advanced by science and profoundly transforms the overall reflection, traversing it as a most shattering factor. The view on things that is still in large part dominated by the primacy of thought over actual, material, and bodily reality and is grounded on a conceptual apparatus still based on abstract categories is replaced with a dynamic and fluid perspective that compels to a radical reconfiguration of reality in its entirety and the modalities through which one thinks of it. Philosophy quickly becomes the interpreter and source of transmission of this distinct change of paradigm. I will not dwell on the profound influences that the intense scientific debate occurring between the eighteenth and nineteenth centuries exerted on philosophers such as Kant, Hegel, Schelling, and others, who followed such a discussion with great attention and acknowledged its most fecund positions.[11] The thinkers who, with uttermost clarity, have accepted the revolutionary contributions of the discussion have undoubtedly been Henri Bergson and, with him and after him, Georg Simmel and Vladimir Jankélévitch.

Bergson shows, for the first time and in a clear-cut and unequivocal manner, the complete turnaround that has occurred by his time. The temporal living dimension and its continuously transformative development, which up to that point had been regarded as marginal or merely an illusory substratum, reverse and come to the foreground as the originary and inescapable dimension of reality. Correspondingly, the dimension that for centuries had been regarded as *the* Truth, *the* real Substance—the network of eternal Ideas supporting the real—is now revealed as pure pretense, as an artificial layer that, for reasons of mere human usefulness, has been cast on something that, in itself, is mobile and ungraspable. Therefore, the ideal and immobilized vision of reality is replaced with another view that operates in the form of temporality—*sub specie durationis*, in Bergson's famous words—and is marked by a metamorphic, unpredictable, and nonuniversalizable dynamic that takes place in the corporeal fibers of the organisms. One must note that this should not to be mistaken with the unilinear, pixelated, and geometric time that is produced by calculative reason. On the contrary, this time is the pulsation of infinite rhythms, living matter that is qualitatively differentiated and vibrant within bodies. As Deleuze remarks commenting on Bergson, "this breaks with the whole philosophical tradition."[12]

Bergson thus offers the conceptual coordinates to think of the theoretical reversal that has taken place within the historical-cultural process. This gives birth to a robust philosophical lineage, which starts with Simmel and Jankélévitch up to Deleuze, just to mention the most significant and famous names within this legacy (next to them, one should also mention some Italian thinkers of the early twentieth century such as Giuseppe Rensi and Adriano Tilgher).[13] There is, however, a definite gap between the first two thinkers, that is, Simmel and Jankélévitch, and the third, namely, Deleuze. Deleuze fundamentally follows Bergson's entirely affirmative approach—as is well-known, for Bergson, death is simply a moment of transition between two affirmations of life. On the contrary, Simmel and Jankélévitch retrieve the inherence of death *in* life, which was already at the center of Bichat's vitalism, and turn it into the pulsating core of a different philosophical way of thinking and, thereby, of a different view on things.[14]

Simmel immediately grasps the subversive relevance of Bergson's reflection on life and becomes its acute interpreter and committed continuator. Equally immediately, though, he re-establishes the role of the negative, that is, the other side of life that is constituted by death; thereby, Simmel gives his discourse a decisively tragic intonation. As he says explicitly in *The View of Life*, life is constitutively traversed by a double, contradictory movement. On the one hand, in order to manifest itself, life must determine itself and close itself up in rigid forms, which therefore negate life as moving life, as life-in-movement. On the other hand, though, these "life forms" are destined to be negated in turn, to be swallowed up by life—that is, they are destined to die—so that life may keep alive its own incessant dynamism. Hence, Simmel's paradoxical claim: "As life, [life] needs forms; as life, it needs more than a given form. Life is thus caught up in the contradiction that it can only be lodged in forms and yet cannot be lodged in forms."[15]

Jankélévitch follows these acquisitions when, ever since the beginning of his philosophical path, he assumes Bergson's theoretical framework as his own constant background. Yet he mitigates Bergson's entirely affirmative "optimism" through Simmel's "tragic" sense of life.[16] What emerges from this combination is a view on things that is certainly marked, according to Bergson's major "revolution," by an irreversible and ungraspable temporality, void of an absolute and eternal ground. Yet this temporality is also continuously fractured by the abysmal interruptions provoked by death, which cannot be reabsorbed within the compact flow of duration. This pushes Jankélévitch's reflection to acknowledge the sense of precariousness, of fragility with respect to life and the entirety of reality; and this casts an unmistakable trait of melancholy on his philosophy, even though—or perhaps precisely because—this is hidden behind its often-lavish aspects. Melancholy is here to be understood in the sense of Albrecht Dürer's 1514 engraving *Melencolia*, which was inspired by the *facies hyppocratica*, the Hyppocratic face of life: that is, by the presence of death that life contains within itself as if it were the "black hole" around which life constantly wraps itself. What is generated here is one of the most powerful reflections on death that the previous century has bestowed on us. We should remember, however, that such a century has witnessed two world wars and a pandemic (the Spanish flu) that have caused millions of deaths.

The "Black Hole" around Which Life Wraps Itself

The "Internal Contradiction" of Life

Jankélévitch had devoted an impressive reflection to the theme of death, which is present throughout his works but condensates in the weighty volume *La Mort*. His is a lengthy, acute, painful meditation, due also to the Shoah (as he was of Russian Jewish descent). Such a reflection situates itself, with an even greater speculative power, as we shall indicate below, side by side with Heidegger's considerations. It is of particular interest for us, here, because—in a period like ours, characterized by strong "biopolitical" tendencies empowered by the current pandemic—Jankélévitch succeeds in tying in single plexus considerations that have a biological-vitalist provenance with reflections that broaden that horizon and touch on the ultimate borders of existing. Thereby, he discloses to us their inseparable and insurmountable bind.

Jankélévitch was the child of two medical doctors, one of whom, Samuel, the father, had been deeply influenced by the vitalist school of Montpellier. Since his youth, Jankélévitch was well acquainted with the biological-scientific environment. This theoretical family rooting is probably the cause of his initial fascination with Bergson's vitalism, which then became a convinced subscription to the French thinker's positions. Retrieving Bichat's famous assertion and interpolating it with considerations that he had heard from his father, Jankélévitch claimed, "It is life itself that carries within itself its own internal contradiction. . . . To live is to keep oneself in an unstable balance between such contradictory forces. Bichat used to say that life is the set of forces that resist death. Yet in order for that to make sense, one should add that life resists something that is life itself . . .: my very own death comes and hits me just like a stranger and from the outside—that very same death that, nevertheless, operates within my own life."[17]

The incandescent core of the question is perfectly focused. It seems to echo equally shocking achievements attained a few decades earlier by

Freud, who also had adopted the most advanced theories in biology. One should also recall that the first translator into French of Freud's works was Jankélévitch's father. In his most shattering text, *Beyond the Pleasure Principle*, Freud maintains that in order to be able to explain some behaviors that can be observed daily but are otherwise incomprehensible (for example, the compulsion to repetition), one must arrive at a "hypothesis" that has never been mentioned before and that introduces one into "the most obscure and inaccessible region of the mind."[18] The hypothesis is that there "*is an urge inherent in organic life to restore an earlier state of things*" and that such an earlier state is "the inertia inherent in organic life."[19] According to Freud, this is "an *old* state of things, an initial state from which the living entity has at one time or other departed and to which it is striving to return by the circuitous paths along which its development leads."[20] The outcome is as inevitable as it is explosive: "*the aim of all life is death.*"[21] What we call life is therefore nothing else but the ensemble of "ever more complicated detours" that the organic substance is forced to make "before reaching its aim of death."[22] From this point of view, the only function of the conservative instincts of self-preservation is "to assure that the organism shall follow *its own path* to death, and to ward off any possible ways of returning to inorganic existence other than those which are immanent in the organism itself." That is, such self-preservative instincts ultimately amount to "the fact that the organism wishes to die only *in its own fashion.*" Thus, Freud's conclusion is that "these guardians of life, too, were originally the sentinels of death."[23]

The disruptive power of Freud's passages is evident. They bring us to the core of the problem, of which Jankélévitch is well aware as his considerations come very close to Freud's. These considerations concern us greatly for various reasons.

First of all, for us too, in these historic times, the horizon of meaning within which we frame the question of life and death is biological. This is inevitable, and not simply because of the historical-conceptual transformations we have addressed earlier. Indeed, currently such transformations enable us to see, in an undeniable manner, that life and death pertain, first of all, to our bodies and our embodied existence with no possibility of overcoming such a level and sublimating it into alleged spiritualisms or consolatory forms of transcendence. Equally undeniably, this has definite biopolitical consequences in terms of the general management of the matter. Who could deny that, in the global political agendas, the first and fundamental problems are, and duly so, health, environmental conservation in connection with our lives, the care of bodies, and material subsistence in terms of our existence? The current pandemic has revamped and strengthened such an evidence in an exponential manner both through the prophylactic measures that have been implemented and through the regulations of high "immunitary" character that have ensued at all levels—at the medical-healthcare but also at the social and even economic ones.[24] Combined with Freud, Jankélévitch thus helps to frame within the correct historical horizon what has happened, and continues to happen, at the global level. He does so by calling out attention to the corporeal and organic aspect, which is *primary*. This level cannot be neglected or simply stepped over in the name of "higher rights," which in fact can only exist because their roots are grounded in such an organic and material terrain.

This takes us to some other radical evidence that is completely sidestepped by the traditional view of things. There is, in fact, another remarkable aspect that we can discern in its entire relevance only thanks to this conceptual framework. Let us start again from what we said earlier. Life carries death *within itself*. More precisely, ever since we are born, in addition to our own life, each of us carries within ourselves our own death—our "own fashion" of dying, as Freud phrases it. As Rilke claims, with birth, everyone acquires a double condition, namely, life *together* with death. As paradoxical as this may sound, one could even say that death belongs to us more than life itself. Birth may be contingent, whereas death is certain. In this sense, death is not something that awaits us at the end of life. Death is that which continuously accompanies us, that with which we are always contemporaries; it is like the *basso continuo* that constantly lies in the background of our living.

This means that death constitutes the perimetral margin that continuously marks off our life; it is that which seals it and makes it be that specific *"unique life"* that exists *"only once."* In this sense, the inseparable bond between "my own life" and "my own death" is what turns me into *a specific and unmistakable life form*, an individual in flesh and bone who is unrepeatable. The uniqueness of the individual is not, of course, a novel concept. Yet here it acquires a more definite and specific relevance. It is not a matter of a simply "spiritual" or "cultural" acquisition, or it is not just that. Rather, it is something that belongs to life itself. As Bergson and Simmel already claimed, in order to live, life needs to gather, to be "instituted," as it were, in specific forms that are unrepeatable and live *only once*.[25] The consequences are radical. What is here literally undone is the modality of viewing beings within an abstract logical frame, according to which each of us is merely the interchangeable expression of an eternal universal essence. Undone is the strategy according to which, far from being "my own" death, death becomes the impersonal "one dies," that is, a death that does not affect anyone in particular because it affects everyone in general. The strategy that is undone is, moreover, the one according to which death is removed as "the ownmost death" of a unique life that exists only once and according to which death is instead made—in an entirely consolatory manner—the "transition" to access a superior immortal life.

The "Infinitely Precious" Fragility of Existing

We reach here a last set of reflections that, still through Jankélévitch, may prove to be quite significant especially in light of what we said at the beginning regarding the *annus horribilis*. It is certainly true that death is "one's own" even since birth. Yet there is a paradoxical side to this, which Jankélévitch observes very clearly and which breaks all attempts at inflecting the discourse on death in an appropriative direction as Heidegger does when he speaks of death as that which delivers every being to its "uttermost potentiality-for-Being—that is to say, the possibility of *authentic existence*."[26] As it is something I can *never* either master or choose, my own life—and likewise my own death—is indeed what, in me, can be least possessed or appropriated and yet constitutes me in my very being. This condition is even more emphasized and becomes emblematic in the case of death. I can somehow know my life by living it. I cannot do the same with my death. The simple and trivial reason is that I am not the one who decides when to die. Moreover, though, when death is here, I will no longer be. Whereas I can live my life, I can never die my death. Therefore, I, the I that is me, never truly dies, and the death that "befalls" me is something so completely "external" to me that it does not belong to me at all. In this sense, death is the "absolutely other" from me. It is something that is so "extraneous," even though it dwells within me, that it displaces all possibilities of thought thereby revealing the abysmal impotence of our thinking. Precisely because of such a profoundly and insurmountably paradoxical nature, death is even the *unthinkable* par excellence, the unconquerable "outside-all-categories" that undoes all categorizations.

It is here, though, in front of such a "black hole" where our reason collapses, on the edge of the unfathomable abyss, that another kind of view opens up.

Death can neither be regarded "in the third person"—that is, as an abstract modality of universalizing logic—nor can it be grasped "in the first person"—as I am never in front of my own death. If that is the case, then there remains only "the second person," only a "you" to whom "my" death may "belong" or be donated and who only may welcome and live the death of an "I." The "you" is the only one who, well beyond all abstract conceptual generalities, may grasp the absolute uniqueness of that specific life—my life—that the "you" has had in front of itself and with which it has lived its own life (perhaps even fragmentarily). From this side too, which is so closely adherent to the living substrate of reality, we are brought back to the crucial importance of accompanying, burying, and commemorating the dead.

The reason for this is that it is only "in front of the extreme," in front of death, that we become aware of "the profound gratuitousness and extraneousness of life—gratuitousness and extraneousness that would go unnoticed . . . if it were not, indeed, for death."[27] What ensues is a complete reversal of the understanding of ourselves and of things. Against a culture that, in the name of an alleged eternity, has accustomed us to see beings in the transfigured light of everlasting ideal essences—which it then can manipulate and destroy—here, we are offered another path: that of looking at things from the displacing margin of death.

The place where all consoling certainties of future or superior forms of transcendence shipwreck is also the site where an access to the true safeguarding of things and beings opens up. In no other place as the one where their fragile precariousness shines most extremely can we in fact come to the realization that their *"finitude is infinitely precious."*[28]

Translated from Italian by Silvia Benso

Notes

1. This metaphor has been used to indicate the impact provoked by major events whose probability cannot be predicted and whose consequences cannot be calculated. See Nassim Nicholas Taleb, *The Black Swan: The Impact of the Highly Improbable* (New York: Random House, 2007).

2. Giambattista Vico, *Principi di Scienza Nuova* (Naples: Muziana, 1774), 236.

3. Ugo Foscolo, "*Dei Sepolcri*," vv. 1–3 and 88–96. I am quoting from the translation contained in Valentina Bianchi, "Rediscovering Foscolo: A Translation of the 'Sepolcri' and of Three Sonnets" accessed online at https://www.academia.edu/22334674/REDISCOVERING_FOSCOLO_A_TRANSLATION_OF_THE_SEPOLCRI_AND_OF_THREE_SONNETS. The original Italian verses read: "All'ombra de' cipressi e dentro l'urne / Confortate di pianto è forse il sonno / Della morte men duro? / [. . .] Ahi! sugli estinti / Non sorge fiore ove non sia d'umane / Lodi onorato e d'amoroso pianto: / Dal dì che nozze e tribunali ed are / Dier alle umane belve esser pietose / Di sé stesse e d'altrui, toglieano i vivi / All'etere maligno ed alle fere / I miserandi avanzi che Natura / Con veci eterne a' sensi altri destina."

4. Many considerations, from all parts of the world, can be accessed at http://www.thomasproject.net/2020/03/14/coronavirus-map/.

5. See *Il bios dei filosofi. Dialogo a più voci sul tipo di vita preferibile*, ed. Fulvia De Luise (Trent: Università degli Studi di Trento, 2009).

6. See Henri Bergson, *Oeuvres* (Paris: Presse Universitaire de France, 1970), 1392, 1428–29.

7. For this terminology, see Gilles Deleuze and Felix Guattari, *Pour une littérature mineure* (Paris: Minuit, 1975).

8. On this specific point, fundamental is Michel Foucault, *The Order of Things: An Archeology of the Human Sciences* (New York: Random House, 1970); "The Discourse on Language," in *Archaelogy of Knowledge*, trans. A. M. Sheridan Smith (New York: Pantheon, 1972); and *The Birth of Biopolitics: Lectures at the Collège de France 1978–1979* (London: Picador, 2010). On this topic, see also Roberto Esposito, *Bios. Biopolitics and Philosophy*, trans. Timothy C. Campbell (Minneapolis: Minnesota University Press, 2008) and Laura Bazzicalupo, *Biopolitica. Una mappa concettuale* (Rome: Carocci, 2010).

9. The so-called vitalism of the vitalist School of Montpellier, which has greatly contributed to the birth of biology as an autonomous field of knowledge, starts during this historical period. Its theoretical tenets are the discontinuity between vital and inanimate phenomena; and the presence of a specific generative force, an "active principle" that cannot be brought back to inanimate matter as an explanation for the living being as nonpreformed transformation. Scholars such as Georges Cuvier and Xavier Bichat belong to the Montpellier school.

10. Xavier Bichat, *Recherches physiologiques sur la vie et la mort* (1800) (Paris: Masson, 1862), 43.

11. See Stefania Achella, *Pensare la vita. Saggio su Hegel* (Bologna: Il Mulino, 2020).

12. Gilles Deleuze, *Cinema 1: The Movement-Image*, trans. Hugh Tomlinson and Barbara Habberjam (Minneapolis: Minnesota University Press, 1997), 60.

13. See Enrica Lisciani-Petrini, "La vita e le forme. Uno scorcio sul pensiero italiano primonovecentesco," *Agalma* 38 (2019): 35–44.

14. This vitalist line of thinking reaches up to our period with Frédéric Worms, who has become the promoter of a "critical vitalism" attentive to the needs of our current age; see Frédéric Worms, *Pour un humanisme vital. Lettres sur la vie, la mort et le moment present* (Paris: Odile Jacob, 2019).

15. Georg Simmel, *The View of Life*, trans. John A. Y. Andrews and Donald N. Levine (Chicago: University of Chicago Press, 2010), 15.

16. See Vladimir Jankélévitch, "Deux philosophes de la vie: Bergson et Guyau," *Revue philosophique de la France et de l'étranger* 2 (1924): 402–49 and "Georg Simmel, philosophe de la vie," *Revue de Métaphysique et de Morale* 2–3 (1925): 213–57 and 373–86. For a comprehensive presentation of Jankélévitch's thought, see Enrica Lisciani-Petrini, *Charis. Essai sur Jankélévitch* (Paris-Milan: Vrin-Mimesis, 2013).

17. Vladimir Jankélévitch, *Quelque part dans l'inachevé* (Paris: Gallimard, 1978), 178–80.

18. Sigmund Freud, *Beyond the Pleasure Principle*, trans. James Strachey (New York: Bantham Books, 1959), 22.

19. Freud, *Beyond the Pleasure Principle*, 67–68.
20. Freud, *Beyond the Pleasure Principle*, 70.
21. Freud, *Beyond the Pleasure Principle*, 70.
22. Freud, *Beyond the Pleasure Principle*, 71.
23. Freud, *Beyond the Pleasure Principle*, 72; italics added.
24. See Esposito, *Bios* and Roberto Esposito, *Immunitas: The Protection and Negation of Life*, trans. Zakiya Hanafi (Cambridge: Polity Press, 2011).
25. On the relation between life and institution, already at the biological level, see Maurice Merleau-Ponty, *L'institution, la passivité. Notes de cours au Collège de France (1954–1955)* (Paris: Belin, 2015).
26. Martin Heidegger, *Being and Time*, trans. John Macquarrie and Edward Robinson (San Francisco: Harper & Row, 1962), 307.
27. Vladimir Jankélévitch, *La Mort* (Paris: Flammarion, 1977), 454.
28. Jankélévitch, *La Mort*, 463.

Twelve

What Finitude Does Not Say
Rethinking Life beyond Nihilism

Roberto Mancini

Beyond Nihilism

Within the context of Western philosophy, especially starting with Heidegger, the category of finitude (*Endlichkeit*) has been regarded as particularly crucial and compelling. Such a category has been interpreted in various ways. The underlying presupposition, however, has always been that, for us, life is the arc of experiences that begin with birth and end with death. Finitude appears as a category that says what is essential. Everything that one can articulate within philosophy seems to be a set of variations internal to the perimeter circumscribed by this notion.

In the time marked by the attack on humanity by the Covid-19 virus, such precomprehension has been reinforced. Life is constantly subject to the threats of disease, suffering, and death. Thus, one can, at most, hope to survive as best as possible and as long as possible until our enemy's final victory. People often argue that death is not really an enemy but rather a natural given, which we would be wise to accept. In this perspective, we look at life as temporary guests, who have a residence permit eventually due to expire. When we try to consider universal life, nowadays we rely purely on the natural sciences. Philosophy, and especially metaphysics, seems to be unsuitable to say anything that is not abstract and rhetorical.

In actuality, it is we who end up being "abstract" when we are compared, on the one hand, with the concrete processes of universal life and, on the other, with the inexorable power of death. We are marginal, ephemeral. We are a detail in the universe. What is thereby consolidated is the perception of a structural gap between universal life and our own life. The result is that the philosophies of finitude end up considering death as the truth of life itself and read all experiences in terms of life consumption. Caducity and mortality become the implicit or explicit coordinates within which one is to interpret all situations. The global Covid-19 pandemic pushes us to be even more vigilant as death can arrive invisibly and simultaneously for a large number of human beings.

From this perspective, the hermeneutics of finitude that are typical of contemporary thinking simply take to its logical consequences a sentiment of radical distrust that underlies the entire Western philosophical tradition. I am referring to the conviction according to which, more than an irreversible gift coming from a mysterious origin, life is a sort of loan for which we have to pay dearly. The Italian expression that speaks of the *usura del tempo*, literally the "wear of time" (but *usura* also refers to money borrowed at an exorbitant interest), exemplifies well the idea that, with birth, we contract a loan that we need to pay back with high interests in terms of anxiety, suffering, and despair. According to some Christian theology, for example, even the Son of God, Jesus Christ, had to pay a very high price in order to gain salvation not for the entire humanity, but only for those few who will not be condemned at the end of times.

The belief in the annihilation of life has been a guiding thread for a long time and has been modulated in various ways in the different periods of Western philosophy. In most of Greek thought, life appears not as a gift but rather as a dereliction. Aristotle sanctions the insurmountable fact of the extinction of our being. Christian thought should have brought in the idea of a saved life. This happened, however, in such a selective and meritocratic manner that the announcement of salvation has been experienced more with anxiety than with hope. Not only are all human beings marked by a hereditary original sin, but few will receive final salvation by the inscrutable divine sovereignty. All the others will find peace not even in death, as they will be subjected to the eternal sufferings of hell.

The Lutheran Reformation introduces the theory of predestination. On its basis, one may wonder whether we are already lost regardless of what we do in our lives. Modern thought, tired of such forms of subjection, sets the topic increasingly aside and replaces the reference to salvation with the notion of progress or, in Hegel's case, with the idea of reconciliation (*Versöhnung*) according to which the real life is only the life of Spirit, not ours.

When we take into account this evolution of the dialectics of anxiety and hope in the history of Western consciousness, we immediately realize that what the various hermeneutics of finitude do is simply to weaken the expectations for transcendence of the finite and recall human beings to a head-on confrontation with the limits looming over them. The ungrounded mythology of the economic culture of globalization, which pursues the fantasy of unlimited growth on a planet with finite resources,[1] is the most recent expression of the neurotic need to compensate for the deep persuasion regarding what is deemed as the elementary truth of life: that for living beings, there is no salvation.

In the vocabulary of classical metaphysics, one could say: nothingness tailgates being and, in the end, absorbs being within itself. The metaphysical scandal par excellence is then not nihilism but, rather, faith in the possibility of a saved life; that is, faith in salvation understood as universal and final liberation from all evils, including death. This is the leading thread of an unsuspectedly nihilist precomprehension of life that underlies many philosophies in all periods of the Western tradition, including those that, at least verbally, criticize nihilism.[2] Criticisms always move against forms of relative nihilism (radical relativism, the denial of values, atheism), but they hardly scratch the paradox of this latent transcendental nihilism. It is sufficient to recall, for example, that within the culture to which we have been accustomed for thousands of years, the idea of victory that is celebrated refers historically not to victory over death, but to victories of death, to deadly victories, that is, victories where some individuals are eliminated. According to Pier Paolo Pasolini, this form of nihilism misrecognizes that "what is insignificant, *is*"; rather, "it has as fundamental proposition that 'which is, *is insignificant.*'"[3] Those who consider everything from this point of view take for granted the plausibility of the notion of finitude.

Life and Living Beings

Finitude as the recapitulating philosophical category, however, *does not say the essential* of life as it is experienced by humans. First of all, it does not account either for the experiences of transcending mere life consumption or for the actual values that we can acknowledge. Even if we die, we are still capable of acts of freedom, creativity, love, and knowledge that go beyond the temporal dimension in which they occur. This shows that we can renew and transfigure life, thereby elevating it beyond the measure imposed on it by death. Death is a universal and unavoidable fact; yet it cannot aspire to posit itself as the very meaning of existence. Believing in death is a profession of nihilism; it is not an act of philosophical discernment.

The alliance among generations and all expressions of human creativity produce outcomes that have resisting endurance. As Ernst Bloch writes, death "is not and *per definitionem* cannot be anyone's true death (for our space is always life, or something more, but not what is less than life)."[4] A product of the nihilistic precomprehension of life is also the misrecognition of *living values*. Living values are those that are embodied in people, in relations, in nature. When we tie ourselves to one of these values, especially with regard to interpersonal relations, its death does not mark the cancellation of the meaningful presence of such a being; the reason for that is that we have interiorized our relation with such a living value. And we do not accept that death puts an end to the value and meaning of the life of a deceased person who has been dear to us. The simple experiment of contemplating the face of a beloved is enough to grasp how unconditional that person's value is.

Only a nihilist society and culture, in their economistic obsession, can think that real values are exclusively use-value (that is, the usefulness of an object) and exchange-value (that is, money). Persons, relations, nature, works of art, and ideals of truth, goodness, beauty, justice, and freedom certainly are neither use values nor, even less, exchange values. Phenomenological attention to forms of experience and of elaboration of finitude should imply, on our side, both listening to living beings' aspiration to self-elevation above mere mortality and recognizing the opening that characterizes their being. Finitude is not a delimited and self-sufficient space. Finitude is a *relation* with that which grounds and surpasses finitude itself. As Hegel remarks, the absolutization of finitude is as illegitimate as the rhetorical evocation of an infinite taken to be demonstrable.[5]

A philosophical program invested in rethinking life should thus overcome the habit of conceiving of the relation between life and living beings always and only through the model of contraposition. The new path instead brings us to think of this relation in terms of the mutual implications of the one—life—with the others—the living being. This relation of possible convergence becomes evident if we keep in mind that, biologically, life is caught in the parabola between birth and death; yet life carries within itself the drive toward forms of success and harmony that do not coincide either with death or with the end. Life is a reality that is not only biological but also metaphysical, that is, entrenched in the mystery of its own origin and destination, and thus rooted in the immemorial past and the unforeseeable future.

Because of its being open to the beyond, life has borders that are not boundaries, but thresholds. This opening is clearly manifested in human beings' modes of existing. All of us can see that there are individuals who live so closed up within themselves that they are already dead even while they are still alive. On the contrary, there are individuals who are so generative and passionate that, even after their death, they continue to nourish our lives.

Philosophy must give an account of this complexity. It cannot get by simply by evoking finitude as the explanation for everything. Much more honest and promising is the program of a new inquiry into the borders of life—borders to be understood not simply chronologically or biologically but rather in terms of the question of the source of meaning of life and even of its possible fulfillment. What this program also requires is, to my mind, an in-depth exploration of the questions of origin and of salvation.

The Philosophical Memory of Birth

When, where, and from whom did life begin? The development of life can be retraced by science up to its earliest stages. Yet the origin of life in itself remains a mystery. For this reason, religions and philosophies try to provide an interpretation of it within the frame of a legitimate pluralism. What is rarely the topic of reflection, though, is the fact that living beings experience the relation with the origin by passing through the experience of birth. Thus, for all living beings, the beginning of life can be understood as a relation between *origin and birth*. In particular, for a human being, the experience of being born implies, together with the relation with the woman who carries him or her in her womb, a progressive participation in the relation with the metaphysical origin of our existence.

Two conceptual alternatives find their rooting in the comprehension of the meaning of the origin: one is a conception that emphasizes the power to make something be, and the other is a conception that highlights relationality. Most of the Western metaphysical tradition addresses the question of the beginning and the origin along the first line of research and adopts the method of the logical elaboration of the most general categories and of reflective abstraction as the tool to penetrate the reality of the absolute. This logical game takes up ontological value and gives access to a systematic explanation regarding the identity of the origin.

The conviction has been that through the method of pure abstraction, one could explain origin and reality by following the indications that emerge from rigorous logical argumentation, in the belief that the categories of thought can mirror them both. There has been no patience for keeping together the unfolding of the dynamics of meanings and the development of the dynamics of experiential givens. Keeping these two dynamics together would instead allow us to cultivate a concrete understanding of life, where reflection and contact with reality can join rather than exclude each other.

An essential consequence of the method of abstraction has emerged in the habit of thinking of the relation between the origin and the human or, more broadly, between the infinite and the finite in terms of systematic contraposition. Yet when one restores the link between concepts and experience, as well as between the origin and what has originated from it, then one realizes that there is no reason to conceive of the origin as if it were at the antipodes of our life condition. The irreducibility of the origin to what is human does not at all imply blocking out its relationality. The whole matter lies, rather, in grasping what kind of concrete link exists between us, life, and the origin.

If we acknowledge this relation as an indirect source of discovery and comprehension of the meaning of the origin of life itself—given that the meaning of the origin is implied in life—a different path opens up. Such a path is an alternative both to naïve, positive anthropomorphism, which projects onto the origin typical features of our own being, and to reactive, negative anthropomorphism, which claims that it can grasp the absolute by eliminating all aspects having to do with us.

Some paths in contemporary metaphysical anthropology offer an important contribution to a rethinking of life. These perspectives are in fact capable of approaching the meaning of the origin of life by putting down the claim to objectify life in pure abstraction and deepening instead the suggestions that emerge from the study of the relationality that connects the origin to living beings. I am referring here to those conceptions that delineate an anthropology of the subject in terms of birth (nascent being) and therefore offer an alternative perspective to the tradition of anthropology focused on the subject as a lacking being (Mängelwesen).[6] The philosophical memory of birth enables us to understand that there is an originary generative power that does not simply aim at dissolving into nothingness that to which it has given birth and life.

According to Hannah Arendt, human abilities are rooted in everyone's birth, which is the true and real event of freedom. When a child is born to life, the face of the Earth and the entire human community are renewed by this birth. The reason is that what comes to existence is a unique subject, irreducible to what already is; it is a being that is, in itself, freedom. Freedom is the ability to inaugurate a still unknown reality, generating a *novum* in society and in history. Birth, to be born means to be this novelty, which launches a creativity that is, in turn, also generative.

To be born also enables other acts of birth. By acting, human subjects make social relations, situations, and dynamics become generative too.

This is in opposition to the inertia of the natural course of things and to violence, which tends instead to destroy the human and natural world. Arendt writes that "the miracle that saves the world, the realm of human affairs, from its normal, 'natural' ruin is ultimately the fact of natality, in which the faculty of action is ontologically rooted."[7] Arendt delineates an anthropology where the opening to the eternal is constitutive of the human: "Men, though they must die, are not born in order to die but in order to begin."[8]

According to María Zambrano, birth is the existential dynamism that expresses our dignity and coincides with the success of our life. To be born is a carnal and concrete experience of the origin, even though the origin remains mysterious. Entry into life requires an acceptance of "the wound in one's being,"[9] that is, one's detachment from the mother and the separation from the origin. What matters for us, though, is to unfold biological birth into existential birth, which consists in realizing the uniqueness of the individual and thus succeeding in being fully oneself. This freedom to be actualizes itself in an existence where one feels confirmed in one's dignity and gratuitousness, where one willingly accepts one's being as living gift even though the origin of the gift remains mysterious. In this perspective, to fulfill one's birth amounts to leaning beyond, to transcending one's subjection to evil (*male*), thereby coming to develop a personal adhesion to the relation with the truth.

As we look deeper into the possible meaning of being born, Luce Irigaray's contribution offers various important indications concerning the link between existential birth and the spiritual elevation of men's and women's natural condition. Irigaray stresses how a constant spur in everyone's path of life is the fact of being able to discover the mystery of one's origin. When we are born to the world, the beginning actually coincides with a separation. The detachment from the maternal body means that being in the world corresponds to being isolated. Even though relation and alterity are constitutive of one's person, to the point that each of us is the embodiment of an act of love—at least at the physical level—nevertheless each of us must exist starting from ourselves. She writes, "Our existence cannot be the outcome of a mere chance, and our will to live clearly manifested itself at the time of our birth."[10]

The experience of being born begins with the acceptance of oneself as being in separation and of separation as being within oneself; that is, it begins with the awareness of one's being separated. This is an essential passage, because if we accept our condition of separation, we will not treat the other as an object that must fill the void in which we find ourselves. On the contrary, what will be freed in this way is our desire to go toward the other with respect for the other's alterity. Listening to the meaning of desire attests our transcendence of, but also our rootedness in our own origin and it opens us to the other's transcendence: "To desire means longing for uniting a bodily conjunction with what transcends us, for uniting here and now with a beyond, within ourselves and between us."[11] The metaphysical implications of this phenomenology of existential birth emerge when we realize that the origin of life is to be sought in the intimacy of the flesh, in ourselves and our relations with all forms of alterity, and not in abstraction.

Overall, the paradigm of birth moves us in the direction of a radical rethinking of the metaphysical, and hence metabiological, status of life. We do not come from nothing. In our existential being-born, we partake of the relation with the origin, regardless of how we qualify it. This solicits an acknowledgment of the meaning of our being-in-the-world beyond the limitation of death, which therefore appears more as an interruption than as a fair fulfillment. The habit of delegating the question of the origin either to religion or to science interrupts the aspiration, which belongs to philosophical research, to understand the meaning of things in the light of truth. Rethinking life in its relation with the origin is an unavoidable task for twenty-first-century philosophy. A similar and related task is that of rethinking in what ways there may be, for us, a saved life.

The Ethics of Salvation in the Age of the Contagion

Does critical reason truly need to eliminate the very idea of a complete and universal liberation from all evils (*male*)? Is what the aspirations of human consciousness have always evoked under the term "salvation" so unreal as not to warrant any examination? Is it not true that, nevertheless, we do indeed have experiences of salvation?

A small opening appears when we start to differentiate the various stratifications of this concept. Despite the prejudice for that salvation is by definition only eschatological, based on divine initiative, there exist in truth other meanings of salvation that correspond to related experiences accessible to anyone, regardless of whether they have religious faith.

We use the term "salvation," first of all, to refer to *physical salvation*, when we escape a lethal danger. The use is here partly inappropriate because, in this context, the matter is simply one of survival. Yet the use indicates some kind of resistance to death. More congruent is the concept of *interior salvation*, legitimately used to indicate the preservation of the integrity of an individual's conscience despite possible pressures exerted by the external environment toward the dehumanization or alienation of the individual in question. Additionally, we speak of *existential salvation*, which consists in succeeding in escaping meaningless existence. Even if death were the end of everything, a life might still be deemed "saved" if it had meaning and brought something to others. Many authors, such as Emmanuel Levinas,[12] highlight also the notion of *ethical salvation*. This refers to the fact that by helping someone who is in danger, we save such an individual from the evil that might sweep that person away. Within the context of intersubjective relationships, the experience of saving someone or needing to be saved is a daily recurrence, which can be misrecognized only by a conscience steeped in banality.[13]

At the two extremes of this semantic field, we have physical and eschatological salvation; at the center, though, the meanings of interior, existential, ethical, and historical salvation have emerged. Philosophy must ponder on these. In this way, philosophy can be reminded of the fact that life assumes meaning on the grounds of the quality of one's response to life itself. To live means to take up the responsibility of welcoming life, of transforming it in such a way as to honor its value and share it. What unexpectedly begins to emerge here is an *ethics of salvation* that demands that we exist with critical consciousness, responsibility, and creativity. It also requires that we progress beyond the egocentric regression that leads us to say "Me first!" or "Us first!" Life is, actually, togetherness. It is the community of living beings. Only those who keep this in mind are capable of opening spaces of salvation, that is, experiences of liberation from evil and suffering *male*.

How can we not see evidence of this when confronted with the aggression of the Covid-19 pandemic? The lesson from this global health emergency teaches us that the lethal mistake, whose consequences we are paying for, is to ground the existence of oneself as an individual, of families, of nations, and of the global society on egocentrism. Ultimately, egocentrism is even too easy a target, though, and risks remaining an unexplained word. Egocentrism is the final effect of a deeper distortion. Its root is anxiety toward death, the nihilism that belongs to a spirit that is scandalized by the vulnerability of life. One who surrenders to this anxiety starts living with a closed, self-referential attitude, without understanding that such an attitude is the real cause of irremediable precariousness and mortality. Life is such that, when one self-isolates, one's existence implodes and resembles an experience of death even prior to one's passing. The contrary is the case for the one who is dedicated to cultivating the life of others. Even when such a person dies, such an individual lives on in the shared good and in the existence of those who sustain themselves on that person's dedication. The access to this form of eternity is not a surrogate for those who do not believe in God. On the contrary, it is the discovery of the true texture of life. This ethical passage holds true also for those who do have religious faith.

The aggression of Covid-19 should teach us to rethink life by overcoming the dogmas that so far have prevented us from understanding life's meaning and value. Jared Diamond has studied the recurrent causes of past societies' extinctions. He has found that the reasons are always two: devastation of the natural environment and inability to develop a new way of thinking when confronted with a new challenge.[14] These are the mistakes that weigh on us today. If we wish not to end up like the societies that went extinct many centuries ago—and the difference is that, this time, no one would be saved—we must develop an authentic culture of salvation. To this goal, we must tear down the seven dogmas that currently are still the pillars of our necrophiliac society.

The first dogma is the primacy of capital over living beings. We must begin again with the United Nations' Declaration and the commitment to an integral democracy, where all people can live with dignity. It is absurd to go on subjecting ourselves to an economic model that only cares for money accumulation, trespasses the rights of humanity, and destroys natural balances. At the same time, we must stop thinking of ourselves as the masters and dominators of other nonhuman living beings (which are, in fact, oftentimes more humane than we are). What must surface is a society based on social justice and alliance with nature—the only society that can preserve the future.

The second dogma is the primacy of the West on other cultures and peoples. Europeans and North Americans must rediscover the better core of their traditions (which has been swept away by technocratic capitalism), learn from the better cores of other cultures, and collaborate in the spirit of chorality—all sing together while, at the same time, each voice remains distinguishable.

The third dogma is the primacy of nations over humanity. We must rid ourselves of all nationalisms and racisms as life is a universal relation tending toward community. Isolation and segregation are dynamics of death. There is salvation only in a form of solidarity that does not exclude anyone.

The fourth dogma is the patriarchal primacy over women. Male domination continues to mortify the entirety of humanity at the same time as it vilifies women, and it impedes the flourishing of all vital relations.

The fifth dogma is the primacy of the older over the younger generation. The adult world (especially the adults who are in power) continues to sacrifice younger generations. Currently, we must support the younger's peaceful rebellion and make room for their initiatives in order to build a society where no one is penalized because of age. This is the only way to ensure that any season of life may be lived with dignity.

The sixth dogma is the primacy of violence over dialogue, solidarity, and nonviolence. We must recover from the tenacious superstition regarding the allegedly greater efficaciousness and indispensability of violent manners. Due to this deadly prejudice, war has remained the first human institution. The experience of Gandhi and of various other struggles around the world have shown us that political action produces outcomes only through nonviolent conflicts and the capacity of caring for society without causing victims.

The seventh and last dogma is the primacy of ignorance over knowledge. The arrogance of those who manage world power is often on par only with their ignorance. We can no longer allow narcissism and ambition to be the principal motivations of those who are candidates for public roles. We can live well only if we develop awareness through authentic knowledge, which is always inspired ethically.

For the reasons I have highlighted in this reflection, I think that the task of rethinking life may be actualized only if, at the same time, we are willing to transform our way of existing. The transformation will have to mark the passage from nihilism to the spirituality of shared life, learning no longer to oppose responsibility with freedom, justice with individual initiative, and living beings with universal life.

Translated from Italian by Silvia Benso

Notes

1. See Serge Latouche, *Farewell to Growth*, trans. David Macey (Cambridge-Boston: Polity Press, 2010).

2. For a critique of nihilism in the nuclear age, see Karl Jaspers, *The Atom Bomb and the Future of Man*, trans. E. B. Ashton (Chicago: University of Chicago Press, 1964). See also M. A. Gillespie, *Nihilism before Nietzsche* (Chicago: University of Chicago Press, 1994) and Karl Löwith, *Martin Heidegger and European Nihilism*, trans. Gary Steiner (New York: Columbia University Press, 1998).

3. Pier Paolo Pasolini, *Heretical Empiricism*, trans. Ben Lawton and Louise K. Barnett (Washington: New Academia Publishing, 2005), 243.

4. Ernst Bloch, *Traces*, trans. Anthony Nassar (Stanford: Stanford University Press, 2006), 30.

5. See Georg Wilhelm Friedrich Hegel, *The Science of Logic*, trans. George Di Giovanni (Cambridge: Cambridge University Press, 2010), vol. 1, 101–103.

6. See Arnold Gehlen, *Man: His Nature and His Place in the World* (New York: Columbia University Press, 1988).

7. Hannah Arendt, *The Human Condition* (Chicago: University of Chicago Press, 1958), 247.

8. Arendt, *The Human Condition*, 246.

9. María Zambrano, *Delirium and Destiny: A Spaniard in Her Twenties*, trans. Carol Maier (Albany: State University of New York Press, 1999), 7.

10. See Luce Irigaray, *To Be Born: Genesis of a New Human Being* (London: Palgrave Macmillan, 2017), 1.

11. Irigaray, *To Be Born*, 75.

12. See David F. Ford, *Self and Salvation: Being Transformed* (Cambridge: Cambridge University Press, 1999), 90–105.

13. See Hannah Arendt, *Eichmann in Jerusalem: A Report on the Banality of Evil* (New York: Viking Press, 1963).

14. See Jared Diamond, *Collapse: How Societies Choose to Fail or Succeed* (London: Penguin Books, 2005), 486–525.

Thirteen

Writing Life

Biography, Autobiography, and the Remainder

Claudia Baracchi

Stage

How is one to attempt any remarks on life? How is one to venture a first word on what is always already first? In recent years, within diverse philosophical circles, intense debates have developed around life. Yet its mystery abides closed, uncircumscribed—despite its evidence, its indestructible unfolding around and across us. Not even scientific research has succeeded, up until now, in providing an uncontroversial definition of it. The consequence is that crucial issues remain undecidable (for example, whether viruses, or viroids, are living organisms or not) and, with them, the line of demarcation between living and nonliving. We are thus in the realm of storytelling, of myth, and of metaphoric discourse.[1] And metaphors are discourses that overwhelm us, always transport (*pherein*) us beyond (*meta*), and wander uncontrollably, exerting irresistible power.

One might begin by acknowledging two things. First, the locution "the discourse of life" tends to convey a subjective genitive. Discourse, *logos*, belongs to life. In all senses, it is owned by life. In Aristotle's formula of the human being as *zoon logon echon*, the intimation is that the living being holds *logos* within itself, that *logos* inheres in the living being. *Logos* is carried by life—like a graft, an interpolation. Any discourse that thematizes life can be said to be "on life" quite literally, as if riding on the back of an animal. Discourse moves out of that animal movement, in that living transport that is, at once, elation and rapture. Recall the pawing horse through which, in the *Phaedrus*, Plato images impulsive, desirous life. Or think of the mosaic from Pella, the old Macedonian city: a rampant panther carrying Dionysus on its back, naked and languidly reclining. Even the god belongs in that motion without dominating it, although, to be sure, he appears less apprehensive than a mortal probably would.

The second thing to be acknowledged is that, indeterminately prior to our exposing life in words, it is life that exposes itself—saying, writing itself, carving its graphemes on the skin of the world. It is life that, in unfolding its course, conveys its discourse (*discorrere*). Well before any story we may tell, life has always already told its own story, has always already articulated itself in its forms and transformations, in its actions and vicissitudes. Life moves through living beings, lives in them, uses them up. One might then, perhaps, grasp something about life in the tales of the living, in their stories, in the twists and turns of their ventures.

Such peripeteias are, in and of themselves, a kind of writing, systems of signs. The passing of life across living beings writes. Have we grasped the deep syntax of this language? It has carved the lineaments of the world and engraved its otherwise hard surfaces since immemorial time, ever since the absolute prehistory of planetary events. And even if we were to narrow the field and shift from such a geo-astrophysical vertigo to a focus on the experience of mortal individuals, we may perhaps still perceive our own living in linguistic terms, as a text. Whatever "we" and "our" may mean (and this is the issue), we may think of our acting, of our motions and behaviors in the course of our existence as writing of the world, in the world, as writing (on) the page that the world is. The choreographies that we draw step by step, our paths, and our gestures cut through the world and leave a mark. In the singularity, in the minutiae of every living mortal, life takes shape, takes its shapes. From ineffable invisibility, it yields to vision, at least in part. It gives itself a face, takes on an appearance.

It looks as if the realm of life is theater—the place of vision where it is possible to witness acts, actions performed by actors, on the stage.[2] Life unfolds on stage, on a stage as broad as the world. Yet what is at stake in the transition from writing actions on the page of the world, from writing as action, drawing our course across the world, to the writing made of linear swirls on paper or on screen? How do we bring the life on stage, the part we play, to words on paper or on any other more or less material support? How do we gather and transcribe actions, happenings, events that make up a life, whether my own or someone else's?

There are indeed things that can be seen, that can be observed while they unfold, even though always in a finite, perspectival manner. Yet we also sense the evasiveness of certain issues. For example, who is the one who writes, who composes the work that we call biography or autobiography (in both cases, it is a matter of listening to the other)? Who, what animates the hand that writes? Who is the storyteller, whether myself or another or both? Who is written? We are immediately faced with serious difficulties—we contemplate the implausibility of writing life. Upon careful consideration, what strikes us is what slips away, what eludes us, what seems not to enter the stage—the backstage of life.

Clandestine

In his short film *Critique de la séparation* (1961), Guy Debord evokes "the clandestinity of private life," which is unrepresentable, "intransmissible" because, with regard to it, we possess nothing but documents that are "laughable [*derisoires*]" in their insufficiency.[3] Recalling this piece, Giorgio Agamben situates what he calls the "incommunicable, almost ridiculous clandestinity of private life" within the dichotomous logic established by the "medical or philosophico-theological or biopolitical machine."[4] To private life Agamben associates biological life, its physiology, its metabolic functions from nutrition to excretion, as well as the attempts at recounting it.[5] He then sets it in sharp contrast to public discourse and its sovereign, ordering power.

Consequently, Agamben considers with curiosity, almost with amicable condescension, the fact that Debord returns multiple times and "apparently without shame" to biographical and autobiographical narration, even when he understands the insufficiency of it.[6] As if, despite everything, "there was, in [Debord's] own existence or in that of his friends, something unique and exemplary, which demanded to be recorded and communicated."[7]

In fact, it seems to be so. In Debord's words, it is documents (and not the "clandestinity of private life," as Agamben says) that, due to their inadequacy, are laughable. And, no matter how laughable, even documents are not banal.

Agamben's decisive preoccupation regards releasing life from the discursive, conceptual, and operational apparatus of biopolitics so that bare life may not be impoverished, deprived of world, of manifestation, of discourse. Yet discourse (account, narration, symbolization) does not necessarily reduce life, does not necessarily contain or confine its overflowing. Indeed, following life, its trajectories, and writing its singular stories may let life transpire precisely as it furtively follows us, finding protection in us, without documents. The unfolding of discourse, in its shortcomings, allows for the possibility of the experience of an excess of life that cannot possibly be spoken, of an intensity from which we even have to protect ourselves (for we seldom, if ever, encounter it).

So perhaps, far from remaining implicated in (and complicitous with) the logic of biopolitics, and precisely by virtue of their insufficiency, the attempts at documenting life, at biographic or autobiographic writing may be seen as initiating a destitution of biopolitical control and unsettling its strategic dichotomies (public life vs. bare life, politics vs. animality, *bios* vs. *zoe* . . .). Because they are incapable of grasping elusive life at the very moment they undertake to say it, because they are destined to document their own impotence, the documents of life may, not unlike relics, be reminders of the immensity of life, begin to disclose the private life of mortals as other than deprived of world, the animal as other than deprived of political life.

These documental efforts could be seen as documentations of the fact of life (*to hoti*, the disarming evidence of the given, as the ancient Greeks would put it), even as we do not know *what* it is. We stand out, in the lack of definitions. We stand outside definitions, in the open of existence. Despite its improbability, because it is improbable, the attempt at writing life constitutes a nascent disclosing of the question of life as such—a disclosure of life as enigmatic and unbound.

Credits

In 1972 (a time when the subject and its sovereign integrity are under full challenge), Jacques Derrida writes: "I say *I* [*je dis* moi], I say that to myself because everything I write, as one can tell very quickly, is terribly autobiographic. Incorrigibly so."[8] Beyond any ideological slogan, and only apparently against himself, Derrida affirms that discourse is rooted in life, in *this* life—this one singular life, me. *Logos* is not, and has never been, one. It has always been disseminated in an infinite multitude of languages, idioms, declensions that are so radically singular as to call into question signature, author, and various institutions of writing and intellectual property. This rootedness in life, however, is not an answer but rather the formulation of the most obstinate, arduous, and profound problem. That is, "*Who* thinks? Who signs? What do we make of singularity in this experience of thought? And what do we make of the relation between life, death, and *psyche?*"[9] As Italo Calvino noted, "every line presupposes a pen that draws it, and every pen presupposes a hand that holds it. What is behind the hand is a controversial question: the drawing I ends up coinciding with the I that is drawn, not a subject but rather an object of drawing."[10] There is a hole at the center of the story. The texture of the text is torn apart. Diction and knowledge, of oneself as well as of any other, make up a desperate project.

The project seems desperate not so much or not only because it is impossible (which it is) but also, markedly, in its affect. Far from abstractly epistemological considerations, which are indeed a consequence, what is here at stake in the first place is the desperately vital experience of recognition, without which life becomes basically unbearable. In the 1976 lecture "Otobiographies," Derrida analyzes the first paragraph of the preface of Nietzsche's *Ecce Homo*.[11] As his contemporaries deny him credit, Nietzsche finds himself giving his very self an advance payment, forced to stipulate a debt with himself in order to receive that on which he can live. *Ecce Homo* is this operation:

> Seeing that before long I must confront humanity with the most difficult demand that has ever been made of it, it seems indispensable to me to say *who I am*. Really, one should know it, for I have not left myself "without testimony." But the disproportion between the greatness of my task and the *smallness* of my contemporaries has found expression in the fact that one has neither heard nor even seen me. I live on my own credit; it is perhaps a mere prejudice that I live . . . I need only speak with one of the "educated" who come to Upper Engadine in the summer, and I am convinced that I do *not* live . . . Under these circumstances I have a duty against which my habits, even more the pride of my instincts, revolt at bottom—namely, to say: *Hear me! For I am such and such. Above all, do not mistake me for someone else* [Verwechselt mich vor Allem nicht!].

Nietzsche advances a credit to himself by gathering his own story and writing himself, writing his own life and books—writing himself to and for himself.

Nietzsche's debt with himself can only be paid back by the other, by the other's attention and listening: as my contemporaries do not know *who* I am, as they have not heard my scream, they have not written my story, I must do that myself. As the educated vacationer in Engadine does not pay any credit to me, I must give myself such credit. I, that is, the other than myself who, in myself, listens to me, and writes (of) me. The other's recognition, at the limit the recognition of the other that I myself am—this is the only thing that can dissipate the impression that my being here, alive, is merely a prejudice, a sort of dogmatic as well as ungrounded belief.

And yet, despite everything, it happens. The writing of life happens, the fabric of the text is woven. Certainly, there is no lack of lacerations and desperate deficiencies. Yet the one *who* writes, *who* weaves, keeps doing it, even and precisely in the continuous dissipation of oneself. For while persevering in this exercise, the one who (due to the void, to the questioning one harbors within oneself) does not know how to carry on, nevertheless still carries on. As in Samuel Beckett: "I can't go on. I'll go on."[12] Or as in Penelope's plot, with her permanently open construction site—nighttime deconstruction, daily repetition and variation.

It happens, and the action holds. Writing articulates. Even without certainties regarding who, or what, is at the center of the stage. Or is hiding behind it all. One writes. One weaves. And, little by little, the gaze broadens, deepens. Hearing becomes sharper. All perceptions become more finely attuned. In a field that appeared desolate and unstructured, languages start to emerge, speak, converse with one another, and intertwine—rhizomatic connections of words, writings, sounds, images, and matter configurations. Something lets itself be grasped, gathered, known, pursued. Something. Not nothing.

In some way, thus, life is said and says itself. It is written and writes itself. Sometimes it gets canceled, and then it gets rewritten. Never entirely, never fully translated into discourse. Never fully symbolized—a writing in a dotted outline, evanescent, yet *not* nothing. After all, it might be possible (this is what Nietzsche desperately shows) to say "I" without thereby invoking a sovereign subject.

Psyche

Life moves as clandestine in this world of phenomena. It flows subterranean, furtively traversing the surface of appearances (stories, masks, clothes, covers, shifting guises). It crosses borders, transgresses, passes from a physiognomy to the next, without belonging to any. A fugitive. Fugitive life. At once *bios* and *zoe*.

One of the names of life is *psyche*. The task (*ergon*) of *psyche* is to live (*zen*), according to Plato in the *Republic*. In the most elementary sense, life is the work of *psyche*—*psyche* in act.[13] This distinguishes a living (animated, *empsychon*) from an inert body. Even intellectual, reflective functions (and hence the entire architectonics of character and existential deportment, of *bios*) are rooted in corporeal metabolism, that is, in the living, the animal.

The fact of life is so evasive, so ungraspable that the entire articulation of Plato's dialogue attests, time after time, its unspeakability and enduring mystery. Or, when Plato does speak about it, he does so as if in a dream. First, he stipulates the isomorphism *psyche-polis*, given that *psyche* is inaccessible and one can try to understand it only by turning to the visibility of shared (communal, public) life. From the visible dynamics of individual and collective acting, *polis*, one may then imaginatively seize life's invisible and silent structures, *psyche*. That is, one may imagine that the invisible manifests itself in visible acting. This is a daring, indeed reckless turn, for Plato (Socrates) says he can say nothing of the invisible as such. Yet he attempts some definition of it by transposing it into the visible. To be able to fathom some feature of the invisible, he conjectures that it is not radically discontinuous with respect to the visible; that it may even be in perfect continuity with the visible, only written in somewhat smaller characters, so that it is not legible. Reading the larger characters one can thus return to the initial ones—via proportion or poetic simile.[14] *Psyche* is nothing except a hypothesis or a supposition, as Lacan once said.

It would seem, then, that life (*psyche*) is what we do, acts carved on the stage of the world. The rest eludes us, so much so that, at the end of the dialogue, in the myth that narrates how, after a passage through death, the *psychai* are called to choose once again in what guise they will reenter the life cycle, Plato has Socrates say that "an ordering of the soul was not in them, due to the necessity that a soul become different according to the life it chooses."[15] In this sense, to live would be to manifest oneself in action. The transit of existence would be such a standing out, such a brief hesitation in the exteriority of the world, in one's exposedness and visibility, before fading away. Existence is *ek-stasis*, an unstoppable reaching out. And this is also, always already, a mask. This is the form, these are the forms that *psyche*, life, takes up. And this is, more or less, the measure of life's knowability.[16]

Anonymity

Agamben too, toward the end of *The Use of Bodies*, encounters the myth concluding Plato's *Republic*. A close reading of his interpretation exceeds the reflection outlined here, particularly because this encounter engenders more than one perplexity and would deserve a sustained engagement.[17] But, leaving aside the destiny of Plato's text in Agamben's work,[18] let it simply be underlined that the myth is especially remarkable for the visionary clarity with which it stages the impersonality of *psyche*, its passing through different lives, different names, profiles, and fatal turns.[19] *Psyche* is impersonal because, as in the archaic intuition, it is nothing except the principle of animation, the enlivening breath. It is that nothing that always wears new clothes, new masks, before undressing anew and always again, in cycles. Psyche images undying life, dispersed in infinitely many lineages and visages. Especially when seen as a multitude, "in the company of many (*meta pollon*),"[20] *psyche* indicates one cosmic life. Indestructible *zoe*, as Kerenyi will say—the ground of individual mortal life; the immortal life that always returns, immortal precisely because it never rests, in its constant movement of self-differentiation.[21]

This vision is vertiginous, intoxicating as it restores individual life to an entirely new situatedness. Those who are captured by such a vision will, to be sure, experience themselves as individuals (at once in their irreducible originality and as children of their time). But they will also sense their own belonging to the cosmic life in which all space-time is recapitulated; they will perceive cosmic life breathing through them, transporting them, unstoppable. At that point, mortal life will be what it always was—minuscule and vulnerable—yet nothing will ever be the same. The *pathos* of separation and individuation will assume a different tonality.

Such is the register of awareness, the *Stimmung* that the myth favors. This myth especially emphasizes the cultivation of (self-)reflectiveness, of that spacing between the self and itself, of that non-coincidence with oneself that awareness requires. Particularly striking in the myth are the scenes in which the *psychai* that have just returned from their paths through Hades, before leaving for their new reincarnation, linger for a bit in a meadow, recounting among strangers their own adventures, as if they were refugees or illegal immigrants, without either documents or known history. Here surfaces the therapeutic power of self-narration, of giving oneself to be known to another, and to oneself—the festive joyfulness or even simply the relief of that exchange.[22]

The reference to Odysseus, at the conclusion of the myth, points in the same direction. All souls have chosen their next life; the soul that lived as Odysseus comes to the foreground last and, after carefully considering the various options, chooses to be reincarnated in a "private" life, away from the clamor and the intrigues of public positions (*apragmon*), finally free from the passionate love of glory.[23] The choice is deeply surprising because, already in the idiom of the times, the private, *idiotes*, has strongly privative connotations. Indeed, remaining outside political life indicates a dull (if not even plebeian) obtuseness, an ordinary life in the sense of unremarkable, even vulgar, dark.

Yet Odysseus's *psyche* claims to be glad of that generally despised selection. It says that many disgraces have made it relinquish its love of fame and yearning for heroic sparkling. But there is more to this. It is not pain in itself that brings the shadow that once was Odysseus to this turn. Rather, it is the *memory* of pain, the retention of lived experiences, and, thanks to such a retention, the possibility of working through them. This is the only way to begin to try to interrupt automatisms and mechanical or reactive responses. Suffering by itself is not transformational. However, when it leaves marks and scratches, when it inheres unforgettably and builds up, then it can become conscious material and, as conscious, transmutable. This becoming conscious may change the entire game.

More or less felicitous inclinations aside, memory and becoming aware do not occur without long cultivation, exercise, and distillation. It is through such a path that the memory of the challenges one has undergone becomes a properly philosophical orientation. With respect to this, the highly original Platonic interpretation not only appropriates the Homeric legacy, but it also subtracts Odysseus to evaluations that, in antiquity, were less than flattering, due to the far-from-luminous nature of the aged king of Ithaca (suffice it to recall, by contrast, the figure of dazzling Achilles). The hero, by definition longing for the everlasting glow of the consideration of others, in Plato emancipates himself from images and their ensnarement, from confirmations and glorifications that never suffice, and knows how to choose without being dazzled by vain semblances. Being, as a survivor, an astute deceiver, he is no longer easily deceived. And he chooses to live, "just" to live. Anonymous, private life is "just" life, demanding nothing in return—no prize, reward, recognition. However, past hardships have taught him that life, "just" life, is boundless—due to what one ends up experiencing, due to the palette of affections, thoughts, numinous encounters, and infinite other vicissitudes. The private thus appears to him quite different from the impoverished opposite of public splendor. Odysseus recognizes, in what is private, the thickness and depth of life, which mostly escape the public—thick life, quite different from ridiculous or banal. Or maybe ridiculous, but then also moving, simultaneously comic and tragic in the sense of "worthy of wonder."[24]

Life has worked on him harshly. Like a goldsmith, it has finely chiseled him. The lover of immortality has given immortality up, when it was offered to him by Calypso. He has learned to cry "like a woman"; that is, he has learned to contact himself, to speak to himself and to his heart.[25] In order to survive, he has learned to be no one, nameless. And he has learned to narrate himself. For four books in the *Odyssey* (IX–XII), he narrates himself in first person, repeats his errancies, and exposes himself aloud, no less to himself than to the court of the Phaeacians. In this repetition, he awakens, begins to grasp something about himself, and confronts the Sphinx, exactly like Socrates in the *Phaedrus*, when he faces the Delphic imperative.[26] He begins to remember himself. To heal the fractures and the imbalances between interiority and the exterior. He is king without being either sovereign or tyrant. He expresses a power that is completely other than violence and irreducible to the dichotomy between sovereignty (with its violent logic of exception) and bare life. Instead, Odysseus's power is here similar to what Ralph Waldo Emerson calls the "hieroglyph" of that conscious dignity or regality that is, ultimately, "the right of every man."[27]

In self-narration, beginning to write myself, and writing about the other—I describe the immense movement of life in me, its invasion, its excess, and its unfathomability, which pierces me from side to side. The work of writing about oneself is not only tracing a path, the adventures and misadventures that have marked me; it is also the creation of oneself, the effort to give a profile, albeit mobile, to the flowing of life that floods me and slips away, that simultaneously supports and dissipates me, that is and is not me. It barely allows me to say "I" and to say it meaningfully. It makes this pronoun as dubious as it is urgent. Almost a prejudice. A biography is always already zoography. It is an ephemeral mark on a life that keeps fleeing, untracked. It is, at the same time, auscultation and construction. It is as if one liberated a form from the formless that, while exceeding form, constitutes it.

This work may broaden one's consciousness as well as freedom in choosing, even though according to the myth such choice is then rigorously taking place according to necessity. What, in the final perspective of the *Republic*, the philosophical excavation seems to give us to think is this: an existential bearing that is freer, the more it is aware of being inscribed in necessity.[28] In Nietzsche's words: "Free in most amorous constraint." Where freedom comes to mean something entirely other than caprice and self-indulgent arbitrariness.

A Sensing Multitude

To complement what we have been saying so far are three very brief highlights. First, the essential ingredient of self-reflectiveness is listening to the other, the resounding space that welcomes, understands, and gives back. This availability is the distinctive feature of friendship more than of any other relationship. It is not by chance that Aristotle, in the *Nicomachean Ethics*, notes that friendship "enhance[s] our ability to think and to act";[29] that is, it favors a growth in being, an intensification of living.[30] Here is the power of the amical climate, here is what it enables and empowers. In the absence of any other goal that is not the pleasure of being together, friendship promotes as wide a sharing as possible, a self-narration that is a little less contrived. One dares to share the secret, the unacceptable traits at the core of ourselves, the silence that seems nothing and that, more often than not, we undergo as unpresentable. This fundamental attitude toward the other should then be explored also in its political inflection. Aristotle associates to it the attitude of benevolence (*eunoia*). It can also be discerned in welcoming the stranger as, for example, in the hospitality Odysseus is granted at the court of Alcinous, who encourages Odysseus to unveil himself and surrender to the unarmed *pathos* of narration.

Second, the sharing that is made possible in friendship is not only civil participation in discourses but also sharing of life, of silent and unstoppable *zoe*. Friendship embraces the animal that we are so that it becomes as much a matter of sensibility, of co-sensing or sensing together (*syn-aisthesis*) as of *logos*—not only knowing but also sensing oneself being, sensing oneself living, and feeling alive thanks to sensing together.[31] Aristotle's insight seems here to come from afar, reverberating, in its own characteristic way, the myth of Plato's *Republic* according to which reincarnation involves passages from one life form to another, from the human to other animals and vice versa, thereby adumbrating the common ground of all mortal lives, regardless of their form.[32] Or it echoes even earlier Pythagorean motifs, as for example the fragment in which Empedocles recalls having been born, "at one time," as "boy, girl, plant, bird, and dumb sea-fish."[33]

Third, this nameless life, which flows in a nomadic manner underneath and across names and guises, like the life of the companions who, organized in guilds, anonymously set up the age of cathedrals, is remembrance of one's participation and belonging in a chorality with no aspiration to eternalized glory and reputation. It is memory of the fact that not everything—or rather, almost nothing—depends on me; and this is so without deposing responsibilities but rather setting them on a ground completely different from my omnipotence. Here lies the freedom finally to die. And in this way, perhaps, one may live. Because it is life that is living, that is alive, and not names, signatures or the dream (or delirium) of everlastingness.

Echoes

Rather than venture a conclusion, I will leave these considerations open and let them resonate with a remembrance of Ernst Bernhard, Jewish doctor and psychoanalyst from Berlin who, in 1936, in his forties, sought refuge in Italy. There, he boosted an original development of the discourses of psychoanalysis and analytic psychology. Interned in 1940–41 in the concentration camp at Ferramonti di Tarsia, near Cosenza, in Calabria, he lived in Rome until his death, in 1965—but he lived there as a stateless individual, therefore steeped in the excess of the living human being with respect to the citizen. His thought, which remains ahead of us in the future, grasps the work on individual evolution in its collective-planetary potentialities (and responsibilities). Here are some passages from a reflection he dictated in summer 1964:

> Indeed, in this earthly life of ours, we must represent a pre-allotted part with all the commitment of which we are capable as interpreters. Good and evil, positive and negative—these are inherent in the part and they are not to be attributed naturally to the actor. Human beings, however, are irresistibly prone to identify with the part. . . . However, similar to actors who, no matter how much they identify with their role, nevertheless do not believe to be the person they are supposed to represent, [human beings] may acquire some distance from their part. . . . This way, they are progressively released from the conceptions of the author of the drama of which they have been interpreters and become, simultaneously, authors and actors in a new work. In it, they represent the part that corresponds to themselves and the conflict between the part and their individuality is annulled. They identify with the author's idea, that is, the author identifies with them. They are the representational function of the author who, through them, manifests him or herself in the drama. "Free in amorous necessity."[34]

Notes

1. One could think of the mytheme of the tree of life, ubiquitous in the most diverse traditions and disciplines, or of the mobilization of the language of life, vitality, and liveliness to connote anything vibrant, joyously generative, touching, moving, and expansive.

2. Here I can only recall the stunning *oeuvre* by Charlotte Salomon, *Leben? Oder Theater?* (Cologne: Taschen, 2017), a collection of 1300 sheets in which painting, poetry, and music intersect to form an unprecedented *Gesamtkunstwerk*. Shortly before dying at Auschwitz in 1943, at the age of 26, Charlotte gave her work to a friend saying: "*Sorg gut dafür, es ist mein ganzes Leben!* [Take good care of it, it is my entire life!]."

3. Guy Debord, *Oeuvres cinématographiques complètes 1952–1978* (Paris: Gallimard, 1994), 49.

4. Giorgio Agamben, *The Use of Bodies*, trans. Adam Kotsko (Stanford, CA: Stanford University Press, 2016), xv, xx. Here and in the rest of the chapter I provide references to the English translations of Italian, German, French, and Greek texts, although I often significantly modify them.

5. Agamben asks, "What does it mean that private life accompanies us as a clandestine? First of all, that it is separate from us as a clandestine is and, at the same time, is inseparable from us to the extent that, as a stowaway, it furtively shares existence with us." He then goes on to say: "Thus, the one that accompanies us as a clandestine in our long or short voyage is not only private life but also corporeal life itself and all that is traditionally inscribed in the sphere of so-called intimacy: nutrition, urination, defecation, sleep, sexuality. . . . And the weight of this faceless companion is so strong that each seeks to share it with someone else—and nevertheless, extraneousness and clandestinity never completely disappear and remain unresolved even in the most loving life together"; see Agamben, *The Use of Bodies*, xx–xxi, translation modified.

6. Agamben, *The Use of Bodies*, xvii.

7. Agamben, *The Use of Bodies*, xv.

8. "Avoir l'oreille de la philosophie. Entretien de Jacques Derrida avec Lucette Finas," *La Quinzaine Littéraire* 16–30 (1972), later published in *Écarts. Quatre essais à propos de Jacques Derrida* (Paris: Fayard, 1973), 309.

9. Jacques Derrida and Maurizio Ferraris, *A Taste for the Secret*, trans. Giacomo Doni (Cambridge: Polity Press, 2001), 36.

10. Italo Calvino, "La penna in prima persona (Per i disegni di Saul Steinberg)" [1977], in *Saggi 1945–1985* I, a cura di M. Barenghi (Milan: Mondadori, 1995), 362.

11. Jacques Derrida, *The Ear of the Other: Otobiography, Transference, Translation*, ed. Christie McDonald (Lincoln: University of Nebraska Press, 1988), 8–10.

12. Samuel Beckett, *The Unnamable* (New York: Grove Press, 1958) ends with these words: "I can't go on. You must go on. I'll go on. You must say words, as long as there are any—until they find me, until they say me. (Strange pain, strange sin!) You must go on. Perhaps it's done already. Perhaps they have said me already. Perhaps they have carried me to the threshold of my story, before the door that opens on my story. (That would surprise me, if it opens.) It will be I? It will be the silence, where I am? I don't know, I'll never know: in the silence you don't know. You must go on. I can't go on. I'll go on."

13. Plato, *Republic* 353d.

14. Plato, *Republic* 368c–e.

15. Plato, *Republic* 618b, trans. Allan Bloom (New York: Basic Books, 1991).

16. On this ground one may also understand the reasons for the philosophical-biographic turn in psychoanalysis. Instead of postulating and hypostatizing psychic (or intrapsychic) structures while groping in the dark, such a turn rather follows the structures of action, of manifestation, and of history, which is irreducibly individual and, at the same time, collective, despite what remains unexpressed in expression, despite what remains unsaid in each story yet is deposited at the bottom

of all stories. See, for example, Romano Màdera, *La carta del senso. Psicologia del profondo e vita filosofica* (Milan: Cortina, 2012).

17. Here I limit myself to signaling the strange (and, from a textual point of view, altogether awkward) topology of the *psyche* positioned "between" *bios* and *zoe*; see Agamben, *The Use of Bodies*, 261.

18. For a particularly incisive assessment of Agamben's reading of this myth, see Catherine Malabou, "Odysseus' Changed Soul: A Contemporary Reading of the Myth of Er," in *Contemporary Encounters with Ancient Metaphysics*, ed. A. J. Greenstine and R. J. Johnson (Edinburgh: Edinburgh University Press, 2017), 30–46.

19. I have analyzed this Platonic text on various occasions. To name but two, see Claudia Baracchi, "Exile in the Flow of Time: On Memory and Immortality in Plato's *Republic*," *Research in Phenomenology* 47, no. 2 (2017), 204–19 and "Animals and Angels: The Myth of Life as a Whole in Plato's *Republic* X," in *Plato's Animals*, ed. Michael Naas and Jeremy Bell (Bloomington: Indiana University Press, 2015), 209–24.

20. Plato, *Republic* 614c.
21. Plato, *Phaedrus* 245c.
22. Plato, *Republic* 614b–616a.
23. Plato, *Republic* 620c–d.
24. Plato, *Republic* 620a.
25. Homer, *Odyssey* VIII, 523–31.
26. Plato, *Phaedrus* 229e.
27. Ralph Waldo Emerson, "Self-Reliance" (1841).
28. But, of course, the work of self-reflectiveness can undergo various drifts. It can become alienated fixation, inflation or construction of the self as a cult object. This is the inferno of social networks, whose phantasmagorias often concern us more than our very selves, so that we abdicate ourselves in order to take care of our self-representation and reproduction, in a caricatured reversal of life into spectacle.

29. Aristotle, *Nicomachean Ethics* 1155a.
30. Aristotle, *Nicomachean Ethics* 1170a–b.
31. Aristotle, *Nicomachean Ethics* 1170b6–19.
32. Plato, *Republic* 619e ff.
33. Empedocles, DK 117, Hermann Diels and Walther Kranz, *Die Fragmente der Vorsokratiker* (Zürich: Weidmann, 1968).

34. Ernst Bernhard, *Mitobiografia* (Milan: Adelphi, 1969), 211–12. The final quotation proposes yet again the question of freedom according to necessity which, as mentioned in the previous pages, is also at the core of Plato's *Republic* as well as, later, of Spinoza's thought. The quotation evokes an expression in Nietzsche's *Ecce Homo* (1888), *Frei im liebevollsten Muss*, "In most loving constraint, free." See Friedrich Nietzsche, *On the Genealogy of Morals and Ecce Homo*, trans. Walter Kaufmann and R. J. Hollingdale (New York: Random House, 1969), 293. The formula appears in the section on *The Gay Science*.

Fourteen

With the Finitude of Life beyond the Phenomenon

Phenomenology, Hermeneutics, and a Metaphysics of the Finite

Ugo Perone

The Entanglement of the Finite

Many years ago, when my daughter was in second grade, I was invited, just like all other parents, to illustrate what my profession was about. To explain to such young children what philosophy is and who a philosopher is, I got hold of the arguments from the dawn of the philosophical discipline, and I went to class with a bucket, appropriately filled with water, and a stick. In front of the children, I performed the famous experiment of the stick that, in the water, looks as if it were broken, whereas as soon as you take it out of the water, it presents itself in its previous, intact form. What I meant to show the children was the origin of that typically philosophical distinction between appearance and being. Philosophy begins, as matter of fact, from this distinction even though, unlike what is suggested by the little trick, what we usually experience is not being (the intact stick) but appearance (what, in the experiment, is represented by the broken stick immersed in water). Philosophy in fact suggests that the whole of what we experience is appearance, whereas the ascent to the truth of being is granted only to a skilled gaze. Briefly, we are all immersed in the fluid of appearance, and it is practiced reason alone that elevates us to the firm truth of being.

Philosophy begins more or less in this way; that is, by telling us that, usually, we are prisoners in a cave, and it is only by exiting the cave that, according to the well-known Platonic image, we can grasp phenomena directly in their truth.

The outcome of a similar operation is simultaneously grandiose and dangerous. The accurate distinction between truth and appearance remains a task that, more than two thousand years after the beginning, still deserves pursuing—this against the confusion of messages that, repeated and amplified, pass off lies as truth and also against individual escapism into artificial, alternative realities. The risk is, nevertheless, that this precious tool of distinction may lead to taking leave of reality, considered in its entirety as a site of appearance.

From Aristotle on—but, in truth, already in Plato—philosophy has constantly searched for correctives to such a risk and has continuously been preoccupied with the nature of this fleeting reality that surrounds and, at the same time, constitutes us. To remind philosophical readers of these efforts is superfluous. What is sufficient for us, here, is to draw a conclusion that is also the premise for what I intend to claim: namely, that the finite—that is, both what surrounds us and we ourselves as finite beings—is the most difficult object for thought, which can find a much quicker resting place in the self-consistent fullness of the infinite. To say it with a formula: it is easier to define God than the human being; it is easier to define what perfection is than what finitude and precariousness are. When we come to ascertain the existence of such two opposed measures, things get however to be reversed: it is indubitable that the finite and precariousness exist, even though in their structural questionability (we can recall Descartes's *cogito* here); on the contrary, that God exists is not immediately included in human reason's ability to comprehend because of the ulteriority attested by God's perfection.

Let us not pursue this direction of thought, at least for now, and let us focus instead on the outcome that the entire philosophical path seems to bequest us: its mysterious object is the finite, and it is around this that we ought to labor. Two elements seem to be a given, at this point: the certainty of the existence of the finite and the difficulty in understanding its nature.

One certainly ought to distinguish among various historical periods. The finite of classical Greek antiquity, as we experience it for example in the art of sculpting, is fixed in its belonging to being. By withdrawing from all individuality and pain, statues simply speak their being-there, the archaic manifestation of their being (so that, at least for Parmenides, the alternative becomes between being and nonbeing). The question becomes more complicated (and it is handed down to us as such) with reference to the Jewish and Christian traditions. In them, God's supreme being withdraws in the unspeakability of the name and, when it reveals itself, it does so in something that God itself is not (for example, the burning bush). What is unprecedented in Christianity is the thought that Christ's divinity manifests itself in the finiteness of Jesus as a human being. The finite is thus, simultaneously, identical to and other than the divine. Through this way, the whole finite is welcome, in its weakness and its mortality. This is the difficult legacy with which we must now reckon. It is understandable that there are some who, in order to rest on the finite as simple modality of being, propose a return to paganism, that is, to a finite that is nothing else than a way of being (the unintentional consequence of this is, however, closing one's eyes to the finite that is poor and defeated).

If we now return to focus on how, in post-Cartesian modernity, philosophy attempts to react to this accentuated problematic character of the finite, we immediately note that certainty of the existence of the finite, on which we thought we could rely, nevertheless leaves unsolved the question of the identity of the finite I. Once again, it is Descartes who provides us with the best tools for understanding this matter. That I am is indubitable, Descartes thinks. Given the way in which we have reached such a certainty of thought, it is not arduous to know what I am—I am a *res cogitans*, a thinking thing. What remains utterly indeterminate, however, is who I am, that is, the application of such certainty to a determined being. It seems that, at the level of the finite, at the very moment when one happens to grasp it, one is faced with the same problems affecting the infinite. As soon as we grasp its indubitability, and we approach its nature, its concrete existence eludes us.

It is not an accident that in the end, even though interested in returning to the things themselves, Husserl proposes the "phenomenological reduction" as the condition to grasp the true nature of the phenomenon. That is, he proposes a gaze that suspends the natural attitude and brackets the value of existence of the phenomenon. Such an existence is what existentialism emphasizes once a complete reduction turns out to be impossible, as a phenomenologist like Maurice Merleau-Ponty reveals without disavowing its importance. In this way, a different philosophy begins, one that is at the same time so close and so distant from phenomenology.

The intention of these brief remarks is certainly not to retrace a more than bimillenary philosophical itinerary but rather to remind the readers of the complex, intricate, and even contradictory aspects of this sequence of events concerning the finite.[1] Such a finite is what, in my own personal philosophical path, I have often identified with the finite-that-says-itself, that is, the subject.[2] After these remarks and cognizant of the many attempts that have already been made over the centuries, we can return to the theme that we have set out for ourselves, which is: How can we speak of this finite, which is fragile, precarious, continuously fleeting, and yet so essential? How can we produce a phenomenology of the finite that does not force us to take leave from existence? How can we speak of a life that not only disappears due to its mortality but is also continuously threatened in its consistency? How can we speak of the now, when the past passes and is subjected to wear and tear, and the future does not come and carries signs not simply of uncertainty but also of a threat? Where and how can we find a point of consistency?

On the Edge of the Finite

The phenomenological gaze accesses phenomena descriptively, yet it claims to say their essential form. We encounter here a difficulty that, at first, seems unsurmountable and allows us to understand the reasons for resorting to the method of reduction. Through the reduction, the intention is to sidestep the marker of reality of the phenomenon and thereby dissolve the knot between phenomenon and appearance that philosophy, ever since its beginning, had meant to set off. The appearing [*apparire*] of the phenomenon is not its appearance [*apparenza*]. The matter is, rather, that of establishing a relation between different modes of appearing of a phenomenon (the broken stick and the intact stick) by considering them adumbrations of a single act of consciousness capable of retaining different stages—stages that are nevertheless related to the same single phenomenon—as subsequent moments capable of compenetration. Description is not to be mistaken for a flash of immediacy. Rather, it must be understood as the insertion, within the horizon of consciousness, of a phenomenal given that occurs within time—within the time of the perception of consciousness (intuitions do not happen all at once) and in the perception of temporality of the thing itself (the phenomenon is a given endowed with multiple strata and stages, just like a wave). The essence that is thereby attained is not an abstract and unrelated form but, rather, the self-manifesting of a consciousness that perceives a happening. More precisely, we should even say: that perceives the happening of a happening. For this reason, as Merleau-Ponty correctly understood, phenomenology is always, originarily, thought of birth, of the birthing of birth.

These considerations, which configure a possible development of phenomenology—the development that seems to me most appropriate and productive—have the merit of bringing us back to the question that we raised at the beginning. If we do not employ this approach, how could we describe the finite, which is so precarious and fleeting while being simultaneously so urgent and ineludible? There are many things one ought to take care of. If the finite cannot explain or understand itself by itself as it is neither self-sufficient nor self-referential, then if we wish to grasp its nature, we need to wonder about its origin, investigate the complex contradictoriness of its being, and hypothesize the sense of its finite course. We could, of course, limit ourselves to acknowledge the punctual scansion of all the moments compounding this adventure, which, as one may have noticed, comprises the times of life: the past of birth, the present of life, and the future of death. But this would be nothing else than chronicle. And if, taking somehow a step forward, if, limiting ourselves precisely to description, we tried to turn the description into a desperate explanation, we would raise ourselves beyond ourselves, and the conclusion would be the meaningless sense of living. That is, we would provide a phenomenology of the finite that ends up with its *nihil esse*, its being nothing. This is a possibility that is always possible and that is even made plausible by the fugacity of experiences, the meaninglessness of evil and suffering, and the load of injustices and inequalities. It is an explanation that explains nothing and yet can justify everything. While offering neither tears nor laughs, it makes us understand the meaningless and indifferent neutrality of nature.[3] It may even teach us to enjoy, in this desolate land of the neutral, those fragments of positivity that life nevertheless grants us.

As I said, this is a possibility that is always possible and can never be excluded with contempt. It is a possibility that is even reasonable. Yet it is not the only one. One can in fact attempt a phenomenology that exceeds chronicling and draws on what is not there in order to describe what is there. The appearing of the phenomenon is quite consistent in its multifarious manifestations; it is not mere appearance. As we realize with surprise, being is that which is not there and yet is capable of letting appear, in the phenomenon, something more than what is immediately given while, at the same time, remaining capable of accounting for the given in its present givenness. It is a double movement, which says "the same" and "more." This movement is reversed in comparison with the nihilistic movement, which draws "more" from "the same" and is therefore analogous to the muteness of tautology. In the case we are proposing, the "more" discloses a "same" that is simultaneously loyal to itself—it is *that* very same—and yet is inscribed in a view that opens it to unprecedented significations.

To take a stand in favor of meaning rather than nothing is quite similar to Descartes' decision, in his *Meditations*, to exclude madness (*amentes sunt isti*, these are insane). At the very moment when we begin to think, we cannot avoid such a decision because thinking as such is an overcoming, and not a mere mirroring, of the given. The overcoming cannot result into nothing though, as nothing does not even explain the negative that it was intent on expressing. The venerable metaphor of knowledge as the light that illuminates the dark already contains within itself the asymmetry of a darkness that cannot overpower but only dispel light. On the contrary, the turning on or off of the light explains both itself and the dark. The real challenge to which thought is exposed—here, I employ the term "exposed" in the same sense in which Paul Celan speaks of poetry as exposing itself—is not the choice between meaning and absence of meaning.[4] Even when tormented, this choice is contextual to positing a question, which demands not a negation but rather an answer. The challenge is to configure a form of meaning that neither has the features of mere illusion nor dismisses the seriousness of the negative experienced by the finite or resolves it dialectically as the condition for a higher good.

To bring this interrogation to completion requires that one practice quite an amount of naivety. Despite the reassuring protection of the fictional procedure, what is at work in art is a process of unveiling of the narrating self, which ultimately entrusts itself, without protection, to the artistic consumer. Likewise in philosophy, despite the protection of a huge argumentative apparatus and the aid of quotations—which, as Benjamin said, are similar to mercenaries hired to launch the attack—the rational process implies an ultimate decision that, without protections and naively, exposes itself to the acceptance or the refusal and, even earlier, to the understanding or the misunderstanding of the one who faces it. One must be aware of this. The speaker must know that, in conversations, one delivers oneself, and not merely one's own smart knowledge. Therefore, the speaker must be anxious and humble. The listener must protect this self-communication with his or her own respect. Briefly, every philosophy is a confession that speaks of our own being in the world.

Finitude contains a double movement. It is precarious and fragile but also tenacious and consistent. Its precariousness is easy to acknowledge. It is not simply the case that life passes; as Francesco Petrarca memorably writes in the *Canzoniere*, "*la vita fugge, et non s'arresta una hora, / et la morte vien dietro a gran giornate* [life flees, and does not halt even for an hour, / and death follows with great steps]." Additionally though, all experiences undergo a same destiny as they are exposed to consumption and fading; they are predisposed, as it were, to being forgotten. This is so much the case that one may romantically try to live each experience already with the awareness of its caducity—one may turn experience into a memory at the very same moment in which one lives through it (this is the romantic love perfectly well portrayed by Kierkegaard). Yet the aspect of finitude of the finite makes each moment most precious. Marked by its caducity, each moment is, in some way, the last, and, therefore, each is not only precious but cannot also be renounced. One holds onto it tenaciously and entrusts its consistency to memory—without this consistency, existence would have no power. One clings to memories to the point of becoming their victim; that way, the terrain of finitude is protected from all landslides and becomes a fortress. Enclosed in the fortress, one lives ready to risk everything: it is either this existence or nothing. Pascal describes this well, namely, the duplicity of human beings that makes their misery really miserable at times and their greatness really heroic at others. Moreover, one aspect is not without the other, so that, in the end, it is necessary to choose one's standing in favor of the one in order to unfold the other, and vice versa. A good phenomenology cannot simply list possibilities. It must push itself to explain what opportunities emerge from which choice. It is here, on this extreme edge where the finite applies to itself, questions itself, and thinks about itself, that phenomenology gestures beyond itself—not toward existentialism but, rather, toward hermeneutics.

Phenomenology and Hermeneutics

The phenomenological gaze is essential but is not enough. The finite can be pursued only by a perceptual ability capable of grasping all the various nuances that comprise it. A comprehension based on a priori apodictic certainties can only end up with annihilating finitude by ultimately assimilating it to mere appearance. A cheerful passing from finitude to finitude in search of the essential aspect that connects the discrete phenomenal manifestations into a continuity—what phenomenology is actually in search of—cannot, however, overcome the natural attitude and its inability to exceed the awareness of its own participation in the natural cycle. Thinking is not merely gathering, though. Rather, it is knowing how to gather and search for an answer to the very question of why to gather. To think is to transcend. It may very well be, as in Bloch, a transcending without Transcendence. Any decision with respect to this question surpasses philosophy and concerns the freedom of the individual, the entirety of one's own existence. Yet to renounce transcending means to deny oneself the possibility of understanding, creating, and hoping. Art does that, aware that it is creating a fictional world but also convinced that, in the fiction, there is a ground from where to interpret the real. Religion does that also, by trusting that it can give a name to the principle of transcendence—a principle that becomes creator and consoler. Philosophy too does that through the metaphysical invention, by creating a world of ideas capable of accounting for the world of facts. Each of them transcends, in its own way and within its own limits. All of them are ultimately confronted, however, with the need to reduce that world of transcendence by measuring it up against the experience of life. When compared to one another, which of the three forms of transcending comes out better? Each exhibits its own benefits. What would we be, were we not to experience a successful form, a form that, even when it portrays ugliness and pain, nevertheless grants them an even heart-wrenching possibility to be a trace that cannot be erased? Dostoevsky, who does not renounce depicting the pain and evil [il male] of the world, does not hesitate to claim that only beauty can save us; he is in fact convinced that, in artistic representations, the form allows that even the most terrible contents be given a chance of redemption. Religion, on the contrary, through faith relies on a reality that is believed capable of subverting the world. Its myths are not fictions, that is, fictions that are known as such, as is the case in art; rather, they are realities, realities of faith, truer and more profound than any daily reality. As Habermas notes, on the one hand, faith contains more certainty than knowledge because it is vital; on the other hand, it entails a cognitive deficit.[5] One has reasons why one believes, yet what is at stake is an act of will. One believes on the grounds of the communicative trust based on another person. This is the reason that precedes belief; it is what finds expression in Schleiermacher's feeling of dependence. Furthermore, we add, one believes in another person (for Christianity, it is Jesus of Nazareth) who is the most proper content of belief.

Thus, both art and religion give us, each in a way that mirrors the other, a transcending [trascendimento] of the natural factuality in which we nevertheless partake in everyday life. In so doing, they prepare us for rethinking the customary conception of reason, which is experienced in a deeper connection with feelings and the will.

Can philosophy learn from art and religion? Can it do so when it knows that the reasoning on which it relies can neither be fictional nor depend on faith? The answer is already contained in the opening part of the current chapter, where we retrace the initial steps of philosophy. Philosophy can learn from art and religion if it undertakes the risk—the risk is beautiful, the ancients used to say—of marking a separation between appearance and being (without falling into the equivocation of turning all manifestations into semblance), between remaining in the world of opinions and venturing into the differences of truth. Here resonates the decisive word: the finite—the mysterious matter that intrigues us in existence, in imagination, and in thought—can be grasped, albeit in its fleetingness, only if we abandon its mere description, and we dare the freedom of attempting an interpretation. As phenomenology searches for essences, it gets into trouble when trying to grasp the essence of that which, by nature, is constant change and caducity. The essence is more nonbeing than being; better said, the essence of a finite whose being is inseparable from nonbeing can only be said by an act of freedom that, by separating being from nonbeing, turns one into the filter to understand the other. The finite is being and nonbeing. Having said this, which is what phenomenology shows us not only in its factuality but also in its ineludible connection, one must take a step further, engage in an act of choice.[6] Currently, hermeneutics is the only position that is capable of taking this step and giving birth to a renewed metaphysics (which, elsewhere, I have named an "a posteriori metaphysics")[7]—a metaphysics capable of welcoming and redeeming modernity. The solution I see is in the link between phenomenology and hermeneutics. A help on our way can only come from a phenomenology that opens to the ultimate step of hermeneutic freedom and from a hermeneutic that has enough patience to dwell phenomenologically by the finite.

For a Metaphysics of Modernity

I will conclude with some considerations that recapitulate points made more extensively in various other places.

Any authentic philosophy is a metaphysics and, as such, it implies the explosive power of transcending that metaphysics enshrines. This does not turn philosophy into a crypto-religion or an illusory portrayal of another world. While remaining loyal to reason and its earthly limitedness, philosophy strives to delineate the horizon within which the existing reality can finally be understood. To do so, it must exceed reality and then test this exceedance against reality itself. Classical metaphysics accomplished this by feeding itself on wonder, which provided an encounter with the fleetingly abysmal character of that which is. It did so by moving from wonder to wonder until it delineated a world of perfection. In this doing, though, it left behind the precariousness of the existing finite. During modernity, which wanted to start anew and, in various ways, experienced a form of diffidence against the world of the a priori, the finite returned to being the inevitable reference from which to draw, with diffidence against any attempt at pursuing truth to the detriment of certainty. Metaphysics therefore became highly suspect. The cost of this was the weight placed on the finite as well as on the subject and existence—a weight that became burdensome to sustain. Hence the various renunciations belonging to contemporary thought, which has been intent more on deconstructing—on playing with materials from an edifice that has been dismissed yet not abandoned—than on building. With the nexus of metaphysics and hermeneutics as we propose it, it becomes possible to avoid what, according to Habermas, brings together scientism and metaphysics, namely, the possibility of a gaze that is "objectively" transcendent, a gaze that occurs from "nowhere" or from the standpoint of a divine observer.[8]

For this reason, we have stated that the first step to approach the precariousness of the finite is a phenomenological gaze that is, first of all, capable of welcoming the varied, fleeting, and even contradictory modulations of the finite. Such a gaze thinks them to their extreme, without reducing them to mere appearances but, rather, taking seriously their character of manifestations. The essence, in fact, never coincides with the immutability of a substance but is, rather, the inexorable belonging of a predicate to a concrete existence. Unlike substance, the essence is not the property of a substantive; rather, it is the property of a proposition and the marker of a nexus. Yet when, as in the finite, predicates are in conflict and opposition with one another, are we allowed to interrupt our research and stop in front of the realization of such paradoxical contradictoriness? Or should we take a step further? And on whom or what do we rely for such a move forward?

What intervenes at this point is the freedom of hermeneutics, that is, the procedure of a reason that does not surrender to the duality of intellect and will that is handed down to us by the tradition. As is well known, such a duality appears in Descartes in order to explain the insurgence of errors, which are due to the greater extension of the will.[9] Already in Kant, however, in its practical use, reason incorporates free will within itself. We are here confronted with a reason that not only posits the boundaries of its own jurisdiction but also ventures to delineate, from its location at the edges of its own domain, that which it claims it needs to presuppose in order to understand a more complex reality. This more complex reality is not only the horizon of that which can be known but also the terrain of acting and living. It is Schelling who then advances a real ecstasy of reason, an ecstatic reason that, by exceeding the limits of negativity, reverses itself and turns into what we would currently name hermeneutic reason.

Hermeneutic reason explicitly acknowledges its venturing on a terrain that is not granted by empirically verifiable certainties; yet it does so while providing plausible arguments and resulting into deeper elaborations that would not be possible otherwise. As already stated, it becomes explicitly metaphysical, but it is a metaphysics of modernity as it does not produce an a priori and self-subsistent edifice. Instead, it embarks to delineate a horizon within which to inscribe and understand the real as it gives itself, a real that has undergone a phenomenological interrogation. The ultimate question underlying any philosophy is whether there is meaning. As we have suggested, though, this question has already received an answer in the very act of beginning to philosophize, which, as such, is the search for a meaning based on the presupposition that there is meaning. In choosing in favor of meaning, philosophy justifies itself first and foremost. How can we still sing and write after pain and suffering? How can we not do so, though, unless we give up self-affirmation and declare as a defeat a match that is in fact still happening? Even if meaning were simply the permanence of a memento in the memory of others, it would still be something that would deserve preserving and for which a fight would be worth. It would be a transcending without Transcendence.

Philosophy does not go beyond this and awaits an answer. The finite is an open question for infinity.

Translated from Italian by Silvia Benso

Notes

1. The thinkers and concepts we referred to are undoubtedly well known to all philosophical readers. In general, our references suggest a line of continuity between Descartes' *Meditations on First Philosophy*, Husserl's *Cartesian Meditations*, and Merleau-Ponty's *Phenomenology of Perception*.

2. See Ugo Perone, *Trotz/dem Subjekt* (Leuven: Peeters Verlag, 1998); the original Italian edition was published in 1995.

3. On the notion of ontology as a knowledge of the neutral, see especially Emmanuel Levinas, *Totality and Infinity: An Essay on Exteriority*, trans. Alphonso Lingis (The Hague: Nijhoff, 1979).

4. Paul Celan, "La poesie ne s'impose plus, elle s'expose" (March 26, 1969), in *Gesammelte Werke in sieben Bänden*, ed. B. Allemann and S. Reichert (Frankfurt am Mein: Suhrkamp, 2000), III, 181.

5. See Jürgen Habermas, *Auch eine Philosophie der Geschichte*, vol. I (Berlin: Suhrkamp, 2019), 718–19.

6. The reference is, once again, to Celan and what he says in the discourse he gave on occasion of the acceptance of the Georg Büchner Prize for literature. See Paul Celan, *The Meridian*, ed. Bernhard Böschenstein and Heino Schmull, trans. Pierre Joris (Stanford, CA: Stanford University Press, 2011).

7. See Perone, *Trotz/dem Subjekt*, 35.

8. See Habermas, *Auch eine Philosophie*, I, 473.

9. For this, see René Descartes, *Meditations on First Philosophy*, Meditation 4.

Contributors

Claudia Baracchi is professor of moral philosophy at the University of Milan-Bicocca. She is a founding member of the Ancient Philosophy Society. Among her publications are *Aristotle's Ethics as First Philosophy* (2008 and 2011), *Amicizia* (2016), and *Filosofia antica e vita effimera. Migrazioni, trasmigrazioni e laboratori della psiche* (2020). Her research focuses on ethics and the question of nature; philosophy in relation to myth, poetry, and theater; Asian (especially Indo-Vedic) traditions; and psychoanalysis. She teaches at the Philo School of Biographical Analysis with Philosophical Orientation and is a practicing analyst.

Silvia Benso is professor of philosophy at the Rochester Institute of Technology. Among her areas of interest are ancient philosophy, contemporary European philosophy, the history of philosophy, ethics, and aesthetics. She is the author of *Thinking after Auschwitz: Philosophical Ethics and Jewish Theodicy* (1992, in Italian); *The Face of Things: A Different Side of Ethics* (2000); and *Viva Voce: Conversations with Italian Philosophers* (2017). And she is the coauthor of the volume *Environmental Thinking: Between Philosophy and Ecology* (2000, in Italian). She has also coedited various volumes such as *Contemporary Italian Philosophy: Between Ethics, Politics and Religion* (2007); *Levinas and the Ancients* (2008); *Between Nihilism and Politics: The Hermeneutics of Gianni Vattimo* (2010); *Thinking the Inexhaustible: Art, Interpretation, and Freedom in the Philosophy of Luigi Pareyson* (2018); *Open Borders: Encounters between Italian Philosophy and Continental Thought* (2021); and *Contemporary Italian Women Philosophers: Stretching the Art of Thinking* (2021). During the past decade, she has devoted herself to the promotion of Italian philosophy; she is the general coeditor for the SUNY Press series on Contemporary Italian Philosophy and the codirector of the Society for Italian Philosophy (SIP).

Lorenzo Bernini is associate professor of political philosophy at the University of Verona, where he founded the PoliTeSse (Politics and Theories of Sexuality) Research Center, which he now directs, and where he teaches political philosophy and sexuality. He is one of the major voices in the Italian gender and queer debate. He is the founding member of the Italian network of Gender, Intersex, Feminist, Trans-feminist, and Sexuality Studies (GIFTS). His interests range from classical political philosophy (especially Thomas Hobbes) and twentieth-century French thought (especially Michel Foucault) to psychoanalysis (especially Sigmund Freud), contemporary theories of radical democracy, feminist philosophies, critical race theories, and queer theories. Among his publications are *Le pecore e il pastore. Critica, politica, etica nel pensiero di Michel Foucault* (2008); *La sovranità scomposta. Sull'attualità del* Leviatano, with Mauro Farnesi Camellone and Nicola Marcucci (2010); *Queer Apocalypses: Elements of Antisocial Theory* (2017), previously published in Italian (2013) and Spanish (2015); and *Queer Theories: An Introduction. From Mario Mieli to the Antisocial Turn* (2020), previously published in Italian (2017) and Spanish (2018) and forthcoming in French. His most recent book is *Il sessuale politico. Freud con Marx, Fanon, Foucault* (2019).

Alessandro Bertinetto is professor of theoretical philosophy at the University of Turin. He was Alexander von Humboldt Fellow at the Freie Universität Berlin and a member of the Executive Committee of the European Society for Aesthetics. His main research interests include contemporary aesthetics, philosophy of art, philosophy of music, image theory, aesthetics of improvisation, hermeneutics, and German idealism. Among his publications are *Il pensiero dei suoni* (2012), which was published in French as *La pensée des sons* (2017), and *Eseguire l'inatteso. Ontologia musicale e improvvisazione* (2016). His current projects include the edited volume *The Routledge Handbook of Philosophy and Improvisation in the Arts* (2021, forthcoming) and *L'estetica dell'improvvisazione* (2021, forthcoming). He is also the coordinator of the philosophical seminar ART—Aesthetics Research Torino.

Luisa Bonesio has been associate professor of aesthetics at the University of Pavia, from where she retired. She is a scholar of landscapes and geophilosophy and, since 2015, she has been the director of the Museo dei Sanatori di Sondalo (Sondrio). She contributes to various research projects and initiatives aimed at valorizing landscapes and regional and local identities. The designer and coauthor of various edited volumes on geophilosophical themes, she is the author of many publications; among them are *La terra invisibile* (1993); *Geofilosofia del paesaggio* (1997); *Passaggi al bosco. Ernst*

Jünger nell'epoca dei Titani, with Caterina Resta (2000); *Oltre il paesaggio. I luoghi tra estetica e geofilosofia* (2002); *Paesaggio, identità e comunità tra locale e globale* (2007); *Intervista sulla geofilosofia*, with Caterina Resta (2010); and *Il Villaggio Morelli. Identità paesaggistica e patrimonio monumentale*, with D. Del Curto (2011).

Alessandra Cislaghi is associate professor of theoretical philosophy at the University of Trieste, where she teaches courses on philosophy of the person, philosophical anthropology, and philosophy of religions. Educated in the hermeneutic tradition of Luigi Pareyson and Ugo Perone, her research focuses on themes at the intersection of philosophy and theology with a specific interest in the question of the human and, related to that, the cultural transformations occurring in the relations between different languages and spiritualities. She has conducted scholarly work on the hermeneutics of myths, embodied subjectivity, and the notion of the self with specific reference to classical thinkers such as Kierkegaard, Plato, Plotinus, and Thomas Aquinas—authors whom she reads in constant dialogue with the current times. Among her publications are *Interruzione e corrispondenza* (1994); *Il sapere del desiderio. Libertà metafisica e saggezza etica* (2002); *La frattura originaria. Riflessioni sulla condizione umana postedenica* (2006); *Parresìa* (2008); *Essere fuori di sé. Saggio sulla soggettività estatica* (2012); and *L'invenzione della grazia. Sulle tracce di un'idea splendida* (2018).

Rita Fulco is assistant professor of theoretical philosophy at the University of Messina, where she teaches courses in philosophical hermeneutics. From 2016 to 2021, she was postdoctoral fellow in theoretical philosophy at the Scuola Normale Superiore in Pisa. She has worked on the theoretical, religious, ethical, and political entailments of twenty-first-century continental philosophy and, more specifically, on the writings of Simone Weil, Emmanuel Levinas, and Sergio Quinzio. She has presented her work at many seminars and conferences, both in Italy and internationally. Among her publications are *Corrispondere al limite. Simone Weil: il pensiero e la luce* (2002); *Il tempo della fine. L'apocalittica messianica di Sergio Quinzio* (2007); *Essere insieme in un luogo. Etica, politica, diritto nel pensiero di Emmanuel Levinas* (2013); *Soggettività e potere. Ontologia della vulnerabilità in Simone Weil* (2020); and various articles and chapters in philosophy journals and edited volumes.

Olivia Guaraldo is associate professor of political philosophy at the University of Verona, where she directs the Hannah Arendt Center for Political Studies. Her field of research comprises modern and contemporary political thought. She has worked extensively on the thought of Hannah Arendt and contemporary feminist political theory, investigating the theoretical and political relationships between Italian feminist philosophy and Anglo-American gender theory. Guaraldo has also edited and introduced the Italian translations of Judith Butler's works, *Precarious Life* (Rome 2004, Milan 2013) and *Undoing Gender* (Rome 2006, Milan 2014). Among her most recent publications are "Public Happiness: Revisiting an Arendtian Hypothesis," *Philosophy Today* 62, no. 2 (2018): 395–416 and "'The political sphere of life, where speech rules supreme': Hannah Arendt's Imaginative Reception of Athenian Democracy," in *The Brill Companion to the Modern Reception of Athenian Democracy*, ed. G. Giorgini and D. Piovan (2020).

Luca Illetterati is professor of theoretical philosophy at the University of Padua. He is the president of the Italian Society for Theoretical Philosophy, a member of the Board of Directors of the *Internationale Hegel-Vereinigung*, and the coordinator of the Research Group on Classical German Philosophy at the University of Padua. His main research interests are classical German philosophy, especially Hegel; the philosophical understanding of nature; and the philosophy of translation. His publications include *Wirklichkeit: Beiträge zu einem Schlüsselbegriff der Hegelschen Philosophie*, ed. with F. Menegoni (2018); *Filosofia Classica Tedesca: Le parole chiave*, ed. with P. Giuspoli (2016); *Classical German Philosophy: New Research Perspectives between Analytic Philosophy and Pragmatist Tradition*, ed. with M. De Caro (2012); *Hegel*, with P. Giuspoli and G. Mendola (2010); *Purposiveness: Teleology between Nature and Mind*, ed. with F. Michelini (2008); *Das Endliche und das Unendliche in Hegels Denken*, ed. with F. Menegoni (2004); *Fra tecnica e natura. Problemi di ontologia del vivente in Heidegger* (2002); and *Natura e Ragione. Sullo sviluppo dell'idea di natura in Hegel* (1995).

Enrica Lisciani-Petrini is professor of theoretical philosophy at the University of Salerno. She is the coordinator of the ItalianThought Network. Her works are concerned with nineteenth- and twentieth-century thought with special attention to thinkers such as Heidegger, Bergson, Jankélévitch, Merleau-Ponty, and Deleuze. Her research interests focus on the problematic relations and tensions between philosophy and politics and the contributions and role of artistic experiences within twentieth-century culture and philosophical reflection. She has been especially interested in the novel ways in which the abovementioned philosophers address notions of the body, identity, subjectivity, and personhood. Through an ongoing conversation with the thought of Freud, Benjamin, Simmel, Lefebvre, De Certeau, Blanchot, and others, she is concerned with delineating a philosophy of everyday life. Among her publications are *Tierra en blanco. Música y pensamiento* *a inicios del siglo XX* (1999); *Il suono incrinato. Musica e filosofia nel primo Novecento* (2001); *La passione del mondo. Saggio su Merleau-Ponty* (2002); *Risonanze. Ascolto Corpo Mondo* (2007); *Charis. Saggio su Jankélévitch* (2012, translated into French in 2013); and *Vita quotidiana. Dall'esperienza artistica al pensiero in atto* (2015). She is also the Italian translator of various works by Jankélévitch.

Roberto Mancini is professor of theoretical philosophy at the University of Macerata, where he is also director of the philosophy unit in the Department of Humanistic Studies. During his doctoral studies, he studied with Karl-Otto Apel at the Goethe-Universität in Frankfurt am Main. He taught Human Economics and Philosophy of Sustainable Development at the Academy of Architecture at the University of Italian Switzerland in Mendrisio. He is one of the founders of the University for Peace in the region Marche. In November 2009, he received the Zamenhof—Voices of Peace prize from the Italian Association for Esperanto. Since 2019, he has been director of the School of Transformational Economics at the University for Peace of the Marche region. His research interests focus on the dialogical theory of truth, the ontology of the gift, the anthropology of human rights, the ethics of the common good, and the birth of a new economic model. In addition to various articles on ontology, ethics, philosophical anthropology, and philosophy of politics and economics, he has published various books. Among the most recent are *Trasformare l'economia. Fonti culturali, modelli alternativi, prospettive politiche* (2014); *La fragilità dello Spirito. Leggere Hegel per comprendere il mondo globale* (2019); *Filosofia della salvezza. Percorsi di liberazione dal sistema di autodistruzione* (2019); and *Gandhi. Al di là del principio di potere* (2021).

Alberto Martinengo is assistant professor of philosophy at the Scuola Normale Superiore in Pisa. Before that, he taught at the Universities of Turin and Milan. He has published numerous journal articles and book chapters in German, English, French, and Spanish on different aspects of the hermeneutic tradition. His most recent research deals with the philosophy of images and its political relevance. His book publications include *Introduzione a Reiner Schürmann* (2008); *Il pensiero incompiuto. Ermeneutica, ragione, ricostruzione in Paul Ricoeur* (2008); and *Filosofie della metafora* (2016). He also edited *Beyond Deconstruction: From Hermeneutics to Reconstruction* (2012).

Ugo Perone is professor emeritus of moral philosophy at the University of Eastern Piedmont in Vercelli. Previously, he taught at the Universities of Turin and Rome III Tor Vergata. Since 2012, he has been Guardini Professor of Philosophy of Religion at the Humboldt Universität in Berlin. Among his publications are works on Descartes, Benjamin, Feuerbach, and Schiller. His research interests have focused on themes such as the subject, memory, time, feelings, and the relation between philosophy and religion. Among his recent publications are *L'essenza della religione* (2015) and *Il racconto della filosofia* (2016). Several of his works in Italian have also appeared in German or English translations, such as *Trotz/dem Subjekt* (1998); *Endlichkeit. Von Grenzen und Passionen* (2015); "Le principe mémoire," in *Jean Greisch, les trois âges de la raison. Métaphysique, phénoménologie, herméneutique* (2016); "Gegenwart und Gegenwärtigkeit als politische Ideen," in *Italienische Politikphilosophie* (2016); *Die Irritation der Religion, Zum Spannungsverhältnis von Philosophie und Theologie* (2017); and *The possible present* (2011).

Caterina Resta is professor of theoretical philosophy at the University of Messina, where she teaches courses on philosophical hermeneutics and twentieth-century philosophy. She is a scholar of contemporary continental philosophy and focuses in particular on topics such as the deconstruction of the subject, relations of identity and otherness, the notion of the human, the question of technology and nihilism, and geophilosophy (globalization, the Mediterranean, Europe). Some of her books include *Il luogo e le vie. Geografie del pensiero in Martin Heidegger* (1996); *L'evento dell'altro. Etica e politica in Jacques Derrida* (2003); *L'Estraneo. Ostilità e ospitalità nel pensiero del Novecento* (2008); *Stato mondiale o* Nomos *della terra. Carl Schmitt tra universo e pluriverso* (2009); *Geofilosofia del Mediterraneo* (2012); *Nichilismo Tecnica Mondializzazione. Saggi su Schmitt, Jünger, Heidegger e Derrida* (2013); and *La passione dell'impossibile. Saggi su Jacques Derrida* (2016).

Elia Zaru is postdoctoral fellow in political philosophy at the Department of Political Science, Law, and International Studies of the University of Padua after earning a PhD in cultures and societies of contemporary Europe from the Scuola Normale Superiore in Pisa. He also works as a teaching assistant and a member of the examination committee for the course History of Political Thought and Elements of Historiography at the Department of Historical Studies of the University of Milan. He is one of the organizers of the specialization course in critical theory of society at the University of Milan-Bicocca and a member of the editorial board of the international journals *Glocalism* and *Quaderni Materialisti*. In addition to various journal articles and book chapters, he is the author of *La postmodernità di «Empire». Antonio Negri e Michael Hardt nel dibattito internazionale (2000–2018)* (2019).

Index

Action, 45, 46, 101, 121–124, 129, 136, 151, 162, 166, 197, 201, 204, 208, 209
Affectivity, 147
Agamben, Giorgio, 2, 18, 56, 58, 60, 62, 98, 108, 172, 205, 209
Aporia, 121, 128
Aquinas, Thomas, 170, 231
Arendt, Hannah, 2, 16, 58, 97, 102, 103, 123, 172, 196, 197
Aristotle, 2, 9, 17, 85, 122, 127, 141, 163–167, 170, 172, 178, 179, 192, 203, 212, 213, 218
Art, 40, 42, 43, 47, 49, 194, 218, 222–224
Atheism, 193
Autonomy, 26

Badiou, Alan, 134
Baudrillard, Jean, 30–32, 107, 108
Beauvoir, Simone de, 149, 150, 152
Benjamin, Walter, 58, 222, 232
Bergson, Henri, 179, 181–183, 185
Bichat, Xavier, 121, 180, 182, 183
Bioeconomic(s), 2, 15, 54, 63, 64
Biology, 53, 180, 184
Biopolitics, 10, 16, 29, 54, 58, 82–85, 99, 108–114, 153, 154, 173, 205, 206
Bios, 13, 17, 18, 85, 166, 167, 179, 181, 206, 208

Birth, 9, 13, 17, 57, 63, 92, 103, 166, 169, 185, 186, 191, 192, 194–198, 220, 221, 225
Bloch, Ernst, 43, 194, 223
Boccaccio, Giovanni, 2, 6–8
Borders, 33, 60, 64, 73, 110, 111, 153, 194, 195, 208
Boundaries, 12, 13, 78, 80, 109, 110, 139, 142, 152, 194, 226
Breath(ing), 35, 36, 98–100, 125, 138, 143, 163, 165, 166, 169, 210
Butler, Judith, 2, 63, 91–94, 140–142, 154

Capitalism, 63, 111–113, 200
Catastrophe, 26, 28, 143
Cavarero, Adriana, 2, 54–57, 60, 63, 91
Celan, Paul, 222
Christianity, 84, 164, 168, 179, 219, 224
Citizen(ship), 46, 72, 96, 102, 109, 110
Common (the), 16, 113, 114
Community, 39, 45, 56, 60, 63, 64, 72, 84, 112, 114, 141, 196, 199, 200
Compassion, 8, 58, 101, 129, 145, 150
Conscience, 109, 151, 198, 199
Consciousness, 35, 67, 121, 146–149, 193, 198, 199, 212, 220
Contagion, 2, 6–8, 10, 11, 28, 29, 36, 55, 62, 63, 75, 84, 98, 99, 113, 129, 135–139, 154, 198

235

Contradiction, 127–129, 182, 183
Creativity, 7, 15, 41, 42, 47–49, 166, 169, 193, 194, 196, 199

Debord, Guy, 205
Deconstruction, 17, 93, 203
Deleuze, Gilles, 181, 182
Democracy, 15, 55, 57, 102, 200
Derrida, Jacques, 2, 126, 206, 207
Descartes, René, 56, 57, 162, 219, 221, 226
Desire, 9, 11, 26, 33, 39, 43, 97, 102, 125, 126, 128, 130, 161, 197, 198
Di Cesare, Donatella, 11
Dialogue, 45, 56, 163, 169, 201, 208, 209
Dispositive, 77, 79, 84, 135
Distance, 19, 42, 55, 57, 62, 63, 113, 126, 214
Domination, 34, 200

Earth(ly), 13, 27–30, 32–36, 61, 64, 142, 150, 169, 177, 179, 196, 214, 225
Economy, 5, 11, 28, 53, 109, 111, 149
Embodiment, 6, 16, 91, 93, 99, 100, 197
Empathy, 41, 59, 80
Esposito, Roberto, 2, 59, 64, 83–85, 112, 113
Ethics, 18, 94, 97, 101, 113, 149, 198, 199, 212
Evil, 5, 83, 96, 112, 124, 146, 147, 171, 172, 193, 197–199, 214, 221, 224
Exceedance, 10, 13, 18, 19, 225
Excess, 18, 143, 149, 206, 212, 214
Existentialism, 219, 223

Finitude, 18, 19, 187, 191–195, 218, 222, 223
Foucault, Michel, 2, 53, 54, 56, 58–60, 64, 83, 96, 112, 135, 137

Fragility, 3, 16, 17, 19, 30, 93, 113, 130, 137, 142, 182, 186
Freedom, 2, 8, 11, 26, 28, 46, 97, 124, 137, 146, 147, 193, 194, 196, 197, 201, 212, 213, 223, 225, 226
Freud, Sigmund, 134, 184, 185

Gender, 15, 16, 54, 62, 93, 114
Globalization, 14, 17, 27, 29–31, 35, 36, 137, 193
God, 4, 5, 9, 32, 49, 73, 75, 126, 130, 133, 151, 165, 167, 168, 170, 192, 200, 204, 218, 219
Government(al), 4, 8, 54, 57, 58, 72, 74, 85, 95, 96, 108

Habermas, Jürgen, 224, 226
Happiness, 9, 56, 166
Hegel, Georg Wilhelm Friedrich, 2, 16, 127–129, 178, 181, 192, 194
Heidegger, Martin, 9, 27, 122, 123, 142, 164, 183, 186, 191
Henry, Michel, 168
Hermeneutics, 15, 17, 19, 25, 192, 193, 223, 225, 226
Hobbes, Thomas, 100
Home, 4, 12, 39, 40, 55, 56, 59–63, 72, 95, 97, 109, 113, 177
Honing, Bonnie, 56, 57, 102
Husserl, Edmund, 219

Identity, 64, 172, 195, 219
Ideology, 27–29, 32, 33, 114
Imagination, 96, 99, 224
Immediacy, 2, 14, 165, 170, 178, 220
Immunity, 84, 99, 100, 135
Immunitary, 60, 64, 75, 83–85, 153, 154, 185
Improvisation, 15, 43–49
Individuality, 214, 218
Inequalities, 54, 64, 93, 114, 221
Injustice, 8, 12, 143, 221
Interaction, 15, 40–42, 44–49, 85

INDEX 237

Interpretation, 12, 46, 162, 163, 169, 195, 209, 211, 225
Interrelatedness, 13, 94, 101
Interruption, 6, 135, 182, 198
Irigaray, Luce, 197
Isolation, 12, 13, 15, 19, 55, 56, 96, 100, 101, 108, 138, 177, 200

Jankélévitch, Vladimir, 2, 18, 181–186
Joy, 13, 30, 130, 142, 210
Jünger, Ernst, 2, 26, 28–30, 32, 33, 35
Justice, 12, 14, 194, 200, 201

Kant, Immanuel, 42, 181, 226
Kierkegaard, Søren, 169, 170, 223

Lacan, Jacques, 209
Language, 6, 54, 63, 78, 80, 85, 99, 100, 162, 172, 204
Latouche, Serge, 29, 30, 34
Law, 64, 96, 140, 151, 168, 172
Levinas, Emmanuel, 2, 17, 91, 92, 138, 146–152, 199
Liberation, 26, 64, 107, 193, 198, 199
Lived experience, 98, 146, 164

Manzoni, Alessandro, 8
Market economy, 11, 30, 53
Materiality, 77, 97, 98–100, 121, 127, 179
Mbembe, Achille, 2, 110
Media, 30, 34, 45, 55–57, 71, 72, 74, 95, 96, 98
Mediation, 40, 61, 79, 126
Medicine, 4, 33, 75, 77, 114, 139
Memory, 7, 10, 19, 42, 43, 141, 150, 196, 211, 213, 222, 223, 227
Merleau-Ponty, Maurice, 2, 219, 220
Metaphor, 5, 15, 73–85, 91, 99, 101, 177, 222
Metaphysics, 5, 10, 19, 123, 191, 193, 225, 226

Migrant (the), 60, 63, 109–111, 139, 153, 210
Modernity, 14, 16, 19, 26, 27, 32, 36, 53, 54, 60, 83, 84, 100, 112, 138, 162, 169, 219, 225, 226
Mortality, 9, 141, 192, 194, 199, 219, 220
Mourning, 55, 63, 97, 98, 109, 130, 140, 141
Multitude (the), 18, 27, 206, 210
Music, 15, 39–43, 47, 123

Nancy, Jean-Luc, 142
Narration, 77, 165, 166, 205, 210, 212, 213
Necropolitics, 9, 10, 16, 17, 110–112, 114
Negativity, 16, 93, 127, 147, 226
Neighbor(s), 102, 145, 146, 150, 151–155
Neoliberal(ism), 2, 8, 11, 15, 16, 54, 60, 61, 63, 101, 102, 111–115
Nietzsche, Friedrich, 26, 134, 207, 208
Nihilism, 17, 18, 193, 199, 201
Nothingness, 124, 130, 163, 193, 196

Ontology, 86, 92, 120, 138, 145
Openness, 9, 92
Otherness, 111

Pain, 5, 13, 98, 129, 130, 135, 136, 138, 142, 145–149, 211, 218, 224, 227
Pascal, Blaise, 223
Passion, 129, 161, 162
Passivity, 138, 148, 162
Pathology, 63, 77–82, 99
Patriarchal, 15, 56, 57, 61, 93, 200
Performance, 40, 41, 43, 44, 47–49, 114, 148
Phenomenology, 19, 146, 168, 198, 219–221, 223, 225
Plato, 2, 9, 12, 125, 126, 163, 179, 204, 208, 209, 211, 213, 218

Polis, 81, 85, 141, 142, 209
Powerlessness, 14, 137, 138, 148
Practice, 6, 8, 14–16, 29, 41, 43–47, 49, 57, 77, 112, 115, 151, 153, 167, 177, 178
Preciado, Paul B., 2, 59–64
Psyche, 163–167, 169, 206, 208–210

Relationality, 13, 14, 16, 19, 55, 98, 113, 195, 196
Religion, 19, 149, 151, 195, 198, 223–225
Representation, 5, 6, 29, 34, 55, 77, 173
Resistance, 58, 75, 120, 121, 128, 139, 152, 198
Responsibility, 6, 14–17, 19, 93, 94, 112–114, 141, 150–152, 154, 155, 199, 201
Revolution(ary), 31, 53, 150, 182

Sacrifice, 57, 58, 64, 200
Schleiermacher, Friedrich, 224
Schmitt, Carl, 58
Science, 9, 11, 28, 84, 95, 119, 129, 137, 180, 181, 195, 198
Separation, 153, 154, 197, 205, 210, 224
Sexual difference, 93
Simmel, Georg, 181, 182, 185
Sloterdijk, Peter, 2, 31, 35, 36

Socrates, 13, 125, 163, 169, 209, 211
Solidarity, 19, 101, 112, 200, 201
Sontag, Susan, 2, 59, 79–83, 91, 101
Sovereignty, 11, 85, 100, 110, 192, 212
Struggle, 10, 75, 112, 115, 121, 124, 139, 201
Subjectivity, 14, 15, 17, 19, 55, 67
Stranger (the), 17, 81, 82, 126, 143, 145, 146, 150–155, 183, 210, 213
Symbol, 5, 9, 26, 30, 31, 109, 152

Technology, 9, 14, 17, 26, 29, 33–35, 40, 48, 137
Temporality, 42, 108, 181, 182, 220
Theology, 17, 168, 170, 192
Transcendence, 29, 128, 172, 184, 187, 193, 198, 223, 224, 227

Utopia(n), 3, 43, 133, 143, 154

Vico, Giambattista, 10, 178
Violence, 14, 29–31, 36, 65, 91–96, 107, 140–143, 171, 197, 201, 212

Weil, Simone, 17, 149–152
Woman, 32, 60, 62, 130, 195, 211

Zambrano, María, 197
Zoe, 13, 17, 18, 163–169, 179, 206, 208, 210, 213

www.ingramcontent.com/pod-product-compliance
Lightning Source LLC
Chambersburg PA
CBHW020648230426
43665CB00008B/356